The
Moral Measure
of the Economy

The
Moral Measure
of the Economy

Chuck Collins & Mary Wright

ORBIS BOOKS

Maryknoll, New York 10545

Founded in 1970, Orbis Books endeavors to publish works that enlighten the mind, nourish the spirit, and challenge the conscience. The publishing arm of the Maryknoll Fathers and Brothers, Orbis seeks to explore the global dimensions of the Christian faith and mission, to invite dialogue with diverse cultures and religious traditions, and to serve the cause of reconciliation and peace. The books published reflect the views of their authors and do not represent the official position of the Maryknoll Society. To learn more about Maryknoll and Orbis Books, please visit our website at www.maryknoll.com.

Copyright © 2007 by Chuck Collins and Mary Wright.

Published by Orbis Books, Maryknoll, NY 10545-0308.

Queries regarding rights and permissions should be addressed to Orbis Books, P.O. Box 308, Maryknoll, NY 10545-0308, U.S.A.

Manufactured in the United States of America.

Library of Congress Cataloging-in-Publication Data

Collins, Chuck, 1959-
    The moral measure of the economy / Chuck Collins and Mary Wright.
      p. cm.
    Includes bibliographical references and index.
    ISBN 978-1-57075-693-1 (pbk.)
    1. Economics – Religious aspects – Catholic Church. 2. United States – Economic conditions. 3. Christian sociology – Catholic Church. 4. Catholic Church – Doctrines. I. Wright, Mary, 1945- II. Title.
BX1795.E27C65 2007
261.8'50973 – dc22

                                                   2006035190

To Tricia, who walks the Gospel with grace, joy, and humor.

— CC

To Myles and Devin, my two wonderful grandsons,
in the hope that they come of age in a more just economy.

— MW

Contents

Introduction

How do we measure the health of our economy?

Economists have their answer. They use a variety of yardsticks, graphs, rates, reports, and facts. We are accustomed to listening to such indicators as "gross domestic product" and the "Dow Jones." These provide valuable information, but they are certainly not the only measure.

What about the moral measure of the economy? How do we judge the morality of our economic institutions, policies, and practices? What principles or indicators might allow us to take this measure and what would we find?

The economy is integral to our personal lives and community health. It shapes our wages, jobs, cost of housing, health, savings, and so much more. Most of us, however, experience the economy like the weather. It is something "out there" and beyond human control. Newscasters even talk about the economy like the weather: "The storm clouds of recession are appearing on the horizon." We may feel the best we can do is to listen to the forecast and pack an umbrella.

Economic activity happens within a framework created by human beings. That is why the economy of Mexico is so different from the economy of the United States, which is different from Finland. The *rules* that govern an economy shape its outcomes. And our moral values — what we think is right and important — shape these economic rules. *[handwritten margin note: who makes these "rules"?]*

This book looks at our economy in light of Catholic moral principles. Many of these principles are universal and relevant to all Christians and people of other faiths who desire to examine the economy with a moral perspective. It is written for people who have neither the time nor desire to read a dense book about theology or economics. If your eyes glaze over when you hear the word "economy," then this book is for you.

Economics has been called the "dismal science," and many people assume that you need an advanced college degree to understand it or talk about it. Yet whether we understand it or not, all of us share an interest in the economy. You don't need special training to make simple observations based on your personal experience. The starting point of our religious tradition is to read the signs of the times: *What do you notice about the economy? What is working and not working? How is your life touched and shaped by larger economic trends? What do you see in your life, community, and nation as a whole?*

At a church parish hall discussion, one group identified these things that were "working well" in the economy:

- There are many vibrant small businesses in our community.
- Interest rates have been low, allowing many people to become first-time homeowners, including black and Latino neighbors.
- The parking lot at the mall is full of people buying things, which is good for the economy.
- Unemployment seems to be fairly low.

The same group identified things that were "not working well":

- The local homeless shelter and soup kitchen are full.
- There are many low-wage jobs that don't pay enough for people to survive.
- Food banks run out of food before all are served.
- Some families need more than one job to sustain themselves.
- People are buying stuff, but mostly with credit cards, so they are going deeper into debt.
- People are risking their lives to cross our borders and work without legal status.
- There is anxiety that the "bubble" in real estate home values may burst, causing many people's financial situations to change drastically.

Most people are keenly aware of the wide variety of trends affecting the economy. But what does our faith have to say about these economic trends? Here we are less confident in terms of our own experience. Many who have attended church all their lives say they were unaware of specific church teachings relating to economic issues. This is not surprising. As one theologian remarked, Catholic social teachings, especially about economics, are among the church's "best kept secrets."[1]

There are remarkable changes occurring in our national and global economies that call out for greater citizen involvement. Now more than ever we need a moral compass for understanding, judging, and influencing the direction of our economy. *why?*

Our hope for this book is to inspire and enlist you to bring your moral voice to the economic life of this country. Too often, we cede our power as people of faith and citizens to "experts" who make the policies and rules that govern the economy. But these experts often overlook critical factors such as the dignity and worth of humans and fail to bring a "respect for life" perspective to economic decision making.

You may not feel individually "qualified" to speak out about economic issues. Two hundred pages from now, you still may not be able to explain the functioning of the Federal Reserve Bank, but you will be very clear about the moral values that measure economic health. We believe that you are already "qualified" to discuss the moral dimensions of the economy, but this book will give you greater confidence.

Our national conversation is currently very polarized, and readers may desire to know where to position politically the implications of our faith on current economic matters. But this won't be easy. Catholic teaching on economics is neither conservative nor liberal in the traditional political sense.

For example, on the issue of poverty, liberals and conservatives each focus on different aspects of the problem, with differing implications for public policy. Liberals often want to discuss the economic structures that contribute to poverty, the amoral behavior of corporations, individual greed, and the responsibility of government to solve problems. Conservatives generally want to focus on the individual moral choices of the poor, the collapse of the traditional family, and the limits of government as a problem solver.

The implications of our faith teachings, to the frustration of some, cannot be easily pigeonholed. We care both about the structures of poverty *and* individual moral responsibility. We see an important role for government *and* personal and private sector responses. We believe that all humans are sacred and have basic economic rights. We also believe all humans have fundamental obligations. We talk about rights and responsibilities, opportunities and duties. difference?

As the U.S. bishops wrote in their 1986 Pastoral Letter on the Economy, "We know poverty and economic injustice result from discrimination *and* destructive personal behavior, from unwise decisions of corporations *and* the unresponsive behavior of the public sector."[2] In other words, both individuals and the community are responsible.

The Catholic community has historically frustrated many people by robustly denouncing both communism and unfettered capitalism. In opposing communism as an economic system, the church rejected the concentration of power in a central state, the stifling of individual initiative and enterprise, the promise of rigidly enforced equality, and the idolatry of the state itself.

The church is also clear about the importance and limits of private market capitalism. All business activity and private wealth ownership should be balanced with the common good and concerns for justice. As the U.S. bishops wrote,

> The U.S. value system emphasizes economic freedom. It also recognizes that the market is limited by fundamental human rights. ...The market system contributes to the success of the U.S. economy, but so do many efforts to forge economic institutions and public policies that enable all to share in the riches of the nation. The country's economy has been built through a creative struggle: entrepreneurs, business people, workers, unions, consumers, and government have all played essential roles.[3]

Christianity has existed under a variety of economic systems. Church teachings emphasize the importance of balancing individual and community, private and public, and solidarity and subsidiarity.

The teachings of Jesus are very clear on the matter of idolatry, whether it is idolatry of the state, as under communist systems, or idolatry of the market. The dominant secular religion in the United States today is the worship of the market, and there are many points where Gospel values conflict with the values of the marketplace, as we shall discuss further.

Christian teachings on economics are part of our belief that life is sacred and must be respected. Respect for life is a "seamless garment." No political party and few politicians seem able to capture such a holistic focus on life. Some politicians oppose abortion but support the death penalty. Others support a worker's right to organize but vote against nutrition programs for low-income children. Respect for life is not a cafeteria where you pick and choose what appeals to you. Nor does respect for life begin with conception and end at birth. It is a commitment to human life from beginning to end.

The teachings of the Gospel are challenging. On a visit to North America, Pope John Paul II called on all of us who live in the United States and Canada to pay attention to the plight of people living in the poor countries of the developing world — collectively known as the "Global South." Specifically addressing us as North Americans, the late pope told Jesus' parable of the rich man and Lazarus from Luke 16:20. For Pope John Paul II, this parable invoked the northern industrial nations sitting in wealth and splendor ("dressed in purple and fine linen and who feasted sumptuously every day") with Lazarus at our gate ("covered with sores, who longed to satisfy his hunger with what fell from the rich man's table"). The pope was urging those of us in the Global North to face up to our complacency toward the billions in the Global South who suffer.

This book is divided into two parts. Part 1 is a basic overview of Catholic economic teachings and what it means for our lives. Part 2 reflects on the root causes of the changing economy and what can be done to bring our Gospel values into the public square.

Chapter 1, "Economics As If People Mattered," discusses how economic trends touch our lives and why we have a personal stake in living in a more just economy. Chapter 2, "Our Best Kept Secret: Catholic Teachings on Economic Life," summarizes over a century of Catholic social teaching on economics and prepares us to look at the current signs of the times. Chapter 3, "Signs of the Times #1: Life in the New Economy," looks at many of the ways in which the changing economy touches each of our lives in very personal ways.

Part 2 applies Catholic social teachings to contemporary problems, digs deeper into root causes, and suggests ways to approach taking action. Beginning with chapter 4, "Signs of the Times #2: What Kind of Country Are We Becoming?" we explore larger economic trends related to poverty, income, wealth, and growing inequality. Chapters 5 and 6 analyze the root causes of the changing economy. Chapter 7, "The Moral Measures for Our Economy," looks at the values that characterize a more just economy, and chapter 8, "Solidarity in Action: Alternatives for a Just Economy," examines some of the new economic institutions that embody these values. Chapter 9, "Preparing for Discipleship," explores ways to think about our own lives prior to engaging in social action. Chapter 10, "Making a Difference," looks at the ways to engage as faithful citizens and activists. The resources section at the end identifies educational resources and organizations for those of you who are called to further study, reflection, and action.

Many in our country believe that their faith teachings have little relevance to the economy around them. We worship God on Sunday, but Monday through Saturday we worship at the altar of the market. Many followers of Christ fall into a tragic separation between faith and everyday life.

As the U.S. bishops wrote in their 1986 pastoral letter, the economy is one of the most important places for us to exercise our faith.

> Like family life, economic life is one of the chief areas where we live out our faith, love our neighbor, confront temptation, fulfill God's creative design, and achieve our holiness. Our economic activity in factory, field, office, or shop feeds our families — or feeds our anxieties. It exercises our talents — or wastes them. It raises our hopes — or crushes them. It brings us into cooperation with others — or sets us at odds.[4]

We are confronted each day by the ways in which secular society fosters false divisions between our faith life and our economic life. But these false divisions are the source of tremendous human suffering.

> Our faith is not just a weekend obligation, a mystery to be celebrated around the altar on Sunday. It is a pervasive reality to be practiced every day in homes, offices, factories, schools, and businesses across our land. We cannot separate what we believe from how we act in the marketplace and the broader community, for this is where we make our primary contribution to the pursuit of economic justice.[5]

Economic justice work is not a sideshow of the Gospel. It is a main event.

We hope you will find inspiration through these facts, theories, and stories. Little real change will happen without our coming together to worship, to sing, and to be thankful. When we combine our faithful teachings with our creative energy — together we will bind up the broken, heal the sick, and bring forth a just peace to our communities and nations.

Part One

In times of terror and war, of global insecurity and economic uncertainty, of disrespect for human life and human dignity, we need to return to the basic moral principles. Politics . . . should be about fundamental moral choices. How do we protect human life and dignity? How do we fairly share the blessings and burdens of the challenges we face? What kind of nation do we want to be? What kind of world do we want to shape?

—U.S. Conference of Catholic Bishops, *Faithful Citizenship: A Catholic Call to Political Responsibility,* 2004

Chapter One

Economics As If People Mattered

A Human Face on the Economy: Six Families

We begin with several stories of real families as they live and experience the economy. Names and places have been changed, but the stories are true. As you read these stories, consider the ways in which larger economic forces touch, shape, and dictate the seemingly private struggles and opportunities of these people. Also notice your personal response to these stories. You may feel a temptation to make judgments about individual choices or to offer advice. Listen for both the emotions and judgments these stories stir in you — as well as the larger economic forces at work.

"We Lay Up Cash for the Long Winters"

Lucy LeBlanc wears a headset as she sits in front of a computer terminal. "I feel like an airline pilot wearing this," she laughs. "Not that I've ever flown on a plane."

For eighteen months, Lucy has worked at a recently built "call center" for a major credit card company, based twenty-five miles from her home in southern Maine. She fields calls that come in from all over the country. "Sometimes people try to guess what my accent is," she chuckles again. "We're lucky these jobs came here. They almost went to Bangalore, India. And who knows, maybe they'll move there tomorrow."

Lucy LeBlanc is in her late fifties and lives with her husband, Leo, a former paper mill worker. The paper factories closed in the 1990s and Leo lost the unionized job that enabled them to buy a house in the 1970s and to support their family while their children were growing up. The LeBlancs now survive on about $27,000 a year from a patchwork of jobs. Lucy now earns the steady paycheck, though it is only for the Maine minimum wage of $6.50 an hour, which is higher than the $5.15 federal minimum wage.

The LeBlancs live up a dirt road and heat their home with wood in the winter. It's a forty-five-minute commute for Lucy, as it is for many of the workers at the call center. "During the winter, I leave the house in the dark and drive home in the dark," quips Lucy. "I work in a windowless office building, so it isn't until April that I start to see the sun again."

Leo works part-time driving a delivery truck and does some mechanical work. Three months a year, during the summer tourist season, both Leo and Lucy take second shift jobs working for area hotels, Lucy as a kitchen worker and Leo as a security guard. "That's the fat time," says Lucy. "That's when we lay up the cash for the long winters."

The LeBlancs' four children are all adults in their twenties and early thirties. Two are married, and all of them live on their own except their daughter Elsa, who is retarded and lives at home. "We worry about what will happen to Elsa when we get too old to take care of her," says Lucy, in a more somber voice. "But her sister and brothers are all still in the area, thank God. We don't worry about our retirement. We know we're both working until we die."

"We Are an Immigrant Success Story"

Nestor and Letty Rodríguez sit at their dining room table calculating the payroll for their family's ranch. Against one wall is a colorful family altar observing the festival of All Saints and the Mexican tradition of Day of the Dead. It is covered with colorful yellow and orange flowers, votive candles, and a large picture of Our Lady of Guadalupe. "We've been U.S. citizens and lived in east Texas for three generations," Letty says proudly. "But we are still Mexicans when it comes to honoring our ancestors."

Nestor Rodríguez inherited the ranch from his father, who worked over his lifetime to buy several parcels of land and build the business. The ranch now has over twenty employees, and the Rodríguez family find themselves with all the joys and headaches of owning a medium-sized business. "We try to be good to our workers, and we expect them to be good to us."

They've been subject to several raids and fines by the Immigration and Naturalization Service for employing illegal immigrants. "Now we do a better job of checking people's papers," says Nestor. But the topic of immigration is uncomfortable for the Rodríguez family. "We see people every day who cross the border because their family in Mexico or Central America is starving. We need to do something to change the laws. There is something out of balance."

They have five children, all of whom went to Catholic schools. The three oldest have attended college, including their oldest son Hector, who is now in law school in Massachusetts. Pictures of these children adorn the dining room wall, next to the altar. "We are an immigrant success story," Nestor reflects. "My grandparents were migrant workers, and I was the first person in my family to go to college, thanks to the GI Bill. Now all my children are going to college, thanks to our family business. We have been blessed."

"We're Living the Re-Lo Life"

It is Friday night and Jim Murray is sitting in the United Airlines executive lounge, saying goodnight to his three children on a cellular telephone. When he finally arrives home later, it will be well past bedtime. Rita Murray is used to Jim traveling two to four nights a week for his job as a regional sales manager with a national real estate company.

"We're corporate nomads," observed Rita. "We're living the 'Re-lo' life," referring to frequent relocations the family has made. Jim's salary is over $150,000 a year and it affords them a very good life, albeit at a frenzied pace. The Murrays have moved three times in the last ten years.

The Murray family currently lives in Naperville, Illinois, a suburban city of subdivisions, apartment complexes, and recently constructed large houses forty minutes from downtown Chicago. They own a four-bedroom house in a recently developed subdivision, and many of their neighbors are families like their own — also living the "re-lo life." Many have lived in the new sprawling transient suburbs of the booming Sun Belt. These are communities that don't have town centers or Main Streets, but generally have good schools, green lawns, and plenty of parking.

The neighborhood is homogeneous: almost entirely white, higher-income professional families who aren't able to put down deep roots in any community for long, but make the best of their situation. The Murrays have a few friends, but none they would consider close relationships. They don't know anyone well enough to do child care swaps. Both Jim's and Rita's extended families live in other states. "We try to get involved in a new church community and local soccer leagues for the kids," observes Rita. "But it's difficult knowing we'll be packing up again in a few years. It is hard on the kids, especially as they get older."

She has spent the week shuttling kids through heavy traffic in her Eddie Bauer Edition Ford Explorer between school, soccer games, music lessons, and tutors. Each child has a different schedule, but she finds a few hours each day to squeeze in exercise classes, volunteer work at their church, and social gatherings.

To make up for the busy life, the family splurges on several vacations a year, including a recent trip to a Club Med in Mexico. With a big mortgage, two car payments and steep recreation expenses, the Murrays don't save a lot of money for the future. "When you move around a lot in the fast lane," Rita reflected, "you tend to think about the moment, not the future."

"The Bright Future Has Been Slow in Coming"

Candice Charles sits at a tidy desk in her living room, doing her homework on a computer that she bought at a church rummage sale. Her teenage son, Martin, is also doing his homework, though at the moment he is composing a love poem to the girl who sits near him in his ninth grade classroom. "He used to write his poems to me," jokes Candice in his presence. "But he is a bit distracted these days!"

Candice emigrated from the island of Trinidad to Jersey City in 1992, when her daughter Cleo was only four years old. Cleo's father had abandoned them in Trinidad — so Candice moved to be closer to her mother, who was living in New Jersey. Martin was born a few years later to an out-of-wedlock relationship that also soured. "Of course, it would be nice for these children to have a father in their lives," says Candice frankly. "But not those two men. We are better off without them." She leaves it at that, but adds that she gets no child support from either of the fathers.

Candice gets some welfare assistance for the children, but not for herself, as she is not yet a U.S. citizen. Candice has gone in and out of the labor force, attending community college when she's been unemployed. Life is a constant struggle and as she pulls out two letters threatening to shut off her electricity and telephone.

Her daughter now attends college at the state university, and her son is still in Catholic school on scholarship. She proudly shares that this week she successfully sold forty raffle tickets for her son's school. "I don't have much money," she says, "so I try to volunteer all I can. The parish has been so good to our family." Candice says she is hopeful for her children, but not so sure about her personal future. "I'm studying accounting, so someday I pray I'll get a good job. But I try not to think too much about the future. It just keeps me awake at night. The bright future has been slow in coming."

Tale of Two Families after Hurricane Katrina

Hurricanes Katrina and Rita hit the Gulf Coast in September 2005, exposing the serious race and class fault lines that exist in our nation. This is well illustrated by two contrasting family stories.

On the day before Katrina hit New Orleans, both the Rice and Preston families evacuated their homes. Donald and Renee Rice have three children, ages seven, nine, and twelve. John and Lenore Preston also have three children, ages four, six, and seven. Both are long-time New Orleans families and are of African American heritage. Hurricane Katrina uprooted both families, causing enormous heartache, dislocation, and trauma. But despite their many similarities, their experiences were very different.

A week after the hurricane, Donald Rice unpacked several boxes in a newly rented apartment in Alabama. "This has been hell," Donald remarked. "But we're lucky that Renee's family was only a few hours away and her uncle found this house we could rent." The Rices immediately enrolled their children in a school that several of their cousins attend. "We wake up every morning and wonder where we are," said Donald.

The Rices had loaded up their two cars, one with valuable objects, and drove in caravan north and east to Alabama, where Renee had family. There they were able to ride out the storm. When it became apparent that their house was badly damaged, they made arrangements to stay in Alabama.

The fate of the Preston family, however, was quite different. "I would like to take a long, hot shower," growled John Preston, as he sat forward on a folding chair. One week after Hurricane Katrina, the Preston family was living in the Houston Astrodome and waiting for a more permanent placement. The Preston children dozed on cots, except the youngest, who wrestled to escape from his mother's sweaty grip.

The Prestons had no car, so as Hurricane Katrina approached they walked with hundreds of other families to the New Orleans Superdome, the giant football stadium that would become a notorious symbol of mismanagement in the aftermath of the hurricane. "My children have seen and heard things I'd never want them to see," said Lenore, describing dead bodies, screams in the night, and crushing crowds. Later, they were bused with thousands of other people to Houston. "We don't know anybody here in Houston, and it was scary to leave home, but we had to get out of there."

The Prestons have no clothing or mementos and little money. They started their journey with $150 in cash and two garbage bags of rapidly assembled clothes and toys, but shared what they had with even more desperate families they met along the way. Now their future is uncertain. They have no relatives they can turn to, as most of their extended family lives in New Orleans and is suffering the same fate. They are still trying to find John's mother, who lived with his sister. "We write messages and read the postings, but haven't learned anything yet," said John somberly.

Both the Rice and Preston families have suffered trauma, but the Rice family was buffered from major discomfort by their larger family connections and financial resources. The Rices have cell phones, two cars, credit cards, a bank account, health insurance, and an extended family and social network outside of New Orleans. They are not rich, but Donald works as a ticket agent for a major airline and Renee is a public school teacher. Donald's employer has continued to pay him and will be transferring him to another job in the region. The national affiliate of Renee's teachers' union is working with her to find a placement for a teaching job.

The Preston family, on the other hand, has no car, no bank account, no cell phone, and no credit card. They are not destitute, but they have little to fall back on. Lenore ran a home day-care center and John worked at a convenience store. Like many low-income working families, they have no health insurance or savings safety net to fall back on.

The Rice kids come home from school with their knapsacks and colored papers flying. They head for the new swing set that several of Renee's cousins brought over and assembled for the kids. "We're confused, but lucky to have family," says Renee. "Tonight, we're invited to dinner at another cousin's home. We're on the dinner guest circuit." Donald shakes his head in amazement. "Renee is planning a big party to thank everyone," he says. "But I can't get over that we're here in the first place."

Meanwhile, the Prestons are still waiting in Houston for various overstretched government and charity agencies to help them with their next move. "Yes, I'm angry," said John Preston. "You would be too if you suffered such indignity and watched your children go through what they have."

Perhaps you can identify with the experiences of some of the families — or know families with similar situations and struggles. Most of these families share a feeling of not being in control of their economic lives. Even an affluent family, the relocating Murrays, seem to feel like they are leaves being tossed by the wind.

Did you feel any judgments stirring inside you about the choices that different families were making? Did you feel critical of some families' consumption habits or decision to have children out of wedlock? Did you want to offer advice? Our Catholic tradition is very clear that individuals are responsible for their own lives and that individual morality and choices make a difference in terms of individual economic prospects.

Were you able to listen for the changes in the economy that were beyond anyone's control? One challenge of Gospel economics is to try to understand how individual choices and decisions fit into a set of larger — even global — economic forces and frameworks that shape our individual lives.

Changing Signs of the Times

Underlying these human stories is a narrative about the evolving and changing U.S. and global economies. In the two decades between 1985 and 2005, there have been dramatic changes. Here is a brief comparative sense of the signs of the times, trends that we will examine in much greater detail.

- In 1985, the U.S. savings rate was 9.0 percent. In 2005, it was *negative* 0.4 percent, which means that for the first time since the Great Depression, Americans spent more than they earned.[1]

- In 1985, the number of people in the United States in poverty was 33 million, or 14.0 percent of the population. By 2005, the number of people in poverty had increased to 36.95 million, although as a percentage of the population, it had declined to 12.6 percent.[2]

- In 1987, 31 million people in the United States did not have health insurance (13 percent of the population). By 2006, over 46.6 million had no health insurance (16 percent of the population).[3]

- In 1985, the ratio between average CEO pay and average U.S. worker pay was 76 to 1. By 2005, it was 411 to 1.[4]

- In 1985, the wealthiest 1 percent of households had 131 times the wealth of the median household. By 2005, they had 190 times the wealth of the median U.S. household.[5]

- In 1985, the average income of the top 5 percent of families was 13.5 times as much as the average income of the bottom 20 percent. In 2004, the top 5 percent made almost 21 times as much as the bottom 20 percent.[6]

- In 1985, there were fourteen billionaires on the Forbes 400 list of wealthiest Americans. The average wealth held by a member of the Forbes 400 was $335 million. By 2006, there were four hundred billionaires on the list, with an average wealth of $3.13 billion.[7]

- In 1985, the number of children in poverty was 12.4 million, or 20.7 percent of all children. By 2005, the number of children in poverty was 13 million, or 17.8 percent of all children.[8]

Overarching trends of the last several decades include the following:

- The economy has been largely stable, with low inflation and without rapid upheavals or depressions. As a result, unemployment rates have stayed relatively low.

- There is a growing gap between rich and poor. The economic prosperity of the last several decades has been unevenly shared, with enormous wealth and income flowing to the top 10 percent and even 1 percent of households. Wages have been stagnant or even fallen for the middle class and poor.

- Rising fuel costs, and the high cost of basic needs such as housing and health care, are squeezing many working families.

- The nature of work has changed, as more people are working in insecure temporary and part-time jobs, without health insurance or other benefits.

- People are working more hours and extra jobs to survive, leaving people with less free time.

- Individuals have taken on mountains of personal debt, using credit cards and borrowing against home prices. At the same time, our country has undertaken massive public borrowing leading to unprecedented federal debt and annual deficits.

Part of our challenge is to learn how to read these signs of the times through a biblical lens and strengthen the national dialogue about the economy. We will now turn to exploring some of the biblical principles that can guide us in our reflection and choices.

Chapter Two

Our Best Kept Secret

Catholic Teachings on Economic Life

As people of faith, we believe we are one family, not competing classes. We are sisters and brothers, not economic units or statistics. We must come together around the values of our faith to shape economic policies that protect human life, promote strong families, expand a stable middle class, create decent jobs, and reduce the level of poverty and need in our society.

—U.S. bishops' statement on the tenth anniversary of
Economic Justice for All, 1996[1]

As we mentioned in the introduction, some people find that Catholic social teachings are among our "best kept secrets." It may be hard to believe that there are specific and prophetic teachings on economic life that you haven't heard of.

The church's teachings on economics are directly rooted in the Bible, in both the Hebrew texts of the Old Testament and the teachings of Jesus. They are not a footnote in the Bible, but a central part of its teachings. One of our challenges, in the counsel of biblical scholar Ched Meyers, is to "read the economy biblically and read the Bible economically!" In other words, look at the economy through the lens of biblical values and also read the Bible for its economic wisdom.

When Jim Wallis, the founder of *Sojourners* magazine, was a young seminarian, he and members of a Bible study group discussed whether the Bible had anything to say about economics. They decided to scour the Bible for every verse that dealt with wealth, poverty, money, or economic injustice. Wallis remembers,

We found several thousand verses in the Bible on the poor and God's response to injustice. We found it to be the second most prominent theme in the Hebrew Old Testament — the first was idolatry, and the two often were related. One of every sixteen verses in the New Testament is about the poor or the subject of money

(Mammon, as the gospels call it). In the first three (Synoptic) gospels it is one out of ten verses, and in the book of Luke, it is one in seven![2]

Our biblical tradition clearly has a lot to say about economic life. The teachings of Jesus are full of economically oriented parables and stories that serve as the basis for a whole body of religious writings.

Since 1891, when Pope Leo XIII wrote his encyclical letter *Rerum Novarum* on the condition of labor, the church has issued a number of social encyclicals and pastoral letters reflecting on economic life. These have added to a foundation of social teaching that is both inspiring and prophetic.

Our goal is not to trace the history of economic teachings or provide a comprehensive overview of individual encyclicals. We hope this book inspires you to read some of the excellent resources and books we've identified in the resources section (see p. 209). But we do want to offer an overview of church teachings to inform our exploration of contemporary economic life. In addition to a century of encyclicals,[3] we draw primarily from two important documents:

- *Compendium of the Social Doctrine of the Church,* authored by the Pontifical Council for Justice and Peace, published in English by the U.S. Conference of Catholic Bishops in 2005;

- *Economic Justice for All: Pastoral Letter on Catholic Social Teaching and the U.S. Economy,* a statement of the U.S. Catholic bishops, first published in 1986.

Respect for Life and Human Dignity

Our religious teachings on the economy are based on respect for the sacredness of life, belief in the transcendent worth — the sacredness — of all human beings. The dignity of the human person, experienced in community with others, is the yardstick against which all aspects of economic life must be measured.

An immediate implication of these teachings is that we must respect other humans with reverence. And in our interactions with others, we should approach one another with a "sense of awe that arises in the presence of something holy and sacred."[4]

From the Book of Genesis we know that we are created in God's image. Before we see each other as different races and nations, we must first see our common bond as children of God. "As such, every human being possesses an inalienable dignity that stamps human existence prior to any division into races or nations and prior to human labor and achievement."[5] We are each sacred, born with inherent worth and dignity.

Creation is a gift from God, and we are called upon to be faithful stewards of this gift we have inherited. Our work in the world is our contribution to creation. We should justly consider our labors as part of the unfolding of our Creator's work.[6]

As humans, we immediately began to lose our way by forgetting that all the gifts of Creation are just that: gifts. We did not create the blessings that abound. The trouble started early with Adam and Eve's attempt to live independently of God and deny their existence as creatures and stewards. This underscores that the "prime sin" in the biblical texts is idolatry, the tendency to worship false gods and ourselves rather than God, to "praise the creature, not the Creator" (Romans 1:25). The Bible not only condemns the worship of idols, but also rejects other forms of idolatry such as the pursuit of power over others and the desire for vast wealth.[7]

The followers of Judeo-Christian teachings are "people of the covenant." Our practices of prayer and worship are a way of renewing our promise not to forget the gift of Creation. The Hebrew texts describe how the people of Israel gathered in thanksgiving to renew their covenant with God. This promise was to remember what it was like to live as aliens in the strange land of Egypt and to not forget the experience of slavery and oppression, as well as God's mercy and deliverance from that suffering. It is in this memory that God calls on the people of Israel to treat all strangers as he treated them. The scripture states, "They were to imitate God by treating the alien and the slave in their midst as God has treated them" (Exodus 22:20–22; Jeremiah 34:8–14).

The covenant with God is to live in freedom and in caring community. We are reminded that human life is lived in community. We are social creatures, not meant to live alone. The requirement of love and solidarity grows out of our interdependence with one another and the obligations that result from this.[8] In Christian community, justice is measured by our treatment of the most powerless people in the society, often characterized as the orphan, the widow, the poor, and the stranger in the land.[9]

When people forget about this covenant promise, turn away from God, reject their obligations to one another, worship idols, and come to declare that all they have is of their own creation, God sends prophetic messengers to remind them of God's "saving deeds" and this covenant. Micah proclaims the heart of this prophetic message: "to do justice, and to love kindness, to walk humbly with your God" (Micah 6:8 RSV).

God sends Jesus as his own son and most radical of the prophetic voices. In the way he lives, Jesus resists the temptations of power, prestige, and privilege. He breaks bread with the most outcast members of the society, including tax collectors, prostitutes, and lepers. He warns against attempts to "lay up treasures on earth" (Matthew 6:19) and not be so focused on material goods. As Jesus wanders through the wilderness, Satan tempts him with an offer to possess "all the kingdoms of the world and all their splendor" (Matthew 4:8). Jesus responds, "Away with you Satan. Worship the Lord your God, and serve only him."[10]

When asked, Jesus explains that the greatest commandment is to love God with your whole heart, mind, and soul, emphasizing that "you shall love your neighbor as yourself." When he is asked who qualifies as a neighbor, Jesus responds with the parable of the good Samaritan. Your neighbor, the parable tells us, is not a small circle of like-minded friends from your community, tribe, church, union, city, county, state, or nation. Our neighbor is all of humanity.

At the end of his life, Jesus gives the Sermon on the Mount, where he describes the time of judgment (Matthew 25:31–46). At this moment, the nations shall be assembled and divided into the eternally damned and the eternally blessed. Those who will be blessed are those who welcomed the stranger, fed the hungry, gave drink to the thirsty, clothed the naked, and visited those who were sick or in prison. Those who will be cursed are those who neglected these works of love and mercy.[11]

In this sermon, Jesus urges his followers to see him in the form of the outcast, the prisoner, and the hungry. In the faces of the poor, Jesus says he will live on and judge those who adhere to his teachings. Jesus calls upon us to follow him and continue the work he started with his disciples. We are urged to imitate the pattern of Jesus' life by living with openness to God's will and in service to others.

Jesus calls for us to be instruments of peace and justice. Within the Christian tradition, there are three types of justice: commutative, distributive, and social.[12] Commutative justice calls for fairness in all agreements and exchanges between individuals and groups. Distributive justice requires that the allocation of resources such as income, wealth, and power in a society be evaluated in light of its effects on the poor, those persons whose basic material needs are unmet. Social justice implies that all people have an obligation to be active and productive participants in the life of society and that society has a corresponding duty to enable them to participate in this way. Social justice implies a duty to organize society's economic and social institutions so that each person can contribute to society in ways that respect the dignity of their work and freedom. Justice is at the core of biblical teachings on economic life.

Economic Justice for All:
A Framework for Economic Life

In 1986, the U.S. bishops finished a multi-year process of drafting, gathering input, and publishing their pastoral letter *Economic Justice for All*. The letter draws on fundamental biblical teachings as the basis for their moral vision for the United States. Like a companion document on war and peace, it drew in part on testimony from a wide array of experts including ethicists, economists, and business leaders. Both documents emerged from a brief season in which U.S. bishops set out to exercise prophetic and pastoral leadership in bringing Catholic teaching to bear on matters of public policy.

In circulating the letter, the U.S. bishops originally hoped both to provide guidance for Catholics and to add a moral voice to the public debates in the United States over economic policy. In introducing the letter, the bishops noted that the Catholic Church in the United States is uniquely positioned to contribute to this debate with its enormous diversity that crosses lines of race, class, politics, and ideology.[13]

The Catholic community has the potential to transcend traditional political distinctions of left and right. In 1996, in observance of the tenth anniversary of the economics pastoral, the bishops wrote:

> Our tradition emphasizes rights and responsibilities, and advocates greater personal responsibility and broader social responsibility. We recognize the vital roles and limits of markets, governments, and voluntary groups. We hope in this anniversary year we can get beyond some of the false choices and ideological polarization in the economic debate and join in a renewed search for the common good.[14]

The pastoral letter stimulated a great deal of national media attention and educational programs at the parish level. Over twenty years have passed since the bishops' pastoral. Even by most Catholics it is hardly remembered and among many who do remember it may evoke a dim recollection that it was a naïve or failed experiment — which simply proved how pointless it was for church leaders to comment on matters of public policy. But if that is true, that is to dismiss the relevance of faith to the world in which we live, and that goes completely against the clear teaching of Christ and generations of church teaching, right up to the present.

On the tenth anniversary of the pastoral letter in 1996, the bishops rearticulated ten principles for a Catholic framework for economic life.

They provide timeless organizing principles for our discussion of Gospel values.

1. The economy exists for the person, not the person for the economy.

2. All economic life should be shaped by moral principles. Economic choices and institutions must be judged by how they protect or undermine the life and dignity of the human person, support the family, and serve the common good.

3. A fundamental moral measure of any economy is how the poor and vulnerable are faring.

4. All people have a right to life and to secure the basic necessities of life (e.g., food, clothing, shelter, education, health care, safe environment, economic security).

5. All people have a right to economic initiative, to productive work, to just wages and benefits, to decent working conditions as well as to organize and join unions or other associations.

6. All people, to the extent they are able, have a corresponding duty to work, a responsibility to provide for the needs of their families, and an obligation to contribute to the broader society.

7. In economic life, free markets have both clear advantages and limits; government has essential responsibilities and limitations; voluntary groups have irreplaceable roles, but cannot substitute for the proper working of the market and the just policies of the state.

8. Society has a moral obligation, including governmental action where necessary, to assure opportunity, meet basic human needs, and pursue justice in economic life.

9. Workers, owners, managers, stockholders, and consumers are moral agents in economic life. By our choices, initiative, creativity, and investment, we enhance or diminish economic opportunity, community life, and social justice.

10. The global economy has moral dimensions and human consequences. Decisions on investment, trade, aid, and development should protect human life and promote human rights, especially for those most in need wherever they might live on this globe.

1. The economy exists for the person, not the person for the economy. This principle is the opposite of what many of us feel and is a fundamental challenge to the credo of the market. Instead of feeling as though the economy is organized to provide sustenance and enable the flourishing of our families, many find that instead they are serving an invisible God of the market. Recall the stories of the people in chapter 1. They all, even the most affluent, feel that they must contort their lives and values to the external demands of economic survival.

It is worth reflecting deeply about what life would be like if the economy existed for the person, not the person for the economy. When we've asked people the question ("What would be different, if the economy was organized to serve people, not people serve the economy?"), here are some of their responses:

- I'd have more time to be with the people I love.

- I'd spend less time in meaningless toil for money and more in productive work for my community.

- I would not lose sleep over what might happen if I got a serious illness.

- My community would be more ecologically healthy, as there would be less urgency to exploit the earth.

- I would feel less fear for my children and grandchildren's future.

These responses clearly come from outside the values and priorities of the market system.

2. All economic life should be shaped by moral principles. Economic choices and institutions must be judged by how they protect or undermine the life and dignity of the human person, support the family, and serve the common good. The way the economy is organized is not morally neutral. Yet many pretend that somehow the economy exists outside of human values and judgments. State budgets, laws governing trade, tax policy — all are deeply infused with value judgments and decisions. The question is what values are these moral decisions based on?

The church has several "bottom line" criteria in terms of which moral principles we should use in judging the ethical quality of our economy. Does it protect life? Does it promote the dignity of the person? Does it enable the family to flourish? Does it serve the common good?

All these questions measure something fundamentally different from the values of the marketplace with its overriding focus on measurable profit.

3. A fundamental moral measure of any economy is how the poor and vulnerable are faring. We might use a variety of market indicators to measure economic activity — like the Gross Domestic Product or the Dow Jones Industrial Average. But these indicators only measure marketplace transactions — where goods or services are exchanged for money.

They do not measure health, well-being, security, kindness, charity, caring, freedom, or fairness. In other words, they are not *moral* measures. Even an indicator like the "median income" is not a moral measure, though it contributes to our understanding of who is benefiting from the economy.

The measure of health and justice is not how prosperous the wealthy are, or even how the middle class is faring. The moral measure is how well "the least of these" are doing. In the time of Jesus, these were the poor, the widow, the orphan, and the stranger in the land. And these literal indicators remain remarkably relevant in our time.

As we look at the economic picture of our country, we can use the same measures that Jesus did: How are poor people doing? Does a particular economic policy hurt or help the poor? What about orphans and poor children? What is the economy like for elderly widows and single women raising children? How does the society and economy treat immigrants, those who are strangers in our land? Does a proposed tax cut reduce or widen the gap between rich and poor? President Franklin D. Roosevelt put it this way: "The test of our progress is not whether we add more to the abundance of those who have much, it is whether we provide enough for those who have too little."

If we were to develop a moral index for the economy, an alternative to the Gross Domestic Product, it would measure these questions. Perhaps we could call it the COWS Index (Children, Orphans, Widows/Women, and Strangers/Immigrants). It would measure how the most marginalized people in our society are doing including the number of children in poverty.

4. All people have a right to life and to secure the basic necessities of life (e.g., food, clothing, shelter, education, health care, safe environment, economic security). Because each of us is a sacred being, created in the image of God, we have an inherent claim on the necessities of life. In the United States, this birthright is based on a recognition that our society in particular is wealthy and abundant and our economy produces enough for everyone. Note that below in Principle #6, there is a corresponding duty to work and contribute, so these rights are linked to our responsibility to contribute to society with our labor.

5. All people have a right to economic initiative, to productive work, to just wages and benefits, to decent working conditions, as well as to organize and join unions or other associations.

In the Christian perspective, labor is sacred and fundamental to our dignity as humans. Work is the way in which we as humans contribute to God's creation. This is fundamentally different from the view of labor in the marketplace, where work is both a means to earn a living and a commodity, a cost to be reduced.

The economy should be organized, therefore, to enable people to do meaningful and productive work, to earn enough to support the flourishing of families and to contribute to society. Biblical teaching advocates just compensation for a fair day's work, decent working conditions, and rest for "re-creation." The bishops defend the right of workers to form associations, including unions for the purposes of collective bargaining. As we will discuss throughout the book, many people suffer from lack of productive work or inadequate wages.

6. All people, to the extent they are able, have a corresponding duty to work, a responsibility to provide for the needs of their families, and an obligation to contribute to the broader society.

The right to basic needs and economic initiative come with clear responsibilities. Those who are able have a duty to work, provide for their family's needs, and contribute to the common good. Work can be either in the paid labor force or in the "caring economy" of raising children, or providing for elders and disabled people.

The statement that we have an obligation to the broader society is worth stressing. Our duty is not only to earn an income and pay one's own bills, but also to give to charity, pay taxes, and volunteer to address the society's unmet needs. In the credo of the market, the wealthy no longer have to contribute to society's work once they've accumulated or inherited substantial wealth. But in the Gospel lexicon, everyone is a volunteer. As the Pontifical Council for Justice and Peace wrote, "The common good involves all members of society, no one is exempt from cooperating, according to each one's possibilities, in attaining it and developing it."[15]

7. In economic life, free markets have both clear advantages and limits; government has essential responsibilities and limitations; voluntary groups have irreplaceable roles, but cannot substitute for the proper working of the market and the just policies of the state.

We seek a balance between private enterprise and government intervention, the rights of private capital and the common good. Church teachings affirm the importance of free markets, private business enterprise, private property, and entrepreneurship. Private business and free markets are engines of economic productivity, innovation, and efficient distribution.

Christian teachings also state that there are limits on the absolute rights of ownership: "Business and finance have the duty to be faithful trustees of the resources at their disposal. No one can ever own capital resources absolutely or control their use without regard for others and society as a whole."[16] Capital resources refer to substantial investment capital and control of corporate stock, as well as the raw materials, machines, equipment, buildings, and other items that are used to produce goods and services.

Gospel teachings don't subscribe to the fashionable notions of "let the market decide" or "let government decide." Neither are moral agents. Christian teachings affirm the role and limits of government as a force for the common good while warning against too much central state power and the threat it poses to economic initiative and freedom. Christian tradition advocates "subsidiarity," that decisions be made closest to those affected, and that the central government should not usurp decision-making power best left at the local or lower levels (see further discussion in chapter 7). But Catholic teachings underscore that government must play an essential role in defending the common good and ensuring economic opportunity and justice. Government is a defender of human dignity of last resort, when other institutions closer to the problem fail.

Catholic teaching also celebrates the role of "voluntary groups," those institutions that are neither government nor business. This independent or nonprofit sector includes religious charities, civic organizations, universities, labor organizations, research organizations, and political groups. This sector is vital, but not a substitute for either business or government.

8. Society has a moral obligation, including governmental action where necessary, to assure opportunity, meet basic human needs, and pursue justice in economic life.

Christians do not envision a "survival of the fittest" society, with the weak and unlucky living in extreme deprivation. Nor do we envision a society with rigid and enforced equality. Catholic social teachings state clearly that society has a moral obligation to ensure a level playing field with stepping-stones of opportunity in the form of quality education, health care, and productive employment.

The church also believes that society has a moral responsibility to guarantee that basic human needs for all are met. Society in this case refers to all sectors, but especially government and the voluntary sector. The voluntary sector, including Catholic Charities and other faith-based organizations, plays a vital role in feeding the hungry, housing the homeless, running job training programs, and meeting other urgent needs. The nonprofit sector is adept at finding innovative, flexible solutions to poverty, inequality, and social problems. But the church rejects the notion that government has no role to play in solving social problems. The independent nonprofit sector will be the first to declare that it is not equipped to promote and ensure justice on the scale of city, state, and federal government. The government, for instance, is critical to enforcing rules against discrimination, financing public and private affordable housing, and investing in larger-scale research and development. It is hard to imagine the charitable nonprofit sector as able to respond to society's needs on the scale of the food stamp program, Social Security, or children's health and nutrition programs. Each sector has a role to play in promoting the common good. There are no hard or fast rules about who should play what role.

There may be some cases where government should play the role of employer of last resort, as it did during the Great Depression of the 1930s. The Works Project Administration provided jobs and dignity for thousands of unemployed adults, and the benefits of those projects still remain today.

9. Workers, owners, managers, stockholders, and consumers are moral agents in economic life. By our choices, initiative, creativity, and investment, we enhance or diminish economic opportunity, community life, and social justice.

This statement essentially says: "We are all responsible." In our modern society and politics, there is a constant shifting of responsibility and a search for the guilty. In the end, no one claims responsibility for anything. Few say, "The buck stops with me." Large corporations in the market make an art out of shifting costs off their balance sheets and onto someone else or society. But again, our religious teachings turn this cultural tendency on its head.

We are all actors in the economy in multiple roles, and we are *all* responsible. We might be a worker, but through our pension fund we are owners of corporations and responsible for their conduct. We might be a manager of an advertising company, but we are also parents and consumers, concerned about the violent and over-sexualized messages that our children hear and see. We may have little ownership of assets, but as a consumer our choice of products has moral implications. Consumers who have chosen not to buy clothing made in sweatshops or with child labor have transformed the market. We may feel as though we don't have choices, but in fact we make dozens of moral decisions each day that "enhance or diminish" economic justice.

It is true that some people have significantly more power in our economy and democracy, and these individuals have an even greater responsibility as stewards and moral actors. But there is no passing the buck, even if we think we play only a small part in a larger economic drama.

10. The global economy has moral dimensions and human conse-quences. Decisions on investment, trade, aid, and development should protect human life and promote human rights, especially for those most in need wherever they might live on this globe.

While the global marketplace may seem beyond our influence, our Christian responsibilities and duties carry over to the global economy. Those of us who live in the United States have enormous power in the global economy, whether we acknowledge it or not. This means we have a duty to understand our power as consumers, owners, workers, and citizens and to work to protect human life and rights.

The rapid integration of the global economy is probably the most sig-nificant "sign of our times" that we must grapple with. Billions of our neighbors in other countries live in extreme poverty, without adequate food, potable water, or access to health care. Over thirty thousand chil-dren a day die of malnutrition and disease, a fact almost too dizzying to comprehend. Others live in totalitarian societies, without basic human rights and freedoms.

Our religious challenge is take the Christian principle of solidarity into the global context. We must strive to remember that we are "one body" with all of humanity, that the suffering of our neighbors diminishes us, and we must act to protect life and promote human rights beyond our national borders. In the words of John Paul II, "Solidarity too must become globalized."[17]

Looking at the Economy through the Lens of Church Teachings

It is tempting to look at the injustices of our economy and conclude that "this is just the way things are." But our faith challenges us to decode the underlying values of our secular society and to reflect on where we choose to act with Gospel values. This is not easy. The values of the market are the default position of secular society. Almost all of us raised in the United States have deeply internalized the creed of the secular market. Sometimes friends who have immigrated to the United States and are therefore less steeped in our culture can help us see this more clearly.

Our challenge is to learn nothing less than a new way of looking. We are already well trained to look at the economy as shoppers, workers, or investors. We have probably internalized the modern secular religion of the marketplace that is subtly reinforced daily on the news and in advertising. A deeper appreciation for biblical economics will cause us to reassess our accustomed ways of looking at the evening news, financial reports, and credit card statements. It will illuminate the moral issues underlying our life as consumers, employees, business owners, lenders, borrowers, and citizens.

Many of the values of the current economy are in direct conflict with our religious values. We can discern this by reflecting on questions such as:

- Which aspects of our culture and economy affirm life? Which do not?

- When does our economy recognize the sacredness of each person? When does it fail?

- In what ways does our economy distribute its benefits equitably? Where does it concentrate power and resources in the hands of a few?

- When does it promote the common good? When does it encourage excessive materialism and individualism?

- How do our culture and economy value and treasure children and when does it fail?

- Does the economy encourage economic initiative? Provide freedom of choice in jobs, consumer items, and opportunities?

- Do we have the free time to be with the people we love and help those in need?

- How does the economy and society acknowledge and provide support for the important role of parenting? Where are the gaps?

- Do our society and government adequately protect children from exposure to violence and consumerism?

- What are the ways the society protects the environment and ensures public health? Where does it fail?

- Do our communities place adequate emphasis on building parks, on protecting places of beauty and sacredness?

- Do two children born of different races and classes have comparable opportunities to have a decent life?

In reflecting on these questions, you may be wondering whether the larger U.S. culture and economy are operating by a different set of rules and values. Let's look deeper at the conflicting values in our system. One framework to consider is the distinction between "market values" and "Gospel values."[18]

Gospel Values and Market Values

We live in a culture that worships the marketplace. There is a distinction here between respecting the market and understanding its place in our economy — and worshiping it. Market worship is the most prevalent form of idolatry in our culture today. And unfortunately, we have allowed these market values to virtually trump all our religious values, sometimes even in the lives of our parishes.

Theologian Harvey Cox wrote in *U.S. Catholic* a thoughtful and humorous commentary called "The Market Is My Shepherd, and I Shall Want and Want and Want...."[19] After reading and studying the business press and media for many years, Cox discerned a coherent theological framework in the market credo.

> Behind descriptions of market reforms, monetary policy, and the convolutions of the Dow, I gradually made out the pieces of a grand narrative about the inner meaning of human history, why things had gone wrong, and how to put them right. Theologians call these myths of origin, legends of the fall, and doctrines of sin and redemption. But here they were again, and in only thin disguise: chronicles about the creation of wealth, the seductive temptations of statism, captivity to faceless economic cycles, and, ultimately, salvation through the advent of free markets.

One characteristic of the gospel of the marketplace is its tendency to put everything up for sale. Instead of maintaining some noncommercial "no go zones" or even sacred realms of human endeavor, in the religion of the market anything can be a commodity. Cox writes,

> In Catholic theology, through what is called "transubstantiation," ordinary bread and wine become vehicles of the holy. In the mass of The Market a reverse process occurs. Things that have been held sacred transmute into interchangeable items for sale.

Things that it was once unthinkable to consider "for sale" are now traded for Mammon: air, water, human body organs, religious icons, sacred burial grounds, outer space, and more. This "radical desacralization," in Cox's words, changes our human relationship to God's creation.

> The latest trend in economic theory is the attempt to apply market calculations to areas that once appeared to be exempt, such as dating, family life, marital relations, and child rearing. Henri Lepage, an enthusiastic advocate of globalization, now speaks about the

"total market." ... Like the Hound of Heaven it pursues us home from the mall and into the nursery and the bedroom.

The media focus on clashes around the world between Hindus and Muslims, Protestants and Catholics, and the myriad differences between different faith traditions. But the differences between the great religions pale compared to what they all share in common juxtaposed to the religion of the market. At the heart of all these religions is a respect for life, creation, and human potential. There is a common recognition of a sacred reality that cannot be bought or sold. The values of the market and the values of the great religions have radically different perspectives on the human body, the human community, the natural environment, and the importance of life.

The Gospel values tradition, for example, views nature as a gift of creation that we are charged with protecting and being good stewards of. God retains the title, but gives us a long-term lease, as long as we are faithful trustees. The market perspective is that nature is a commodity and its value is measured in what its products can be sold for as real estate, timber rights, minerals, bottled water, etc. We can buy it and dispose of it.

Gospel values respect the sacred and recognize the revered values of human beings and natural gifts. This includes some of the common institutions that we build together, such as religious communities, social gathering places, and institutions to pass on knowledge and protect the natural bounty. Market values do not recognize the sacred, and this has led to commercial encroachment upon the sacred. With Gospel values, there are some things that cannot be sold. In the market, everything is for sale. Everything and everyone has a price.

The values of the Gospel recognize that humans are individuals *within* community, that we draw life from the human community and have obligations to it. Market values recognize only the individual — as worker, owner or consumer. The market does not recognize any duties of obligation or solidarity toward anyone else. To help someone other than one's self is "economically irrational" behavior according to the values of the market.

Market values celebrate the new, the young, and the mobile. Gospel values celebrate old and new, young and old, tradition and innovation, and staying put!

Gospel values affirm a feeling of attachment and a reverence toward certain locations and human artifacts. We find holiness in places, in a mountain, a cathedral, a rural chapel, the site of an apparition, a plaza, a historic shrine. Market values have no attachment to place, except to the extent it provides a market for products or a source of raw materials.

Gospel values treasure the unusual, the irregular, the traditional, and the quirky. A sacred Irish well, the tradition of saying the rosary, a tree trunk in a Mexican chapel, a river bank, a prayer association — they don't conform or add anything to the measurable economy. Market values push the society toward a common mold and a homogenized set of values. The market eliminates twenty varieties of traditional corn or apples and replaces them with one dominant genetically modified version that is easier to harvest, but doesn't necessarily taste better.

Gospel values recognize that the most valuable things cannot be measured or priced. Market values recognize only what can be measured and sold. The raising of children or taking care of a sick relative doesn't count in the Gross Domestic Product. Divorces, however, make the GDP go up, as people set up more households.

Gospel values find security in community and in sharing. The parable of the loaves and the fishes is an example of putting faith in the abundance that comes from sharing. The market finds security only in accumulation. Market values profess to be driven by what the customer wants. Gospel values are rooted in the notion of the greatest common good.

We currently live in a society that does not affirm life, in part because of the internalization of market values in our everyday lives. Gospel values recognize that a person has inherent worth by virtue of being part of God's creation.

Market values do not recognize an inherent worth in people except as workers, owners, or consumers. The market ranks people by their worth in the commercial marketplace, not by their inherent worth. Those who are worth a great deal command enormous salaries, perks, ownership stakes, and privileges in our society. Those whom the market does not recognize as "worth much" are invisible and are marginalized in extreme poverty.

How often do we go through life sorting other human beings into market categories? How often do we forget the holy and inherent worth of all we encounter? Opening our eyes to the ways each of us has unwittingly internalized the values of the market can be shocking and painful, but it helps in our journey to build an economy based on Gospel values.

Chapter Three

Signs of the Times #1
Life in the New Economy

Betty Martin serves up a second helping of lasagna to a young man with neatly combed hair wearing a pullover sweater. She has volunteered at the church's soup kitchen in Tacoma, Washington, for over four years, but the sight of hundreds of hungry men and women still bewilders her. "When I get a chance, I like to just sit and talk to people and hear their stories," she smiles. "People come here for very different reasons. Some are homeless but have full-time jobs. Some have apartments, but live close to the edge of homelessness. This is often the only hot meal they have for the day. I wish I better understood the economic forces pushing people in our doors."

For Betty and others, the process of reflecting on church teachings about the economy begins with their own experience. This is sometimes called "reading the signs of the times." The phrase is a reference to the Gospel of Matthew: "Do you know how to discern the appearance of the sky, but cannot [discern] the signs of the times?" (Matthew 16:3). It has been taken up as a post–Vatican II commitment to reflect on our religious teachings in light of experience. Subsequently, a number of religious groups have adopted the phrase "reading the signs of the times" as part of undertaking critical or social analysis.

You don't have to be an expert to read the "signs of the times." Part of it is simply engaging your curiosity about day-to-day economic activity: What do things cost? Where were they produced? Are people working different types of jobs in one community than another? Who gets paid what? What costs are rising? What are people talking about most? What are they fearful of?

What follows is a brief discussion of the some the "signs of the times" that many individuals encounter in their own lives. Think of these as "home front" indicators of personal economic health and wholeness. Or as humorist Jim Hightower says: "We've heard enough about the Dow Jones. We want to know how Donna and Doug Jones are doing!" Later we will put these personal experiences into a larger context.

Is the Economy Working for People...
or People for the Economy?

In one program we did on Catholic perspectives on the economy, we asked people what were some of the signs of the times they saw in their personal lives or in the lives of their neighbors. They identified a number of experiences, including:

- Being constantly squeezed for time and having less free time for important things
- Having difficulty saving money or getting out of debt
- Feeling squeezed by rising health care costs
- Finding it hard to pay rent or afford mortgage payments
- Fighting a commercial assault on their children
- Dealing with feelings of job insecurity
- Fearing for the future of their children and grandchildren in the U.S. economy

In this chapter, we will begin the process of analyzing the economic trends that underlie these experiences.

The Time Squeeze: "Our Lives Are Going 90 mph"

The Gladney family is feeling the pressure. Fredrick and Nicole Gladney of Milwaukee, both in their early thirties, have two children, two incomes, and two shifts. Nicole works as a marketing coordinator and Fredrick as a deputy sheriff. Their combined incomes make them middle class, but the pace of their lives includes the combined stresses of demanding jobs, children's harried schedules, and a "marriage by cell phone."

Part of their juggling act is necessitated by their working different shifts. Fredrick works a 2:00–10:00 p.m. shift, leaving Nicole feeling like a "single parent with an extra paycheck." A few years ago, Nicole was injured in a car accident and hospitalized. Initially Fredrick's work supervisor turned down his request to take a day off. "My issues are work and family and policies to make sure the nuclear family stays intact," said Nicole.[1]

The Gladney family is hardly unique in today's economy. One of the most powerful clashes we experience between market values and Gospel values is over how we spend our time. The overwork and over busy-ness is a wound, a painful lack of time and emotional energy for the things that matter.

For most households, the amount of time spent in the paid workforce has steadily grown over the last few decades. Since 1972, the overall number of hours worked per household has steadily increased. Average workers now spend 200 more hours a year on the job than they did three decades ago. This translates into an extra five weeks a year.[2] The average middle-income family saw their annual paid household workload rise from 3,331 hours to 3,719 hours, an increase of ten additional weeks a year.

The decline in free time has serious implications for the quality of family life and civic participation. Christian teachings are clear on the importance of work and its essential part in the creation process. But paid work is not the only work we are called to do. Most voluntary work is not included in traditional market indicators, yet it is the real measure of personal and community health. This includes the unpaid and often undervalued part of the economy, the caring economy, for example, caring for children, elders, and those with special needs, and participation in community and civic life.

A caring economy includes making a casserole for someone in need, or providing childcare for a parent in the hospital. Women do most of this unpaid work while also earning wages in the paid labor force and juggling exhausting demands.

The Christian corollary to teachings about the value of work is the Sabbath teachings on the importance of rest and renewal. Declining free time means less time for "re-creation," for vacations, time with family, nurturing marriages, caring for others, and space for prayer and religious life. Overwork leaves less time for friendships and involvement in parish life, children's schools, neighborhood issues, and political organizations.[3]

The time bind for many families is a clear example of how the "structures" of the market economy touch each of our lives individually. Wage laws, technological change, cultural norms, declining wages and savings — all contribute to an environment where households are spending more and more time in the paid workforce.

Some are not sympathetic to those in a time bind that many families are in. They point out that some people are poor managers of their time and resources and are personally responsible for the bind they are in. They observe that people spend too much time watching television or working to buy things. Others suggest that if these individuals had focused on their personal education and training, they might be able to find better paying jobs. Surely there are situations where this might be true. But there are major changes happening in the U.S. economy that are pushing more people to work longer hours and more hours per household.

One of the factors driving the overwork cycle is that wages, factoring out inflation, have remained stagnant while the costs of everything from housing to health care to energy have soared. So many households, in an effort to survive, have taken second jobs or increased the number of adults and youth working. An average family aspiring to purchase a home now needs two incomes to pay a mortgage. The number of households with two income earners has dramatically increased. The percentage of married mothers in the paid workforce grew from 38 percent in 1969 to 72 percent in 2003. This increase was not accompanied by a decrease in hours worked by men. The result is that parents have fewer hours to spend with children. The disastrous effects of this are obvious.

For many employers and companies, the cost of adding an additional employee is much higher than paying an existing worker to work longer hours, even at overtime rates. This is due to the added costs of training, workspace, health care, and other benefits. And most salaried and professional workers don't have clearly defined maximum workweeks. So many manufacturing and professional workplaces have experienced "speed-ups," as the same workers are being asked to accomplish more.

A generation ago, the promise of technological progress was envisioned to be a decline in toil and an increase in leisure. But with the advent of cell phones, pagers, and email, the 24/7 economy squeezes more and more time and attention from the caring economy and recreation.[4]

Given these trends, you'd think that there would be a more public outcry for increased wages and reduced hours. Where is the movement, as there was a century ago, for a shorter workweek?[5] Perhaps it's the overwork trap: people don't have time to be part of organizations pressing for a shorter workweek because they have so little free time in their lives.

In 1993, Congress passed the Family and Medical Leave Act to give unpaid time off to working families in order to deal with newborn or adopted children or family emergencies. The legislation was passed after well-publicized horror stories of parents losing their jobs because they chose to accompany a child with a medical emergency to the hospital and remain by the child's side. But few families can afford to go without paid work for long, so few have been able to take advantage of the law. Instead they are faced with the painful choice between leaving a child in need or keeping their job for family survival.

Even for families not living on the brink of survival, the decline of leisure time results in a serious decline in family, parish, and civic life. Parents return home after ten-hour workdays and long commutes with less emotional and physical energy. This puts enormous pressure for family connection to occur on rare work-free weekends and the periodic vacation.

Not all economies are organized like the U.S. economy. Many countries have different *rules* governing work time, wages, vacations, and paid leaves. As the average work year for a U.S. worker approaches 2,000 hours, the average work year for a French worker is 1,545 hours and for a German worker is 1,444. Many Europeans view the lack of leisure time in the United States as evidence that we are servants to the credo of the market. Defenders of our work hours argue that this explains high rates of U.S. productivity. But many dispute this, pointing to evidence that longer work hours do not necessarily increase productivity.[6] And even if it did increase productivity, what are the social trade-offs? One of the most important "moral measures" of the economy is how a particular policy or practice impacts on the flourishing of the family.

A recently study by the Harvard School of Public Health examined 168 countries and concluded that "the United States lags dramatically behind all high-income countries, as well as many middle- and low-income countries when it comes to public policies designed to guarantee adequate working conditions for families."[7] The study found that:

- 163 of 168 countries guarantee *paid* leave for mothers in connection with childbirth; 45 countries offer such leave to fathers. The United States does neither.

- 139 countries guarantee paid sick leave, but the United States does not; 37 countries guarantee parents *paid* time off when children are sick, a policy that doesn't exist in the United States.

- 96 countries guarantee paid annual (vacation) leave. The United States has no paid vacation policy and has among the shortest vacations in the industrialized world, averaging only two weeks. For many U.S. workers in the "temp" workforce, or who are paid as full-time consultants, there is no such thing as a "paid vacation." Unlike many European countries, where workers are legally guaranteed between four and six weeks of vacation a year, in the United States vacations are not legally mandated.

- 84 countries have laws that fix a maximum limit on the workweek. There is no statutory limit to the U.S. workweek.

There is no reason why the United States couldn't have different rules governing work and leisure. In chapter 8, we explore some of the inspiring work people are doing to address overwork. It is fundamentally a

Figure 3.1

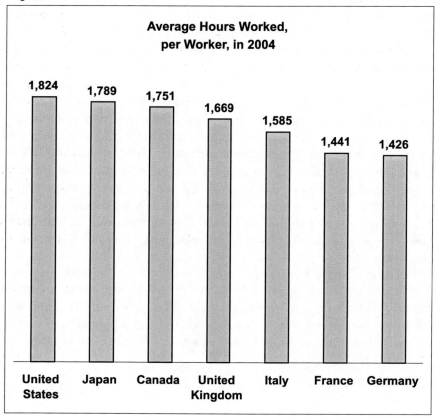

Source: Lawrence Mishel, Jared Bernstein, and Sylvia Allegretto, *The State of Working America 2006 / 2007* (Ithaca: Cornell University Press, 2007), Table 8.7.

moral choice of what we value. As a society, we have allowed the market value of work to trump the Gospel value of family time.

"I've Got Less in My Bank Account and More on My Credit Card Bill"

Rob and Laura are a young couple in their thirties. When they were first married, they felt they were financially stable enough to begin raising a family. Laura had a job working in the business office of a local plastics manufacturing company, and Rob had trained to be an air conditioning and heating technician. With a combined income of $50,000 they were able to live comfortably. Rob's parents even gave them a down payment to purchase their first home.

After Laura gave birth to twins, they found themselves financially and personally stressed. Without affordable childcare, Laura quit her job. Unfortunately, Rob's heating and cooling business took a downward turn at this time, pushing them to the brink. The financial stresses wiped out their savings and forced them to rack up $40,000 in credit card debt. As journalist Tamara Draut described in her book *Strapped: Why America's 20- and 30-Somethings Can't Get Ahead*, Rob and Laura "never dreamed that starting a family would plunge them into such deep financial and emotional straits."[8]

One important economic sign of the times is reflected in our personal bank accounts. In today's economy, a lot of people, young and old, are feeling "strapped." Our national savings rate — the percentage of our national income set aside for savings — has steadily declined over the last two decades. In 2005, the U.S. savings rate was minus 0.4 percent, which meant that for the first time since the Great Depression, Americans spent more than they earned. That minus 0.4 percent rate was down from 4.6 percent in 1995 and 9.0 percent in 1985.[9]

The United States has the lowest savings rate of any advanced industrialized country. In Germany, for instance, the savings rate in 2003 was 10.8 percent and in Japan it was 7 percent.[10]

The corollary to declining savings is the rising level of personal indebtedness and bankruptcy, which have reached all-time highs. The indebtedness of U.S. households, after adjusting for inflation, has risen 35.7 percent between 2001 and 2005. The level of debt as a percentage of after-tax income is the highest ever measured in our history. Mortgage and consumer debt is now 115 percent of after-tax income, twice the level of thirty years ago.[11]

Some people justifiably blame credit cards and other easy forms of debt. Almost 60 percent of all American households are unable to fully pay off their credit card bills at the end of the month. Late payments are at a five-year high.

In 2004, average household consumer debt was approximately $9,000 according to the credit card industry. Yet if we exclude the 40 percent of households that pay off their monthly credit card balances, the remaining households have an average consumer debt of closer to $13,000. Between 1990 and 2004, total credit card debt increased from $243 billion to $735 billion. The number of households that have declared bankruptcy has steadily increased over the last decade. In 2005, 2.39 million U.S. households filed for bankruptcy, a 12.8 percent increase over 2004.[12]

It is easy to focus on the personal causes for declining savings, rising debt, and bankruptcy. Many point to individual irresponsibility as the

Figure 3.2

Source: Bureau of Economic Analysis, National Income and Product Accounts, Table 2.1, Personal Income and Its Disposition.

cause for growing debt and bankruptcy. They argue that people get into debt when they spend too much and get caught up in America's consumer culture of buying the latest gadget. Many adults over the age of sixty remember when people didn't borrow as much and when credit cards were a rarity.

Our Gospel values lens, however, encourages us to look beyond simple theories of personal responsibility or structural change. The reality is there are both *personal responsibility* and *structural economic* causes to the consumer debt and declining savings crisis. There are alarming examples of individual foolishness and irresponsibility. Cultural attitudes toward borrowing have changed, encouraging people to get into debt as if it were a natural state of being.

We must go beyond the individual explanations. There is a very aggressive debt-pushing industry, which combined with aggressive advertising, is a dangerous combination. Also behind the story of declining savings and rising debt are structural changes in the economy that lead many people to borrow for fundamental necessities.

Stagnant or falling wages for middle- and low-income workers is another explanation for increasing indebtedness and bankruptcy. Many families go into debt simply trying to cover their basic needs. More and more, people are using credit cards to purchase groceries, prescription drugs, and basic necessities. According to researchers from the Boston Federal Reserve Bank, the principal explanation for declining savings is not profligate spending, but rising health care costs and other involuntary fees such as child care and interest payments. People declare bankruptcy after unexpected events such as major illness or job loss, combined with low income and little savings.[13]

The number one cause of bankruptcy is catastrophic health care bills that families are unable to pay. A 2005 study of "medical bankruptcy" found that half of individuals who file for bankruptcy, almost 2 million people a year, do so because of health care costs. Three-fourths of these are people who started their illness with health insurance coverage, but were driven to financial ruin after high co-payments, exclusions of coverage, loss of coverage, or job losses resulting from a personal health crisis.[14] As report author Elizabeth Warren described, medical bankruptcy is a traumatic "double-whammy," as families face medical and financial stresses.

> Bankrupt families lost more than just assets. One out of five went without food. A third had their utilities shut off, and nearly two-thirds skipped needed doctor or dentist visits. These families struggled to stay out of bankruptcy. They arrived at the bankruptcy courthouse exhausted and emotionally spent, brought low by a health care system that could offer physical cures but that left them financially devastated.[15]

If rising health care costs are the underlying cause, then current and proposed laws to make it more difficult to file for bankruptcy will do nothing to address the real problem. Placing impediments to filing for medical bankruptcy is no different, in Warren's words, "than a congressional demand to close hospitals in response to a flu epidemic."

While individuals are responsible for their actions, there are aggressive debt-pushing industries that also share responsibility. In 2005, the credit card industry sent out 6 billion pieces of mail to encourage new

DEBTOR NATION
U.S. CONSUMER DEBT STATISTICS

- There were 1.3 billion credit cards in circulation in the United States in 2004.

- The credit card industry mailed over 6 billion credit card offers in 2005, an average of six offers per household per month.

- The credit card industry took in $43 billion in fee income from late payment, over-limit and balance transfer fees in 2004, up from $39 billion in 2003. Credit card late fee penalties totaled over $11 billion in 2005.

- Total American consumer debt reached $2.2 trillion in 2005. Total American consumer debt first reached $1 trillion in 1994.

- Total American consumer debt increased 41 percent between 1998 and 2004. Average household credit card debt has increased 167 percent between 1990 and 2004.

- Average Americans had over seven payment cards in their wallet including credit card, retail store cards, and bank debit cards in 2004.

- The average interest rate paid on credit cards was approximately 14.54 percent in 2005. Average household interest payments were $1,164 in 2004.

- The rate of personal savings in the United States dipped below 0 percent for the first time since the Great Depression, hitting negative .5 percent in 2005.

- In 2004 the consumer debt to net worth ratio was 21 percent, the highest rate in 55 years.

borrowers and expanding borrowing. This is an average of six solicitations per person every month.[16] Students entering college are greeted at freshman orientation by booths offering Visa, MasterCard, and Discovery cards. Many of today's students graduate with three forms of debt: college loans, debts to their family, and credit card debts. As a result, young middle-income families are still paying off school-related debts when they would rather be looking to purchase a home. Surely, if Jesus were alive today he would throw the credit card vendors out of the student union.

DEBTOR NATION (continued)

- A typical credit card purchase is 12–18 percent more than if cash was used (as of 2004).

- 30 million Americans (40 percent of homeowners) refinanced their mortgages during the three years (prior to Q3 2005), with over half applying the proceeds to eliminate credit card debt.

- Seven out of 10 low- and middle-income households reported using their credit cards as a financial safety net, i.e., to pay for car repairs, rent, or housing repairs and medical expenses, rather than relying on savings in 2005.

- According to a national survey, the most significant predictor of financial stress is if households rely on using credit cards to cover non-discretionary living expenses like rent, groceries and medical expenses (Q3 2005).

- According to a 2004 study, the number one cause of divorce is financial stress.

- In 2004, 76 percent of undergraduate college students had at least one credit card in their name with an average of outstanding balance of $2,169. 32 percent of students had four or more credit cards in 2004.

- In 2004, the average college student graduated with $16,500 in student loans, up 74 percent since 1997.

- In 2004, most credit card debt of older Americans was driven by health care expenses and the increased cost of prescription medication.[17]

To address the "bank account" problem, we need to look at a variety of personal, cultural, and structural economic forces. We need to change the culture of permissive borrowing and credit. We need to provide debt-counseling services to assist individuals to cut up their credit cards and plan for their future. But if we focus only on individual behavior, we ignore the complicated structural changes in the economy forcing people to borrow heavily to get an education — or to fill in for declining wages and security. Chapter 4 will dig deeper into these causes.

"Squeezed by Rising Health Costs"

Nick was twenty-five years old when he walked into an emergency room and was diagnosed with neurofibromatosis, a genetic disorder that causes tumors to grow on or inside his body. Unfortunately, in the weeks following his diagnosis Nick missed so many days of work for medical reasons that he lost his job and health benefits.

Because he is a single young adult, he is not eligible for any form of government assistance. So he pays out of pocket for his treatment. Now $20,000 in debt from emergency room expenses, he's changed his phone number to avoid daily calls from bill collection agencies.

Because of his debts, he is postponing treatment and his condition is getting worse. During the past two months, he lost over fifty pounds and has had blackouts that lasted up to six hours at time. Nick told health care advocates at Families USA that he "is losing hope of getting anything done." In the richest nation on earth, a young man is facing a desperate situation.[18]

Do you or a loved one not have health insurance coverage? Have you seen your "out-of-pocket" health care costs rise? Have you paid more to see a specialist? Have you contributed at the local general store or subway stop to the emergency health care expenses of a child who needs a new kidney or suffers from a catastrophic illness?

The United States has the highest percentage of households without health insurance in the industrialized world. In 2005, 46.6 million people had no health insurance at all. The ranks of the uninsured are found disproportionately among people of color. Thirty-four percent of Hispanics have no health insurance compared to 22 percent of blacks and 12 percent of non-Hispanic whites.[19] This does not include the estimated 11 million undocumented workers in the United States, the majority of whom are Latino. The number of uninsured is expected to rise by over 1 million persons a year until 2010, when it will exceed 50 million, or one in five Americans. This is a dramatic increase from 31 million uninsured people in 1995. Over 80 percent of the individuals with no health insurance are employed, though often in temporary or part-time jobs.

As mentioned previously, catastrophic health care expenses are the leading cause of personal bankruptcy, even among families with health insurance coverage. For those families fortunate to have health insurance, medical coverage is taking a bigger bite out of their paychecks. Between 2000 and 2004, the cost of health coverage grew by 35.9 percent, dramatically outpacing earnings. Over this same period, the number of households paying over 25 percent of their earnings on health care rose by 23 percent, from 11.6 million to 14.3 million.

Figure 3.3

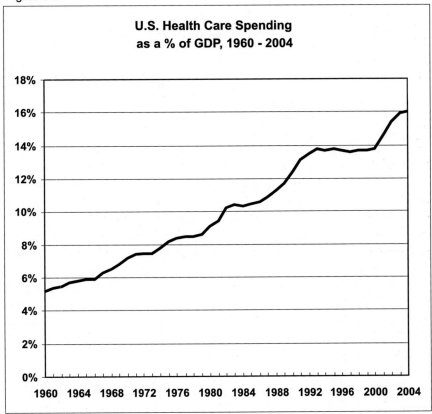

**U.S. Health Care Spending
as a % of GDP, 1960 - 2004**

Source: Department of Health and Human Services, Centers for Medicare and Medicaid Services, 2006.

Some people are suspicious of health insurance statistics. They argue that people have a personal responsibility to maintain health insurance so that the burdens are not shifted onto the community and government. There are, of course, examples of young adults choosing to spend money on things other than health insurance. There is a rigorous debate about the causes of high health care costs, with some pointing to costly litigation and high malpractice insurance.

No one will deny that there is a full-blown crisis in health care costs and insurance coverage. It is not news that health care costs have dramatically risen as a percentage of household budgets, business expenses, and share of the Gross Domestic Product. Expensive innovations in medical technology, the rising cost of prescription drugs, and costly specialist care have pushed the annual growth of health costs way ahead of income growth.

Moreover, the cost of long-term care is exploding as Americans live longer and more independently. These costs include nursing home and home health care services, but also the growing use of assisted living residences, home modifications, new assistive technologies, and adult day care. One study by the Government Accounting Office estimated that long-term health expenditures for the year 2000 were $137 billion.[20] Overall long-term health care costs will continue to rise as the baby boomer generation retires and the average age of the population increases.

Prescription drugs take a growing bite out of the health care dollar. The annual growth in the price of common prescription drugs regularly and substantially exceeds the rate of inflation. This is particularly hard on seniors who spend the most on prescription drugs. The Medicare drug benefit that went into effect in 2006 does little to rein in the cost of drugs, as Congress sided with the powerful pharmaceutical industry in writing the law. The new law prohibits Medicare from bargaining for lower drug prices, as the Department of Veterans Affairs does. A study by Families USA found that between January 2001 and January 2004, the average price for the top thirty brand-name drugs increased by nearly 22 percent, 3.6 times the rate of inflation.[21]

Whatever the reasons, the high cost of health insurance is a drain on the economy. For employers who provide health insurance, the cost of covering employees is an ever larger line item in their budgets.[22] Some employers have eliminated health insurance coverage as an employee benefit. Between 1999 and 2003, the percentage of Americans covered by employer-sponsored health insurance declined from 70.4 percent to 63 percent. Over the same period, lower-income workers with insurance, those who need it most, dropped from 40.3 percent to 35 percent.

Other employers have cut benefits and asked employees to pick up higher deductibles, the cost of medicine, and certain services. Particularly squeezed are retirees, who in many cases gave up wage increases during their work careers in order to have health care in their retirement years. In one recent survey of 458 companies that had retiree health plans, all but 23 now require monthly contributions by retirees age sixty-five or older.[23] General Motors recently cut $1 billion out of their retiree health care program, resulting in dramatic increases in retiree co-payments and deductibles.[24] Rising drug costs are particularly stressful for aging retirees, most of whom are on fixed incomes.

In the wealthiest nation on the planet, 46 million people without health insurance is a national scandal. See the resources section for organizations and efforts that address the need for health care reform.

"It's Hard to Keep an Affordable Roof over Our Heads"

Leonard and Donna are newlyweds, still in their first year of marriage. But instead of living in their starter apartment or home, they are homeless and living under an overpass in Baltimore. There are few shelters in the city that accommodate couples, and they prefer to stay together.

"I was living in an apartment," Leonard explained to a *Baltimore City Paper* reporter. "After we got married, she moved in with me, and then things went downhill. I lost my job at the restaurant. And then city welfare paid my rent for a little while. They stopped. So we had no choice [but eviction]."

Donna and Leonard don't do drugs, and they are able to hold down part-time jobs doing newspaper delivery. But they can't save enough money to get into housing. Donna is pregnant and dreams of becoming a massage therapist.

They face a "Catch-22" when they try to get services, a bind that many people who have hit bottom encounter. Because they are poor and homeless, they don't have the papers to prove they are destitute. They lack state-issued IDs, copies of birth certificates or a marriage license, all of which cost precious money to get. Their only forms of identification are transit passes, library cards and mail. This makes it difficult to open a bank account and to save money, a necessary first step toward putting down an apartment deposit.

Leonard hit bottom in Baltimore before and finds times have changed since his last period of homelessness. "Eleven years ago things were a lot more accessible as far as outreach goes," he says. "People seemed to be a lot friendlier. But now it's like people look [at us] as if we are nothing."[25] The sting of poverty is now accompanied by feelings of isolation, that no one cares — compounded by the meanness and hostility they often encounter.

Homelessness is the most acute and visible housing problem in the United States, and it confronts a surprisingly high number of people. Like Leonard and Donna, many American families face the challenge of keeping an affordable roof over their heads, either by renting an apartment or purchasing their own home. One out of three households in the United States — in rural areas, center cities, and suburbs — faces significant housing problems, including high housing costs in relation to income, overcrowding, poor living conditions, and homelessness. At the core is the crushing confluence of rising real estate values and stagnant wages.[26]

The number of people facing homelessness every year is estimated to be 3.5 million, including 1.35 million children.[27] Many who are about to become homeless are invisible because they are doubled-up or tripled-up with other families in crowded situations. Housing instability and homelessness lead to unacceptable individual suffering and high social costs, especially for children who miss school and lack a stable home life.

Along with health care costs, the bite that housing costs take out of the family budget has steadily increased since World War II. Half of all renter households pay more than 50 percent of their income for housing, a condition referred to as "shelter poverty." In order to stay housed, these families forgo adequate food, health care, and other necessities in order to hold on to their housing. The number of these shelter-poor households has been over 30 million since the early 1990s, an increase of more than 70 percent since 1970. The rates of shelter poverty are highest among families with children.[28]

There are many personal problems that contribute to individual housing distress, including mental illness, addictions, and poor planning and decision making. Some people will not be able to attain housing stability until these underlying personal problems are dealt with. But there have also been dramatic structural changes in the housing market in the last thirty years. Prior to the 1970s, many cities had large stocks of affordable single-room occupancy housing — or "rooming houses" — where people with very low incomes or minor problems could live. While the accommodations weren't luxurious by any means, it was still housing. With the urban renewal and gentrification of the last several decades, tens of thousands of single-room units were eliminated or converted to other uses. The loss of these "bottom rungs" in the housing market has contributed directly to the rise in the number of homeless in our communities.[29]

There are many explanations for the growing gap between incomes and the cost of housing. For more than a century, government at various levels has played an important role in addressing problems of affordable housing, including homeownership assistance. Today, 5 percent of the population lives in low-income rental housing subsidized by federal, state, or local governments. But resources for housing have suffered some of the greatest budget cuts in the last several decades. Between 1980 and 2003, federal housing assistance was cut by almost half.[30] Ironically, the greatest allocation of public expenditures for housing now takes the form of tax breaks like the home mortgage interest deduction, essentially a tax break benefiting middle- and upper-income homeowners. In 2005, the federal government spent $72.6 billion in housing-related tax breaks. Over 36 percent of the tax breaks went to households with incomes over $100,000. This is twice the amount of government housing money spent on households with incomes below $18,500.[31] Heavy subsidies for the highest income households and no assistance for the poor are in clear conflict with Gospel teachings.

Many public policy makers point to homeownership as a national ideal. And the good news is that our national homeownership rate is now at 68.9 percent, its highest point ever. There has also been slow but steady progress in terms of increasing the number of minority homeowners. But there are many people for whom the dream of owning a home is still out of reach.

The most rapid expansion of homeownership and middle-class opportunity occurred in the two decades after World War II, when our nation made an unparalleled investment in homeownership. Between 1945 and 1968, the percentage of American families owning their own home rose from 44 percent to 63 percent.[32] Thanks to federally subsidized mortgage and insurance programs such as Farmers Home, the Veterans Administration, and the Federal Housing Administration, millions of households got on the wealth-building train. Most programs to expand homeownership have since been substantially reduced, explaining why during the four decades after 1965 the United States has increased homeownership by less than 6 percent.

Homeownership, however, is not for everyone. The costs of acquisition, maintenance, and utilities are not always best for very low-income and elderly people. Nor is homeownership always the best investment. There is a serious prospect that home values have been greatly overvalued in the last decade, leading to a "bubble" in housing related wealth. A major adjustment in home values, particularly in high-flying real estate markets on the East and West coasts, could contribute to a serious recession in the U.S. economy. For some, stable, affordable, and well-managed rental housing is the best solution.

Visitors from other countries are often shocked that the United States tolerates such high levels of poverty and destitution. The situation requires a moral commitment to end homelessness and shelter poverty and public policies that reflect these values. Chapter 8 includes stories of organizations working effectively to address housing problems at the local level.

"My Children Are Being Assaulted by Commercialism"

Joe Feagan is like a lot of fathers who worry about the kind of world his daughter is growing up in. One day his eight-year-old girl came into the kitchen singing a tune she heard on an advertising jingle: "Do it to me, do it to me, all night long." In her hand was a girl's magazine with a clothing advertisement depicting young preteens dressed as little prostitutes. Feagan says that was the moment when he blew a fuse. "I know it is my responsibility as a parent to monitor the kind of television, music, and images that my daughter faces," Feagan said. "But it feels like it's coming at her at a million miles an hour. And a lot of advertising seems like it's out to undercut my role as father."

Joe Feagan's outrage is understandable. We tolerate a massive amount of commercialism in our lives. After paying almost $10 to see a first-run motion picture, the movie-going audience is now subjected to fifteen to twenty minutes of movie previews and advertisements. Pull up to a gas station and you can watch an advertisement for a soft drink while you pump your gas. A bus goes by wrapped in advertisements. Log on to the Internet and you are subject to thousands of advertisements in an hour.

The pace of commercial "ad creep" into every sphere of our lives is pressing forward virtually unabated. Children are major targets of these advertising campaigns and the messages aimed at them are frightening. Children are encouraged to buy sodas and sugary foods, which has contributed to an epidemic of obesity. They are exposed to over-sexualized advertising aimed at selling everything from cigarettes and make-up to clothing and financial investment products.

Upon arrival at the schoolhouse, a typical first grader can identify over two hundred brands and will begin to accumulate an average of seventy toys a year. The average eight-to-thirteen-year-old is watching an estimated three and half hours of television a day and viewing forty thousand commercials a year. Children this age make an average of three thousand requests a year for products and services.

Children in elementary school now get math textbooks salted with brand name products. One textbook published by McGraw-Hill includes the following math problem: "Will is saving his allowance to buy a pair of Nike shoes that cost $68.25. If Will earns $3.25 per week, how many weeks will Will need to save?" Next to the text is a full-color picture of a pair of Nikes. Another word problem states: "The best-selling packaged cookie in the world is the Oreo cookie. The diameter of an Oreo cookie is 1.75 inches. Express the diameter of an Oreo cookie as a fraction in the simplest form."[33]

Direct marketing to children has gotten much more aggressive in the last two decades. As long as there has been marketing, there have been efforts focused at children. But what has changed is a shift in marketing strategy and an increase in the volume of marketing resources aimed at children. Twenty years ago, advertising for children's products was aimed at "gatekeeper" mothers, trying to convince them to buy things. But today's advertising is aimed directly at children with the goal of influencing their parent's purchases — not just of toys and sweet cereals, but also of family cars with DVD players, technological gizmos, and other large acquisitions. Children are coached on the potency of nagging and what some marketing experts call "pester power."

There is a health epidemic with 9 million children overweight and obese. Some people are quick to blame parents and children themselves for the problem of obesity. But the problem goes beyond a simple lack of dietary self-discipline. Food vendors are working to load Americans and children in particular with way more fat calories at a time when children are reducing the amount of time exercising to burn those calories. No previous generation has been bombarded with, in the words of journalist Eleanor Randolph, such an "unprecedented wave of sophisticated, multimedia advertising designed to hook them on unhealthy food before they are old enough to understand what is happening."[34]

In 2004, marketing experts estimate that $15 billion was spent on marketing aimed at children, a 1500 percent increase from $100 million spent on kid-focused television advertising in 1983. Marketers have segmented the children's market into dozens of submarkets, each with its own conferences, experts, and tailored messages. The Annual KidPower Food and Beverage Convention discusses how to sell more junk food and sodas to kids while the Annual Hispanic KidPower meeting focuses on marketing to the growing Latino youth market.

Cable TV giant Nickelodeon boasts to potential advertisers that it "owns kids 2–12." Juliet Schor, in her book *Born to Buy*, explains many of the new tactics of the advertising industry, such as enlisting trusted institutions like the Girl Scouts to partner on marketing to girls.[35] Advertising on television has increased, but new avenues are growing rapidly such as promotions, sponsorships, and direct marketing such as museum exhibitions built with the Lego brand.

Christian parents are particularly alarmed by the commercial, cultural, and sexual values that children are being exposed to. Yet we feel we have little power to protect our children from these forms of assault. The solution, in Schor's words, is to "decommercialize childhood." She chronicles some of the movements against marketing to kids and families that have unplugged their televisions and reduced the amount of advertising that enters their homes.

Parents and organized groups have begun to push back against the encroachment of advertising with legislative solutions. Why not outlaw food advertising aimed at kids, just as tobacco and X-rated movies are regulated now? Why not an outright legal ban on advertising and product placement in schools? The consumer organization Commercial Alert has organized a campaign including a poetic "Parents' Bill of Rights." The statement affirms that the primary responsibility for the upbringing

THE MEASURE OF UNEMPLOYMENT

A clear moral measure of the economy is how easy it is for someone to find a job. Therefore the goal of full employment and the measure of the unemployment rate can tell us a lot about the health of an economy from a "Gospel perspective."

In the United States, the Bureau of Labor Statistics measures the rate of unemployment. As of August 2006, the unemployment rate was 4.8 percent. By race, the unemployment rate is 4.1 percent for whites, 9.5 percent for blacks, 5.3 percent for Hispanics, and 2.7 percent for Asians.

The "unemployment rate" however, does not tell us the whole story of how the economy is impacting people because of what is included and not included. There are many personal situations that are not measured that may make the jobless rate appear lower than it actually is. For example, the unemployment rate does not count people who have lost their jobs and whose unemployment benefits have run out. It doesn't include "discouraged" workers who have been looking for work for long periods of time. Nor does it include full-time students and prisoners — the later category masking higher rates of unemployment because, as of 2005, roughly 0.7 percent of the U.S. population was incarcerated.

The unemployment rate does not include people who, for mostly good reasons, are "outside the labor force" — meaning they have no job or are not looking for various reasons including family responsibilities or mental or physical disability. There are many people who are retired or have minor disabilities and still need to work. While these individuals are not measured in the formal unemployment rate, many enter the work force during periods of economic expansion.

of children resides with parents but that "an aggressive commercial culture has invaded the relationship between parents and children, and has impeded the ability to guide the upbringing of their own children." One of their legislative proposals includes the "Child Privacy Act," which gives parents "the right to control any commercial use of personal information concerning their children and the right to know precisely how such information is used."[36]

THE MEASURE OF UNEMPLOYMENT (continued)

Further clouding the picture, the unemployment rate considers people who work part-time, as little as one hour a week, as employed. Those in temporary jobs include workers who would like to work full-time and have a more secure job and seasonal workers who have little job security.

A more accurate moral indicator than the unemployment rate might look at the changes in the total number of full-time jobs in the economy compared to the number of people seeking work. For instance, it is useful to know that there were 8 million people seeking full-time work at the end of 2004. This tells us more than the unemployment rate (4.7 percent at the time). Another more accurate measure would compare the total number of hours people work in a month with the total number of hours people would like to work.

Obviously, unemployment cannot be reduced to zero because there are always people coming and going from jobs and shifts among employers and local businesses. Some economists believe too low a rate of unemployment fuels wage and price inflation because of competition for workers. Because powerful people in the United States care more about containing inflation than reducing unemployment, policy makers have moved away from the goal of full employment and tolerate higher rates of unemployment.

High unemployment, however, often comes with serious human costs. Lack of work, and long and discouraging searches for work, can be damaging to the human spirit and cause unacceptable levels of financial stress, domestic violence, and poverty. This is why many faith activists call for fuller employment policies and for government to play the role of "employer of last resort."

Good news includes the demise of Channel One, the television network that several years ago was planted in over 25 percent of the nation's middle and secondary schools and claimed a captive viewing audience second only to the Super Bowl. Channel One bombarded classrooms with advertising for junk food and other commercial products. After parents and educators rebelled, Channel One now faces extinction. A growing number of states are considering legislation banning junk food sales and advertising in schools, with Maine passing landmark legislation. See the resources section for additional ideas on combating the commercial assault.

"My Job Feels Insecure"

Natasha is a thirty-one-year-old technology worker from Santa Clara, California. She had a good job with Palm, the handheld computer maker. As part of her job, she was flown to India several times to train people she didn't realize would eventually be her replacement. "I was told repeatedly before training my Indian team in Bangalore that my was job safe," Natasha recalled. "Then I got laid off."

For six months she juggled looking for a new job and helping her six-year-old son deal with an anemia problem. It wasn't easy, as even higher skilled technology jobs were being outsourced.

Natasha worries about what kind of economy her son will eventually work in. "The nature of today's economy makes me extremely fearful for his future. I was raised to think that getting an education and working hard assure you a good and steady job. Seeing off shoring [of jobs] run rampant in our country has helped me realize that I need to prepare my son to be a player in the global economy."[37]

Like Natasha, a growing number of workers are feeling the sands shifting below their feet, wondering if their job will be here tomorrow. Even people who have had long-term job security are seeing a growing number of jobs eliminated or outsourced, downsized, or combined with another job. Between January 2000 and 2005, over 3 million manufacturing jobs have been lost.

The good news is that unemployment remains relatively low, at 5 percent, a bit higher than the 4 percent level in 2000. Unfortunately, the United States has only 1.3 million more jobs in 2005 than it did in March 2001, at the start of a recession. This is why people consider the years 2002 to 2005 as "jobless recovery," because if the employment rate had truly returned to pre-2001 recession levels, the economy would have created 3 million more jobs.[38]

But low unemployment doesn't change people's feeling of insecurity. As we shall discuss in chapter 4, the nature of work itself is changing. People may be employed, but they are working as consultants or temporary contract workers, without long-term job security. Wages have been stagnant or falling for the majority of families, and the median household income, adjusted for inflation, has fallen five years in a row between 1999 and 2004. There is legitimate reason for concern.

"I'm Worried about Opportunities for My Children"

Like Natasha, who lost her job to outsourcing, many families look at these signs of the times in terms of work and opportunity and are understandably worried about their children's future. Even families that have attained a modicum of economic stability and affluence still worry about the prospects for their children. U.S. Catholics as a whole have seen their standards of living rise in the last two generations. But the next generation, regardless of their starting points, faces unique challenges in terms of the cost of education and finding stable work in the new economy.

For many people who grew up in the decades after World War II, there was a robust ladder of opportunity. Not only were there subsidies for first-time homebuyers, discussed above, but the larger economic expansion contributed to a sense of a "rising tide lifting most boats."

In the 1950s, returning war veterans received a package of benefits known as the "GI Bill," which included housing, education, and business start-up grants. But the educational benefits went well beyond those who had served their country in military uniform. Millions of people became the first in their families ever to attend college, thanks to grants that made tuition free or very accessible. Reading the profiles of the "greatest generation" of people who came of age during the 1930s Depression and World War II, reveals what a remarkable and prudent investment this was.[39]

Today the cost of college has dramatically increased, while state and federal public assistance has declined. Federal college loans have replaced the grants that were once more widely available. As a result, student debt has increased from an average of $8,200 per student in 1991 to $19,200 in 2005.[40]

These trends not only put enormous stress on families with children in college, but also preclude many of the country's poorest families from attending college at all, especially four-year schools. Fewer than 8 percent of students at private four-year colleges come from families with annual income under $25,000. We would hope that the percentage of low-income students at public and community colleges would be better, but only 20 percent of such low-income families attend community college and only 11 percent are at public four-year colleges.[41] The racial divide in education is also reflected in the profile of who completes college. In 2001, 29 percent of whites had completed four years of college compared to 11 percent of Hispanics, and 17 percent of blacks.[42]

Higher education is, unfortunately, still a privilege that many low-income households cannot reach. In 2004, over 83 percent of high school students from the top fifth of income-earning households, those with family incomes that were greater than $81,529, attended college, compared to 56 percent of students from the middle three quintiles, with incomes between $17,702 and $52,750.[43]

All the experts will tell us that education, particularly higher education and advanced training, is key to participating in the new global economy. Yet at the same time, access to higher education is out of reach or a formidable challenge for a growing number of families. What kind of society are we becoming when the rungs of the ladder of opportunity are being removed?

These are just a few of the signs of the times facing our families. Shrinking free time, declining savings, rising health costs, growing job insecurity, a commercial assault, and shaky future prospects are all symptoms of larger changes in the economy and society. It is important to put these personal experiences into a larger context, as we have begun to do. To stop here, however, would be to act only on the "signs of the times" without analysis.

In Part Two we will analyze the root causes of why our economy is changing and what we can do about it. We will explore the possibilities for thoughtful action that come from a deeper understanding of Gospel values and the economy.

Part Two

If you offer your food to the hungry and satisfy the needs of the afflicted, then your light shall rise in the darkness and your gloom be like the noonday. The Lord will guide you continually, and satisfy your needs in parched places, and make your bones strong; and you shall be like a watered garden, like a spring of water, whose waters never fail. Your ancient ruins shall be rebuilt; you shall raise up the foundations of many generations; you shall be called the repairer of the breach, the restorer of streets to live in.

— Isaiah 58:10–12

Chapter Four

Signs of the Times #2
What Kind of Country Are We Becoming?

Our challenge is to enlarge our picture of the economy as much as possible to analyze the forces shaping our personal lives. What is happening in your community? What is working and not working in your local economy? What are the indicators of health and insecurity? What do we notice about the national economy? What is happening to wages, work, wealth, and poverty?

The underlying trends we see are:

- Stagnant wages for the vast majority of workers.
- A growing disparity between the highest-paid and the lowest-paid workers.
- Poverty that persists even during times of economic recovery.
- A concentration of assets and wealth among the wealthiest households.
- A persistent racial wealth gap.
- New levels of inequality that threaten social stability, solidarity, and democracy.

Income and Wages

Maria Elise Nelson works two jobs, one at a fast-food restaurant in the suburbs of Washington, D.C., and another for an office cleaning company. Both jobs pay a minimum wage. She takes her children to school in the morning and reports for her restaurant job. Her children's school bus drops the children at the restaurant in the afternoon, where her children sit at a table and do their homework while their mother hustles around, periodically stopping by to help them. After dinner, her mother helps her put the children to bed so she can work an additional four hours for the office cleaning company, getting home around midnight.

Maria Elise's life is directly shaped by economic rules such as a minimum wage that is too low to support a family. If she earned a living wage, she wouldn't need to work a second job and could spend more time with her children.

We have already alluded to one of the most troubling trends of the last three decades: the stagnation of real wages. The term "real wages" refers to a way of measuring wages that adjusts for the effect of rising prices. Since 1973, real hourly wages for the vast majority of workers have risen only a little bit, from $15.76 in 1973 to $16.11 in 2005.[1]

This is a marked contrast with the thirty years after World War II, when every income group saw their real incomes double. But since 1979, the bottom fifth of families have seen their incomes decline by 2 percent, the middle fifth has seen a modest gain of 15 percent, and the top fifth has seen incomes go up by 52 percent.[2] Stagnant wages for the majority of U.S. workers, as we shall discuss further, puts enormous stress on working families who face rising prices for many basic human needs.

An important part of the current picture is the way income gains have concentrated among the wealthiest households. In 2004, over half of all income gains went to the top fifth. But as we look closer at the picture, we see that the bulk of these gains went to the wealthiest 5 percent and even 1 percent of households. These are families with incomes over $173,640 a year or, in the case of the richest 1 percent, people with incomes over $1 million a year.[3] According to the IRS, incomes rose fastest among the top 1 percent, and within that group, the biggest gain went to the richest one-tenth of 1 percent. These are the 145,000 taxpayers with reported incomes over $1.6 million who saw their incomes rise by almost 10 percent from 2002 to 2003.[4] These super-wealthy are generally found in fifty affluent urban and suburban zip codes on the East and West coasts and outside a handful of Midwestern cities.

One of the most dramatic trends is the shocking disparity of compensation between chief executive officers (CEOs), the leaders of U.S. companies, and average workers. In 1980, the ratio between highest and average paid worker in a company was 42 to 1. By 1990, this ratio had grown to 107 to 1. But by 2005, the ratio had exploded to 411 to 1.[5]

From 2004 to 2005, executive pay rose by an average of 27 percent to $11.3 million, according to a survey of two hundred large companies.[6] Many of these pay increases were unrelated to the company's performance. For instance, Ivan G. Seidenberg, the chief executive of Verizon Communications, received a 2005 salary of $19.4 million in salary, bonus, and other compensation, a 48 percent increase over 2004. At the same time, the company reported a 5.5 percent decline in earnings and a 26 percent decline in stock price.[7] The paychecks of many chief executives rise even in the years when they lay off thousands of workers, which is a departure from the notion of shared sacrifice that existed in the three decades after World War II.

These trends are even more troubling when top managers personally benefit from war, national tragedy, or energy shortages. Since the 9/11 attack, the CEOs of the top thirty-four military contractors saw their compensation double compared to the four years previous to 9/11. During a time of war and sacrifice, these top managers were paid an average of $7.2 million in 2005, 44 times more than military generals with twenty years of experience and 308 times more than army privates.

As oil prices rose dramatically between 2004 and 2006, the top fifteen CEOs of oil companies also saw their pay rise dramatically. Big Oil CEOs were paid an average of $32.7 million in 2005, compared with $11.6 million for all CEOS of large U.S. firms. CEO William Greehey of Valero Energy took home the oil industry's biggest paycheck in 2005, collecting $95.2 million. But wages for workers in the industry remained stagnant. A construction worker in the oil industry would have to work 4,279 years to equal Greehey's one-year earnings.[8] A growing pay gap between CEOs and workers, especially in the defense and oil industries, is further evidence of a breakdown in solidarity and shared sacrifice in U.S. culture.

Poverty

One of the most important moral measures of the economy is how the poor are faring. Over four decades ago, Michael Harrington wrote *The Other America,* holding a mirror up to America's self-image of affluence with a searing picture of poverty. Harrington's book was widely read, including by President John F. Kennedy, and was credited with contributing to the moral and intellectual resolve behind the 1960s "War on Poverty."

But for over a decade, concern for poverty has vanished from the public dialogue and conditions have steadily worsened. For several years in a row, the number of families and individuals in poverty and economic hardship has risen. The official poverty rate in 2005 was 12.6 percent, up from 11.7 percent in 2001. The poverty rate for children increased from 16.3 percent in 2001 to 17.8 percent. There are 36 million Americans in poverty and almost 13 million of them are children.[9] Among African American children, 33.6 percent are living in poverty. Among all seniors, those age sixty-five and over, over 9.8 percent live in poverty, with 23.9 percent of African American seniors in poverty.[10]

Figure 4.1

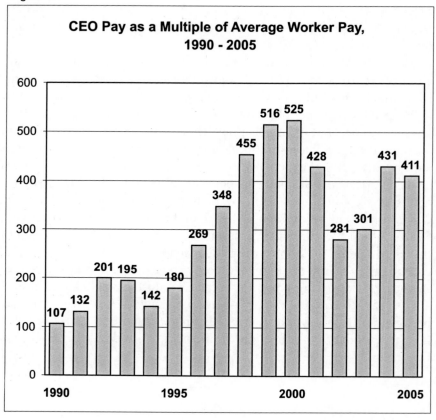

CEO Pay as a Multiple of Average Worker Pay, 1990 - 2005

Source: United for a Fair Economy and Institute for Policy Studies: Executive Excess 2006, based on data from *Business Week* and the Bureau of Labor Statistics.

Poverty usually declines during periods of economic recovery and growth. But in the last few years poverty has grown. According to traditional economic indicators, since 2001 the United States has had three years of economic growth. But during these years, the ranks of our nation's poor have grown by 4 million. In no prior recession dating back to 1960 has poverty increased in the second and third years of an economic recovery.[11]

It is hard to put a face on statistics about poverty, though some writers have done this well (see "The Working Poor" on p. 64).[12] What we generally know is this:

- Children have much higher rates of poverty than adults.

- Poverty among the elderly, thanks to Social Security and other forms of support, has not grown.

- One of five Latinos in America, 9.1 million people, lives in poverty.

- One in four African Americans, 8.8 million people, lives in poverty.

- While there are fewer Asian Americans living in poverty, 1.4 million, their rate of poverty has grown the greatest in the last few years.[13]

Many poor families face hunger, hardship, ill health, and despair. The number of poor Americans who suffer from "food insecurity" and hunger has tracked the poverty rate. Adults in most poor families are employed, though they are not paid enough to lift themselves and their dependents out of poverty.

Gospel perspectives on poverty do not focus only on the economic experience of lacking money, but also on the interaction between poverty and marginalization. Poverty is not only a deprivation of material resources; it is also exclusion from society — a real experience of isolation, loneliness, and disconnection from community life.

When we as Catholics talk about the "preferential option for the poor," we are not suggesting an adversarial slogan or advocating conflict between one class and another. We are simply acknowledging that "the deprivation and powerlessness of the poor wounds the whole community."[14]

If we are "one body," as preached by Jesus, then failing to care for the poor is an infidelity to God. As Fred Kammer writes in *Doing Faithjustice*, "If we forget the poor, we have forgotten God and the truth of our own radical interconnectedness: to God as life-giver and to one another as sisters and brothers."[15]

Wealth and Inequality

For several years, Edgar Proctor lived in a rooming house and worked as a barber in the northeast section of Washington, D.C. The idea of owning his own home was the farthest thing from his mind. "It seemed way out of my reach. I was saving a little, but even if I could get a down payment together, I didn't think I'd be able to afford a mortgage payment every month."

But then Edgar started to participate in a planned savings program with the Capital Area Asset Building Corporation. It required him to reduce his spending and think about saving in an entirely new way.

THE WORKING POOR

In his book *The Working Poor*, David Shipler offers a compassionate and no-nonsense look into the lives of America's working poor. Shipler doesn't try to shoehorn his narratives into an established framework about poverty, so his profiles capture the complex interaction of personal and economic structural forces that contribute to poverty. He spends years getting to know some of his subjects and their circumstances, taking us beyond glib and sweeping theories as their lives and voices speak for themselves.

Shipler tells the story of a woman named Leary Brock who moves from a crack-ravaged life on the streets of Washington, D.C., and drug treatment, to a tough-love job training program and a job with mobility at Xerox. But he also describes the lives of economically precarious sweatshop owners, restaurant managers, social workers, and farmers who are only one rung up the economic ladder from the low-wage workers they employ or counsel.

Some of the portraits are incredibly moving, like Shipler's description of the King family, a working poor family with abundant spirit from Claremont, New Hampshire. Shipler writes, "The fragile life of Tom and Kara King fell apart piece by piece until nothing was left but love and loyalty." With few financial reserves, the Kings and their three children hit bottom when Kara is diagnosed with cancer. Kinship, Shipler observes, "can blunt the edge of economic adversity. When a grandmother takes the children after school, when a friend lends a car, when a church provides day care and a sense of community, a parent can work and survive and combat loneliness." But even with strong family bonds, for the Kings, when their "reverses piled up one after another, they had no defense."

"The biggest challenge was to start denying myself some of the things I wanted instantly — like clothing, jewelry, a new car."

Edgar is excited when he talks about his new home. "I love it. It's just enough house for me, and it's in a real nice section of the city. Most of the people in the neighborhood are retirees, so it's pretty quiet, and everyone is real nice, and we look after each other."[16]

THE WORKING POOR
(continued)

Shipler describes the challenges facing America's working poor as "a constellation of difficulties," including mental and physical health care, education, and job readiness. *The Working Poor* validates an "individual responsibility" perspective that Christians bring to our understanding of the causes of poverty. This includes stories about teenagers having babies out of wedlock, poor parenting skills, and drug and alcohol abuse — personal behaviors that contribute to poverty. But Shipler never slips into a simple "blaming the individual" framework. Rather he shows how individual circumstances and choices interact with larger social forces that keep people poor. For every family,

> The ingredients of poverty are part financial and part psychological, part personal and part societal, part past and part present. Every problem magnifies the impact of the others, and all are so tightly interlocked that one reversal can produce a chain reaction with results far distant from the original cause. A run-down apartment can exacerbate a child's asthma, which leads to a call for an ambulance, which generates a medical bill that cannot be paid, which ruins a credit record, which hikes the interest rate on an auto loan, which forces the purchase of an unreliable used car, which jeopardizes a mother's punctuality at work, which limits her promotions and earning capacity, which confines her to poor housing.[17]

For people of faith attempting to understand the roots of poverty, *The Working Poor* has the poetry to move us, to deepen our individual and national resolve to change the untenable and unjust conditions that many of our neighbors endure.[18]

For most Americans, wealth means the same thing as it does for Edgar Proctor: the ability to save and hopefully to purchase one's own home. Poverty, work, and wages are all key indicators of economic health. But the ownership and distribution of wealth, which is often less visible, is also an important moral measure of well-being. Material wealth can be defined as "net worth" — what you own minus what you owe. For typical families, wealth takes the form of assets like cars, savings, home equity, and maybe a retirement plan. For wealthier families, wealth includes assets like stocks and bonds, businesses, second homes, commercial real estate, and luxury items like fine art or antiques.

How much wealth a person has is a critical indicator of economic security, since assets can be sold or borrowed against during times of need. By this measure, many people are on thin ice. Almost one in six households has zero or negative net worth. They owe more than they own, so they are living with no reserves and great insecurity. The number of households in this group has grown over the last twenty-five years, from 15.5 percent in 1983 to 17 percent in 2004.[19] This corresponds to the growing amount of personal debt that we discussed earlier.

Some individuals and families may appear deceptively wealthy because their income and consumption are high. But a new car or stories of Caribbean vacations may not reflect real wealth. They may actually have little savings and be deep in debt. Others may not appear wealthy, but may have a very high net worth and choose to live simple lives. One popular book refers to these folks as the "millionaire next door."[20]

Most financial planners suggest that individuals and families work to save the equivalent of at least six months of expenses to be able to cope with serious illness, divorce, job loss, or some other unforeseen event.[21] Unfortunately, only about half of the population has more than three months of savings to fall back on.

The lack of savings reserves is most acute in African American and Latino households. Over 80 percent of African American households and 79 percent of Latino households have three months or less of financial reserves.[22] In 2004, 13 percent of white households and 29.4 percent of black households had zero or negative net worth. The median white household wealth was $118,300, but the median black family had only one-tenth as much, or $11,800.[23] While income disparities between different racial groups have narrowed in the area of wealth, the legacy of racial discrimination has left a lasting mark.

A significant amount of wealth is passed on from one generation to the next. Parents help their children purchase homes, help pay for education, and pass on property at the end of life. Wealth-building opportunities grow and compound for some families, while barriers to wealth building can also accumulate over time.

If one group has been historically barred from getting aboard the wealth-building train because of the color of their skin, then this will affect their children's net worth and opportunities. Overt racism in mortgage lending was rampant only one generation ago, and other forms of racial exclusion and oppression are part of our current history. So the racial wealth gap today persists because of discrimination going back several generations.[24]

One of the most dramatic "signs of the times" has been the concentration of wealth at the top of the U.S. wealth pyramid. As with income, the bulk of the expansion of wealth over the last two decades has gone to the wealthiest 1 percent of families. In 1976, this wealthiest 1 percent of the population owned 20 percent of all private wealth. Today, this top 1 percent owns over 34 percent of all private wealth. To join the top 1 percent means having at least $5.8 million net worth. This group has more wealth than the bottom 95 percent combined.[25]

At the pinnacle of U.S. wealth and power, 2005 saw a dramatic increase in the number of billionaires. According to *Forbes* magazine, there are now over four hundred U.S. billionaires. The number of billionaires took a dramatic leap since the early 1980s, when the average net worth of the individuals on the *Forbes 400* list was $400 million. Today, the average net worth is $3.13 billion. The four hundred individuals now on the *Forbes* list have over $1.25 trillion combined wealth, up from $160 billion in 1982.[26]

As we shall discuss later, this trend of growing inequality of wealth does matter for everyone in U.S. society. It influences the kind of society we have and whether there are opportunities for everyone, including Edgar Proctor, to get on the wealth-building train. The dangers of concentrated wealth are also a central theme in the parables of Jesus. In addition to the threat it poses to democracy and stability, accumulated wealth can also become a form of idolatry. As theologian Fred Kammer, S.J., writes "The innate danger of the wealth is that it becomes dominant, it turns the order of creation on its head and our possessions have dominion over us, and not vice versa."[27]

The New Inequality

One overarching sign of the times in the United States is the growing disparity of income and wealth. We've seen changes in wages, wealth, and poverty rates, some dramatic over the last three decades. We've seen how the new inequalities put growing pressure on families — in terms of growing personal debt and bankruptcy, declining real wages, and barriers to opportunity for the next generation.

There is widespread agreement about the data and the picture of inequality. Conservative, liberal, and progressive publications all report roughly the same facts. The *Wall Street Journal, Business Week,* and the *Economist* have all had major features looking at the problem of wealth disparities and inequality. There is, however, some disagreement as to whether inequality matters and, if so, what to do about it.

Some thoughtful religious leaders and economic thinkers have argued that we should focus our efforts on alleviating poverty, not inequality. They argue, "It doesn't matter how rich the rich are. What matters is poverty." This explains the tremendous amount of charitable and governmental resources that are directed toward "lifting the floor," building ladders out of poverty for individuals and impoverished communities.

But inequality does matter, because concentrations of wealth and power distort our democratic institutions and economic system and undermine social cohesion. This section looks at the reasons why we should care about growing inequality. The next section will examine more of the underlying causes of inequality and changes in the economy.

Gospel perspectives on the economy are concerned about addressing both poverty and inequality. As the U.S. bishops wrote in their pastoral letter on the economy,

> This duty [of establishing a floor of well-being] calls into question extreme inequalities of income and consumption when so many lack basic necessities. Catholic social teaching does not maintain that a flat, arithmetical equality of income and wealth is a demand of justice, but it does challenge economic arrangements that leave large numbers of people impoverished. Further, it sees extreme inequality as a threat to the solidarity of the human community, for great disparities lead to deep social divisions and conflict.[28]

Concentrated wealth translates into concentrated political power. As Supreme Court Justice Louis Brandeis observed a century ago: "We can have concentrated wealth in the hands of a few or we can have democracy. But we cannot have both."[29] Brandeis was writing in the context of America's first Gilded Age, around 1890–1915, a period of extreme wealth inequality.

In a self-governing society such as the United States, we should be vigilant about the potential threat that concentrations of wealth pose to our democratic institutions, which in turn shape the rules of our economy. Political scientist Samuel Huntington observed that in the United States, "money becomes evil not when it is used to buy goods but when it is used to buy power.... Economic inequalities become evil when they are translated into political inequalities."[30] The problem is not how many yachts wealthy people buy, but how many senators.

There are, of course, many examples of the good and generous things that have happened thanks to the charity of wealthy individuals. John D.

Rockefeller, founder of Standard Oil, contributed billions to the advancement of medical science. Microsoft founder Bill Gates has funded innovative programs to address global public health. Such donations are to be commended and celebrated. But they do not address the problems rooted in the concentration of wealth.

Our democracy is now at risk because of the enormous power of accumulated wealth in so few hands. The practices of government, legislating and administering for the common good, have been warped by the financial clout of the few against the interests of the many. We now have a Congress more concerned about abolishing the inheritance tax for multimillionaires and billionaires than ensuring no children go to sleep hungry or providing foreign aid to eliminate extreme global poverty in our lifetime.

We can view this concretely in the concentration of media ownership, which inherently narrows the options for open discussion.[31] We witness it in the escalating amounts of money required to run for political office, which leads politicians to spend more time courting wealthy donors and less time relating to their less prosperous or poor constituents.[32] Anyone would have his or her worldview shaped by spending more time with major donors at $1,000-a-plate dinners than talking to constituents at local diners and church soup kitchens. As a result, we get a government primarily concerned with writing rules and administering regulations to serve the interests of its paying patrons. The power of the political contribution now trumps the power of the vote at the ballot box. And in the policy debates over what is really important in our nation, the agenda of concentrated wealth takes precedence six out of seven days a week.

Inequality and the Erosion of Solidarity. Randy Sandowski fondly remembers his childhood in the mid-size city of Appleton, Wisconsin. "When I was growing up, there wasn't such a big division between people," he observed. "Our fathers might have worked in different positions in the paper factory or other businesses, but everyone knew each other. They played softball and cards together and rooted for the high school football team." Randy remembers there being some ethnic divisions, but it wasn't the gulf of inequality that exists today. "All the kids went to the high school together, rich, poor, and middle class and all ethnic groups. Families watched out for each other. Today, it's as if people live in different planets. They don't interact in the same way."[33]

One of the consequences of growing inequality in communities like Appleton is the physical distance that occurs between classes and races. Gospel teachings are concerned about the distance between rich and poor because of the resulting breakdown in solidarity. As the distance widens between haves and have-nots, we forget that we are one body and that we are all in the same boat.

The civic life of an extremely unequal society resembles an apartheid society, with two or three Americas rather than one. People begin to live, work, worship, and socialize with people from only one sector of society and don't have deep connections with people from other sector. This leads to distance, misunderstanding, distrust, and class and racial antagonisms.

High levels of inequality lead directly to the construction of physical walls. A high percentage of new homes are being constructed in gated residential communities where people live behind walls and beyond gates with armed security guards. Over 9 million households in the United States live behind walls, similar to polarized societies like Mexico and Brazil.[34]

Such extremely unequal societies are physically bad for the health of rich and poor alike. A growing body of scientific research shows that the more unequal a society is, the worse its public health indicators.[35] While being poor is often dangerous to your health, you are even worse off if the overall society has wide disparities of wealth. The reason is simple: too much inequality leads to a breakdown in the social solidarity required for good public health.[36] Like Randy Sandowski described in Appleton, Wisconsin, "When people don't know each other, it's harder to take care of one another."

Solidarity is people taking responsibility for one another and caring for their neighbors. But for solidarity to happen, people must know each other or have institutions that transcend differences in class, culture, and race. In communities with great inequality, these institutions don't exist and solidarity is weakened.

How Inequality Erodes Opportunity. Inequality undermines the cherished American value of equality of opportunity. Part of the social dynamic of an unequal society is that wealthy people, those in the top 10 percent, rely less on the institutions of solidarity that are essential to social cohesion and often withdraw their financial support and participation. This is because many wealthy and powerful people "privatize" their family and security needs. Instead of depending on quality public education, vibrant libraries and community centers, and dependable public transportation, wealthy people typically utilize private schools, bookstores, and personal transportation. Instead of public parks and community recreation, the wealthy withdraw to private clubs and personal nature preserves.

There are two problems that result when wealthy families and individuals "privatize" their need for services. First, because they don't depend on "commonwealth" services as much, wealthier individuals would rather not pay for them. They prefer tax cuts and limited government, leaving more money to spend on privatized services. While problems in the area of health care and education are not solely the result of the withdrawal of affluent citizens, it does contribute to a cycle of disinvestment.

Second, the rest of society also suffers when the wealthy don't have a personal stake in maintaining quality public services. In a democratic society, good government and strong public institutions require "all hands on deck," especially those with disproportionate political power, connections, and capacity. For example, if a family doesn't use the public neighborhood swimming pool because they belong to a private club or spend their summers at a private beach house, they don't have a stake in ensuring that the public swimming pool is open all summer, well maintained, and staffed with qualified lifeguards. This lack of stake is even more graphic in terms of public education, where the withdrawal of affluent and even middle-class families has contributed to the severe disinvestment of some school districts.

As the most powerful and wealthy individuals in the society reduce their stake and investment in public services, the quality of these services deteriorates. A vicious cycle begins when it becomes rational, if you can afford it, to abandon public and community services. Non-wealthy families work extra hard to privatize their services as well, until there is a wholesale withdrawal from the public sphere. If you can't depend on the bus to get to work, you buy a car. If you can't rely on the local public or parochial schools to educate your child, then you stretch to pay for elite private schools. If you can't depend on the lifeguards to show up at the public pool, then you join the private pool. If you can't depend on the police to protect your neighborhood, you hire a private security service. The cycle of disinvestment continues and the costs of privatized services rise, trapping the remaining families in poor schools and neighborhoods lacking services.

We can see this disinvestment cycle at work in education, transportation and other services such as libraries, recreation, and policing. We can see it in the declining commitment to inner cities and vibrant urban life after two generations of suburbanization.

For the vast majority of people, their ability to meaningfully participate in society and achieve economic opportunities depends on the existence of a robust "commonwealth" of public and community institutions. As Bill Gates Sr., the father of the founder of Microsoft, wrote:

The ladder of opportunity for America's middle class depends on strong and accessible public educational institutions, libraries, state parks and municipal pools. And for America's poor, the ladder of opportunity also includes access to affordable health care, quality public transportation, and childcare assistance.[37]

Historically, during times of great inequality, there is a disinvestment in the commonwealth.[38] There is less investment in education, affordable housing, public health care, and other components of a level playing field. This vicious cycle of budget cuts and stakeholders pulling out leads to a withdrawal of public support for education.

Inequality does matter. Too much inequality undermines solidarity and equality of opportunity. The issue of poverty cannot be addressed without tackling the root causes of growing economic disparities.

Other Troubling Signs of the Times

Times change and the economy will change. Things may have even changed dramatically after this book went to print. There may be positive signs, such as new jobs being created or new small businesses opening. Or there may be troubling signs of inflation or recession. None of us has a crystal ball to discern the future. How we respond to change, drawing from Gospel values, will be important for what the future holds.

In addition to our discussion of poverty and inequality, there are other troubling "signs of the times" that point to basic vulnerabilities in the U.S. economy. Our household budgets and personal economic circumstances may feel squeezed on several fronts, including rising energy costs, declining home values, inflation risks, and other factors. These are important to notice as they point to deeper structural changes and potential problems. As you read this brief discussion of points of vulnerability in the U.S. economy, try to remember the fundamental questions rooted in Catholic social teaching: How is the economy serving people and supporting families? How are those who are most vulnerable going to be affected by these trends?

Rising Energy Costs. As a result of Hurricane Katrina, increased global demand, and other factors, oil companies have dramatically increased the cost of gasoline and home heating oil. Most families in the northern climates paid as much as 50 percent more for home heating in the winter of 2006 as compared with the previous year. On the positive side, this could lead to bolder investments in energy conservation and independence. But it will also squeeze family budgets and force many people to do without basic needs.

Income Flat and Housing Costs Up. The cost of housing has dramatically risen in the last several decades. For those hoping to buy a home, rising costs have pushed the dream further out of reach. For those who own homes, inflated values have created an illusion of greater wealth (see the discussion of the "bubble" below). There is a very unreal gap between what people can afford and the cost of housing. The ratio of median mortgage payments to median income — a true gauge of affordability — is at the highest level since 1989.[39] This cannot go on forever.

Bursting Housing Bubble. For several years, economists have warned that the price of housing in the United States, and in coastal markets in particular, is inflated. After the decline in stock market prices in the late 1990s, a lot of investors moved their money into real estate. In the spring of 2005, real estate values were 13 percent higher than they were a year earlier. As a result of inflated home values, many people feel wealthier than they really are. People have borrowed against their rising home values to pay for college tuition, vacations, second homes, or sometimes basic needs and living expenses. Almost 80 percent of the increase in mortgage debt over the last couple of years is due to people getting second mortgages on their homes and cashing out equity. The "housing savings rate" — and the amount of equity Americans are saving in their homes — was a negative number in July 2005.[40] Earlier we discussed how inflated home values have masked some of the real problems in our economy, such as stagnant wages. If there is a serious collapse of home prices, there will be a great deal of economic pain.

Inflation. After almost two decades of low inflation, we might start to see a real jump in inflationary pressures. Because of rising fuel prices, the U.S. inflation rate rose to 4.7 percent in September 2005, its highest level since the early 1990s.

Slowdown in Consumer Spending. Any one of the factors above could lead to a dramatic reduction in consumer spending. In chapter 9, we discuss the importance of simplifying our lives and being less susceptible to consumerism. Nonetheless, the trade and purchase of basic necessities is a healthy part of any economy. As working people feel the stresses of inflation, declining home prices, and rising energy costs, they will understandably clamp down on spending. This will ripple not only through the U.S. economy, but the global economy as well, which has benefited from the appetite of U.S. consumers for imported goods.

Pension Crisis. There is a ticking time bomb related to the question of how our society will pay for the retirement security of our elders and future retirees. There are two main reasons for this. First, many companies that promised their retiring workers a pension are now unable to keep their promise due to insolvency, poor planning, or criminal behavior. The Pension Benefit Guaranty Corporation, a federal agency that guarantees private corporate pensions, has stepped in on a number of occasions to fulfill these obligations. This is a potential "budget buster." Second, the federal Social Security system faces some longer-term shortfalls that will require some changes in either benefits or revenue. These shortfalls are not as drastic as some politicians, with an agenda to privatize Social Security, have declared them to be. But the issue is still one that must be dealt with and it will cost money.

Pension Speculation. With future retirement and pension obligations rising, there is increasing pressure for pension fund investors to seek higher returns. This has led more and more pension funds to shift investments into higher risk, unregulated, and secretive investment vehicles such as hedge funds. Pension funds, which account for roughly 40 percent of all institutional investments, have historically shied away from such risky investments. But investment studies forecast that pension funds will invest as much as $300 billion in hedge funds by 2008, up from $5 billion in 1998.[41] In the event of a hedge fund collapse, these pension obligations will land in the laps of the U.S. taxpayer, through the federal Pension Benefit Guaranty Corporation.

Global Speculation. Adding to the potential for great instability is the rapid movement of investment capital at the global level. Because of the concentration of wealth in the United States, enormous corporate profits and reserves, and higher savings rates in European and Asian countries, the world has what Federal Reserve chairman Ben Bernanke calls a "global savings glut." As this money seeks high return investment, it goes to riskier and riskier schemes. "Investors' quests for higher returns can present a dangerous quandary," said Jim Sarni, an institutional investor in an interview with the *Wall Street Journal*. "It makes you continue to invest in higher-yield instruments" even when they don't earn much more than safe investments. "It is a global game of chicken."[42]

Infrastructure Disinvestment. Hurricane Katrina revealed the failure to invest in both infrastructure and emergency preparedness. Three decades of "shrink government" agitation has led state and federal governments to postpone needed investments in infrastructure, such as transport systems, ports, and bridges. After pioneering the Internet revolution, the United States is also lagging behind other countries in making investments in new technologies as part of the Internet era. Some Asian and European countries and regions, for instance, are establishing municipal Internet services to enable the entire community to be connected and lower the cost of access. The U.S. lack of public planning in this area will have a drag on future economic growth and competitiveness.

Imbalance of Trade: More Imports Than Exports. The United States has a troubling and persistent balance of trade deficit, meaning we import much more in the global marketplace than we export. Most economists don't believe trade imbalances are inherently good or bad.[43] Ongoing trade deficits in part reflect growth in the U.S. economy. By a moral measure, however, the trade deficit is bad when it entails an overdependence on oil, food, and raw materials. It is also bad when it leads to the elimination of jobs because U.S. manufacturers cannot compete with imported low-cost goods made in countries with low wages and low environmental standards. The United States has become the world's shopping mall, making us the principal consumer of most of the world's low-cost goods. But we're also seeing our capacity to create goods leaving the country. (See our discussion of globalization in chapter 6.)

Growing National Debt. Each year since 1997, the United States has had an annual deficit, spending more money than it received in revenue. And each year the "national debt" hole gets deeper. As of September 2006, the cumulative national debt is $8.5 trillion.[44] In March 2006, with no plan to reverse the trend, the U.S. Congress raised our national debt ceiling, the amount of money that the government can borrow, to an unprecedented $9 trillion. In 2005, the interest payment on the debt was $352 billion. These annual interest payments are an enormous drag on the economy and crowd out other necessary borrowing and investment. Going into debt, as for individuals, is not inherently bad; it depends on what the debt is for. Borrowing to make a long-term investment in education or to buy a home is prudent. But the federal government policy of borrowing money to give tax cuts largely to the very wealthy constitutes a "borrow and squander" policy. We are guaranteeing that the next generation will have to devote more of their labors to paying off the current generation's debts.

Figure 4.2

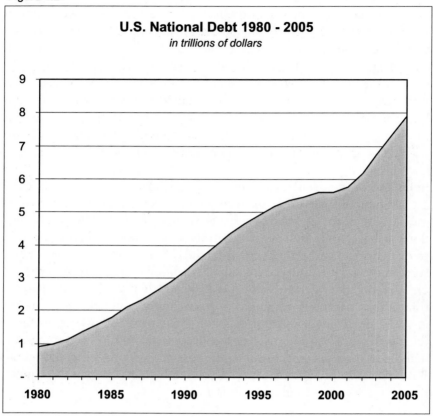

Source: U.S. Office of Management and Budget, The Budget for Fiscal Year 2007, Historical Tables, Table 7.1.

All these signs of the times could trigger serious economic disruptions in the United States. We share a heightened awareness of the risks of terrorist attacks or natural disasters, like Hurricane Katrina. But we typically don't talk about these other troubling economic signs. Given the seriousness of the "signs of the times" we have discussed, why don't we hear more about these concerns at the local coffee shop, at church, or in the news? Or if this picture is accurate, why are the parking lots and stores at the malls full and people are buying more stuff than ever?

There are several factors that keep us from fully engaging in these stories and statistics. First, most of us experience economic life in very private and personal ways. If we are feeling economically stressed out, we

Figure 4.3

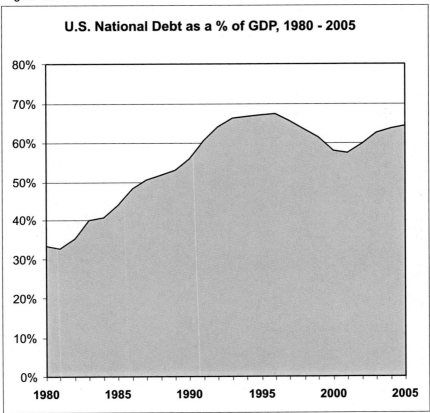

U.S. National Debt as a % of GDP, 1980 - 2005

Source: U.S. Office of Management and Budget, The Budget for Fiscal Year 2007, Historical Tables,Table 7.1.

often keep that information to ourselves and pursue personal solutions. But another reason might be that many of the trends we have discussed are currently masked and invisible. For instance, if real wages for most workers are stagnant or falling, how come a lot of people seem to be maintaining a high standard of living and buying more stuff?

There are three trends that are masking the serious problems in the economy, all of which we have touched on already. The first is people are working more hours per household to survive. The second is people have easy access to credit that enables them to maintain a level of consumption that is sustained by borrowing, not real wage growth. And third, the rise in home prices has enabled people to borrow money unrelated to their income capacity. None of these trends can go on forever. There are limits to how many hours a day we can work. There are limits to how much we can borrow. And there are limits to how much home values will rise disconnected to what people can pay for them.

Once the mask is pulled away, we will see some of these economic trends more starkly. In the event of serious economic disruptions, the framework of Catholic social teachings on the economy will be all the more important to help inform the way our nation responds. Individual solutions will be insufficient, and solidarity will be essential.

Chapter Five

Root Causes, Part I
Values, Wages, and the Role of Government

The most dramatic economic sign of the time, as discussed in the previous chapter, is the acceleration of economic inequality. From a Gospel perspective, we have discussed the reasons why inequality matters to our democracy, economy, and social solidarity. Without social solidarity, there is an erosion in public health, equality of opportunity, and our resolve to eliminate poverty. In this section, we go beyond looking at the signs and signals of the economy to look at the root causes and structural changes that touch our individual lives.

In the United States, we have a strong tendency to understand economic reality entirely through our personal and individual framework. But this individual reality is framed by various "structures" that shape and sometimes dictate our personal experiences and lives. When we talk about *structural forces,* we are referring to the institutions, rules, and norms that frame our economic lives. These include wage laws, government rules and institutions, tax policy, global corporations, the church — all the ways in which we come together in social formations.

Church teachings are concerned not only about individual behavior and personal sin, but also with the role of social structures and institutions. Our church teachings describe both "graced social structures," such as family and some civic organizations, and "sinful social structures," such as the institution of slavery, debtor's prisons, or exclusionary zoning practices.

In some cases, our loyalty to a social norm becomes sinful. At the root of social sins are individuals, and we are all responsible for uprooting social sins, including those of the church. No one is perfect here. For instance, the church cooperated with the system of racially segregated education until the national laws changed in the 1950s. White people were attached to the system of segregated education and considered it just "the way things are."[1]

Our faith teachings call us to go beyond individual morality to examine the systems, institutions, rules, and cultural norms. This is one of the biggest challenges for many of us. There is a certain comfort and simplicity to living in a world of individual actions and personalized morality.

The United States is now the third most unequal industrialized society after Russia and Mexico. Russia lacks much in the way of civic institutions, with a post-Soviet oligarchy enriched by looting. And Mexico, despite joining the rich-nations club of the Organization for Economic and Community Development, has some of the most glaring poverty in the hemisphere.

The causes of inequality have been bipartisan and global. Inequality has grown steadily over three decades under both Republican and Democratic administrations and Congresses. The Gini index, the global measure of inequality, grew as quickly under President Clinton as it has under President George W. Bush. Other countries are also experiencing the pressures of growing inequality, though the pace of widening disparities is faster in the United States.

This prompts several important questions: Why, even during times of economic growth, is poverty growing? Why has inequality grown so dramatically in the last three decades? What are the new dynamics in our society that allow us to tolerate such problems?

A Shift in Power, Rules, and Values

What are the *root causes* of these changes in the economy? Here's a list of some of the explanations, gleaned from a discussion of lay leaders:

- Decline of manufacturing jobs
- Technological change
- Big campaign contributions distorting government priorities
- Globalization of trade
- Individual choices, such as out of wedlock births, divorce, changing family structure
- Declining trade unionism
- Erosion of minimum wage
- Immoral behavior or addiction
- Rising costs of health insurance and housing
- Unbridled greed and the breakdown of responsibility
- Businesses putting profits ahead of people

Our challenge is to distinguish between various *symptoms* and their *causes*. So far, we have talked a lot about the *symptoms* of the changing economy such as less free time, stagnant wages, greater concentration of wealth, and growing personal debt. But what are the underlying causes of these trends? What is the *engine* driving the dramatic economic changes we are experiencing?

There is no consensus about the causes of economic change, particularly in explaining the growth of economic inequality. Even among economists, there is no agreement on how to weight different factors in terms of importance. There are three overarching shifts worth exploring:

- a *power* shift in U.S. democracy
- a shift in the *rules* that govern the economy, changes that have fostered largely immoral economic transformations
- fundamental shifts in moral *values* and cultural norms that have contributed to inequality

Discerning which "came first" is like arguing over the chicken and the egg. All these factors interact and reinforce one another: power, rules and values together shape our economic reality.

The Power Shift

Power refers to who has voice and clout within our democratic society. Few of us are completely without power, though there are those with disproportionate power. While there have always been power imbalances in our history, the dynamics of power have changed a great deal over the last several decades. Certain constituencies have lost power, clout and voice — while others have gained.

Who has lost power?

- **Voters.** With the power of big money in politics, ordinary voters don't command much clout.
- **Religious congregations.** With the exception of right-wing fundamentalists, organized religion has lost influence since the civil rights movement.
- **Civic organizations.** Local community organizations and grassroots civic groups have less influence than they once did.
- **Trade unions and wage earners.** With the tremendous decline in unionized voices for workers, there's a lot less clout to represent the concerns of people who work for wages.
- **Main Street.** Main street businesses have lost clout to the large national chains and global conglomerates.

Who has gained power in our democratic system?

- **Campaign contributors.** The dollars given to elected officials now speak louder than votes.

Figure 5.1

* **Large corporations.** Corporations are huge players in shaping our culture and economic policies. They are not only employers, but through their advertising, purchasing, and political lobbying, shape our economy and our culture.
* **Asset owners and investors.** In our current culture, politicians and advertisers court this "investor class."
* **Corporate lobbyists.** The number of influence peddlers in Washington, D.C., and state capitals has mushroomed.
* **Wall Street.** The power of investment capital and corporate interests is heavily reflected in federal debates. Examples of Wall Street firms include Citigroup Smith Barney, Goldman Sachs, Wachovia Securities, and Morgan Stanley.

The Changing Rules of the Economy

The power shift has resulted in a push for different rules to govern economic activity. Those with greater clout and power have generally pushed for economic policies and rules to their liking. It is important to think about these as *rule changes* because it reminds us that there are human beings making the rules — not invisible hands of the market, God, or weather patterns.

Widening disparities in the United States are the result of three decades of bipartisan public policies that have tilted the rules of the economy to the benefit of large asset owners, Wall Street, and corporations at the expense of wage earners, Main Street, and local communities. Main Street includes locally owned businesses that are rooted in their communities. In the restaurant world, they are the Joe's Diners, Rita's Hamburgers, and the Shady Glen Cafés. Wall Street businesses are nationally owned branches or subsidiaries that are part of large national or regional corporations. They are the McDonalds, Pizza Huts, and Big Boys.

Rule changes that the powerful advocate include:

- **Tax policy.** For over a decade the focus of tax policy has been to shift the tax burden off of income from assets (interest, dividends, capital gains, large inheritances) and onto wages and consumption (income and sales taxes).
- **Changes in job structure.** There has been a breakdown in the social contract between workers and employers that has resulted in a fundamental restructuring of work and benefits. This has led to a rise in job insecurity and reductions in health care and pension benefits.
- **Global trade.** The way recent global treaties have been written, they are focused on reducing barriers to trade for corporations while undermining labor and environmental standards.
- **Wage regulation.** The minimum wage has been maintained at extremely low levels, contributing to wage stagnation.

The Values Shift

We cannot truly understand the causes of economic change simply by reflecting on the shifting power dynamics in our society or the resulting rule changes. Underlying all of these changes are fundamental moral values. For example, there are societies that have considerably less inequality and deprivation than the United States. But this is not necessarily because of government rules and policies. It is because their culture and values are different. The values in U.S. society are changing, and this is shaping and interacting with economic policy and power relations. Here are some examples of our values shift.

Extreme Individualism. One of the dominant values that shape our economic life is *extreme* individualism. Over the last century, we have learned through personal psychology more about our individual identity and uniqueness. There is a *healthy* individualism that recognizes our individual gifts, histories, and importance.

Human beings, as our religious tradition emphasizes, are individuals who exist *within a community*. We are fundamentally social creatures, interdependent and interconnected in physical, social, and spiritual ways. Our individual desires need to be kept in balance and tempered by the community's interest and the "common good."

Extreme individualism denies our social nature and encourages us to live according to a myth of complete independence and self-sufficiency. It denies social obligations and the responsibilities of solidarity. This individualistic worldview holds that individual actions have no consequences for others or society. It views personal success as an independent achievement, with the anti-religious attitude of "No one helped me; I did it alone." In a word, it is a form of idolatry, self-idolatry. And it is perhaps the greatest danger in U.S. society today.

Suspicion of Community and Solidarity. Extreme individualism leads to a suspicion of anything that sounds like a moral obligation to someone other than one's self and immediate loved ones. It rejects and even feels threatened by religious teachings that talk about solidarity and sharing. It reinforces the myth that "we are all on our own."

Market Idolatry. For some, the marketplace has become a god. The "market" has taken on the trappings of a new religion. As a society, we worship at the altar of the market and invoke the language of business in all realms of our lives, including the sacred. The worship of money and the addiction to wealth accompany this idolatry.

Materialism and Consumerism. Another form of idolatry is the inordinate focus of our culture on materialism and consumption. The shopping mall, the commercial strip, and the business district have become the new places of worship. The ownership of material things becomes a central pursuit of our days.

Immediate Gratification. Linked to our consumer society is the value of "immediate gratification" of having one's desires met *now,* immediately, without waiting. This is the "just do it" ethic that applies to consumer purchases, sexuality, and entertainment.

Modernity. We have all benefited from modern advances in medicine, communications, transportation, and material progress. At the same time, we should not overlook some of the important qualities and values of traditional societies and our religion. The danger to our values is when we assume that anything new is better. To deny the wisdom of the ages is to idolize modernity.

Wealth without Work. Considered one of Gandhi's seven deadly social sins, the idea of "getting rich quick" is a cultural value reinforced in the popular media.

People don't often reflect upon the underlying values of our economic life — and the fact that things could be different. We accept these values as norms in our culture. It is in this area of helping change the underlying values of the society that Christians can make an enormous contribution.

The remaining part of this chapter and the next will explore various explanations for many of the negative economic changes in our society. These overarching "root causes" include:

- The breakdown of individual behavior and social morality
- Wage stagnation and the restructuring of work
- The weakening of the commonwealth and government sector by anti-government and anti-tax movements
- The accelerating forces of globalization
- The concentration of corporate power

We will draw on our three-part analysis of causes: looking at power shifts, the rules changes that contribute to the trend, and the underlying values. Our goal is to connect the dots between these various causes. Where appropriate, we will suggest particular responses and even solutions to some of these problems.

Individual Responsibility and Social Breakdown

In our country's broken and polarized political discourse, you will often hear people who talk about "personal responsibility" juxtaposed with "social or societal responsibility." The simple cartoon characterization is that conservatives believe people should be personally responsible for their actions, with government staying out of the picture. When they hear about poverty, low wages, or bankruptcy, they seek causes in an individual's immoral behavior or poor decisions. On the other, the cartoon liberal focuses on society's responsibility for problems and overlooks the importance of individual responsibility and choices.

You have probably figured out by this point that a Gospel perspective can't be captured in a cartoon. We believe in both individual and societal responsibility. In fact, we believe this is a false distinction. Individual responsibility includes responsibility for society and others. And individual morality doesn't exist outside of a social and economic system that we are all part of. We are individuals living in community. Our individual moral choices shape the community, and the social and economic institutions of the community, in turn, shape us.

Individual moral choices matter a great deal. The personal temptation to sin in the forms of idolatry, selfishness, deceit, laziness, sexual promiscuity, and greed can be disastrous for us as individuals, our families, and our communities. So when we talk about the underlying issues impacting the economy, we need to recognize the ways in which individuals and individual behavior matters. We are each personally responsible.

Our church's teachings are unequivocal about the importance of the family. The family is central to the development of the person. It is the "primary place of humanization for the person and society" and the "cradle of love and life."[2] Various Catholic teachings describe the family as the "vital cell of society" and the "first natural society." It is where we exercise a high level of personal responsibility.

From the centrality of the family flows the importance of marriage and parenting. Parents have a fundamental responsibility to provide an integral education to help develop the fullness of their children. Society, in turn, should work to strengthen individuals and families. In accord with the church principle of "subsidiarity," families are the foundation of society and well-being. But when families break down due to reasons of personal immorality or economic dislocation, then extended family, community, and society have a responsibility to step in.

This is why Catholic teachings focus so much on how important it is that the economy enable families to flourish. Society and government exist to serve the family, not the other way around. Individuals might make personal mistakes or fail to plan, but this should not consign them and their children to a life of poverty. Nor should people have to lead the lives of saints in order to have a decent life and minimum security. This is why religious teachings on the economy are concerned about such matters as whether parents have enough free time to parent and whether they can earn a wage adequate to support a family.

Stagnant Wages
and the Restructuring of Work

In previous sections we have discussed the problems related to job insecurity, stagnant wages, and little or no savings. The causes of these problems are rooted in a number of power shifts, policy rules, and value changes. Competition in the global economy, which we will discuss in the next chapter, erodes the bargaining power of workers and depresses wages. There are several causes for this that we'll focus on here:

- The restructuring of businesses and the changing nature of jobs
- The declining clout of labor unions to represent the interests of workers and to advocate rule changes that protect workers
- The failure of the federal minimum wage to maintain a sufficient floor for wages

The Restructuring of Work

The notion of a "job" evolved dramatically over the twentieth century. In 1900, workers in the new industrial economy were essentially day laborers with little long-term security. By the late 1950s, the new norm was that a job had long-term security and benefits such as health care, a retirement pension, and paid vacations. There was a "social contract" between workers and employers that meant the gains of the growing economy were shared with workers.

In the early 1970s, there was a dramatic shift to a more "lean and mean" economy. Part of this was aimed at bringing greater efficiency and productivity to U.S. businesses as they were forced to compete more vigorously in the global economy. But many businesses reduced their overhead costs at the expense of workers, squeezing them in terms of wages and reducing employer-sponsored benefits. Profits became more important than corporate responsibility to employees and communities.

This process of "economic restructuring" moved through the economy, industry by industry: automobiles, meatpacking, textiles, and banking. In sectors that had strong unions the process occurred more slowly and with greater protections for employees. But in many cases the process of restructuring led to the end of union representation and a considerably lower living standard for employees.

The threat of global outsourcing and relocation was an explicit undercurrent in the restructuring process, which reduced the leverage of workers in negotiating for job security, wages, benefits, and dignity. As companies reduced the number of full-time workers with benefits, stock market investors on Wall Street cheered in approval, boosting the stock share prices for "lean" corporations and rewarding their top managers with oversized pay packages.

The restructuring of work and outsourcing of jobs is not limited to the private sector. A growing number of government functions and public jobs have also been restructured and "privatized," meaning replaced with private sector vendors. While in some cases, this has saved money and

improved efficiency, in other cases it has eroded the quality of public services and put public employees in "race to the bottom" competition with
private sector workers over who will work for less wages and benefits.
Different levels of government now outsource many functions that used to
be performed by full-time workers who were paid a living wage and had
benefits like health insurance. These include data management, garbage
collection, driving school buses, cleaning services, and other duties that
are now performed by temporary workers paid a poverty wage.

The effort to reinvent the job and erode job security and benefits
has largely been successful. Today, a shrinking percentage of the workforce has health care coverage and employer-sponsored pensions. An
estimated one-third of U.S. workers are now employed in the "contingent" workforce, meaning they are "temp" workers, consultants, day
laborers, and involuntary part-timers. Most of these workers have no
benefits, paid vacations, or real security. Only 15 percent of male and
11 percent of female full-time temporary workers have health insurance
provided through their employer. And 70 percent of all temporary workers have no health insurance at all. Some workers prefer this flexible
arrangement, but according to the Bureau of Labor Statistics, two-thirds
of contingent workers desire stable and secure jobs.[3]

These changes in the structure of work have meant that growing job insecurity is a basic fact of life for many American workers. Many of us feel
the sands shifting below our feet, knowing that our jobs might be replaced
by technology, temporary workers, or outsourcing. The number of workers who feel anxiety about losing their job rose from 12 percent in 1980 to
61 percent in 2004.[4] This anxiety is borne out by the facts as the pace of
downsizing and outsourcing has accelerated in the last decade. Between
March of 2001 and January of 2004, 2.3 million people lost their jobs.[5]

The basic message about work in the new global economy is "you
are on your own." Don't look to your employer as a source of steady
employment, health insurance, or retirement security. Instead, we are
told, "You need to figure this out on your own." Get your own IRA for
retirement, become a consultant, retool your skills, and sell your labor
in the marketplace. Try to find a minimal health insurance policy, or
take your chances and, if you have an accident, show up and wait at the
emergency room of a free care hospital.

Clearly our values in relation to work have changed. We can see the
idolatry of the market place and the value of extreme individualism
at work throughout any discussion of work in the modern economy.
Human work is no longer viewed as a sacred part of creation, but as a
market cost to reduce or eliminate. Gospel values reaffirm the primacy
of work in God's creation and the high value placed on the dignity of

the individual worker. A job is no longer a source of occupational pride and livelihood, but a transitory source of income. The dignity of the individual has been lost in this equation.

The Declining Clout of Organized Labor

> What does labor want? We want more schoolhouses and less jails; more books and less arsenals; more learning and less vice; more leisure and less greed; more justice and less revenge; in fact more of the opportunities to cultivate our better natures, to make manhood more noble, womanhood more beautiful, and childhood more happy and bright.
>
> —Samuel Gompers, founder of the American Federation of Labor[6]

The power dynamics of work have been altered as the influence of global corporations to shape and reshape work has dramatically increased. At the same time, organizations that have historically defended the dignity of workers and their trades have lost considerable clout. This includes not only trade unions, but also craft guilds, worker and professional associations, and civic associations. The percentage of workers represented by trade unions has declined severely in the last few decades. In 1955, over 34 percent of the workforce was represented by a union. This gave workers significant leverage to enforce a "social contract" with employers and share in fruits of their labors. Today, less than 13 percent of the workforce is in a trade union. And excluding public employee unions, less than 10 percent of the private workforce has union representation.[7]

There are strong feelings about the role of unions in our economy. A sampling of opinion at any church coffee hour will reveal positive and negative experiences with unions and differing opinions as to their relevance in today's economy.

Unions, like businesses and religious organizations, are human institutions subject to sin. In some cases, union leadership may have succumbed to the harmful values dominant in our marketplace, such as individual greed or disregard for others. In some local economies or markets, unions may have more clout than employers. Union contracts should not unjustly enforce compensation without work. A fair day's wage for a fair day's work should be the principle that continues to operate.

Catholic social teachings affirm the basic right of workers to organize and advocate their interests in the workplace. Catholic teaching also holds both workers and employers responsible for engaging in respectful dialogue and negotiation. The fundamental goal of unions is to ensure solidarity among workers in an effort to defend their dignity and liveli-hoods. The decline of worker clout has left an enormous power vacuum that has been filled by the dominance of corporations.

The hard-won rules to protect workers have gradually eroded over the last thirty years. Religious voices and moral values need to be brought into efforts to defend worker rights and policy debates about the future nature of work.

Over the first seventy years of the twentieth century, enormous prog-ress was made to expand the dignity, compensation, and rights of workers. Between 1900 and 1970, the workday was shortened and more jobs had long-term security, workplace safety rules, and health care and retirement benefits. Unions that in the 1950s represented over one-third of the workforce were able to enforce a strong social contract between employers and employees that effectively benefited workers who did not belong to unions. This social contract made possible the broad sharing of wealth in the prosperous years after World War II. But in the last thirty years, we've seen a reversal of these gains. The decline in worker power and the restructuring of work have not only touched individual work-ers, but also have generally weakened participation of those without substantial wealth in the democratic process. This has meant changes in the role of government and a weakening of protections as the U.S. economy enters a new phase of globalization.

Unions have suffered setbacks since the 1950s as a result of the aggressive anti-union tactics of employers and a political environment un-favorable to workers. Since the 1970s, the rules that govern the ability of workers to form unions have been weakened or not enforced. Employers face no moral or timely legal sanctions when they deploy hard-fisted tac-tics to disrupt unionization drives, including the firing of workers involved in organizing and endless maneuvers to delay votes for union recognition.

Labor unions have their own internal work to do to broaden democracy and participation by their members. Gospel principles of participation and respect for the individual apply to the internal culture of unions as well as to the larger economy. Sometimes unions have discriminated against women, people of color, and newly arrived immigrants. But these internal problems do not negate the important historical role that unions have played in expanding economic justice. We must stand with workers in support of their fundamental right to organize. Specific rule change activities that would strengthen worker rights include:

- Prevent anti-worker legislation that denies basic worker rights.
- Support workplace organizing efforts.
- Defend existing labor laws and press for their enforcement.

- Support efforts to strengthen rules allowing the right to organize, including streamlined response to unfair labor practices, bans on strikebreaker replacement workers, and instant recognition when a majority of workers have signed union cards.

There are also other forms of worker organization that need our support, including:

- **Worker centers.** In many parts of the country, new worker organizations and community-based centers are bringing together unionized and non-unionized workers who share a certain bond by virtue of language, ethnicity, or type of employment. Many work in sectors that are not unionized or belong to ethnic groups that unions have not succeeded in reaching.[8]
- **Temp worker organizations.** More than 30 percent of the American labor force are people who work independently, including freelancers, independent contractors, temps, part-timers, contingent workers, and those who work from home. Across the country, there are national associations and local centers providing services and advocacy for this growing contingent workforce.[9]

A Fair Day's Living Wage for a Fair Day's Work

Another reason that wages have stagnated is the political failure to keep the minimum wage high enough to provide an adequate floor below which wages cannot fall.

The federal minimum wage was established in 1938 to create a standard for all non-agricultural workers. One reason Congress passed the legislation was to discourage competition between states and regions within the United States over who would pay the lowest wages. By setting a wage floor, states would have to compete on some basis other than low wages.

During the 1950s and 1960s, the minimum wage was much closer to a "living wage," the earnings required to lift a family of four out of poverty. Today, however, the minimum wage is nowhere near the poverty wage, let alone a living wage. A full-time worker earning the federal minimum wage of $5.15 per hour has an annual paycheck of $10,712 a year, grossly inadequate for an individual or family living in most regions of the United States. According to one calculation, a federal *living wage* would average over $10.00 an hour in the United States.[10] In San Francisco, Boston, Washington, D.C., Seattle, and other cities with expensive housing markets, the living wage would need to be much higher. See the "Family Budget Calculator" on p. 93.

Underlying the debate on wages is a conflict between Gospel values and market values. Market values suggest that the market should set wages,

Figure 5.2

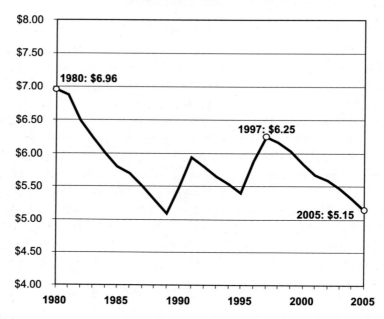

**Buying Power of the Minimum Wage
in 2005 Dollars, 1980 - 2005**

Source: Lawrence Mishel, Jared Bernstein, and Sylvia Allegretto, *The State of Working America 2006 / 2007* (Ithaca: Cornell University Press, 2007), Figure 3X.

that competition over the cost of labor ensures productivity and the best allocation of resources. But in a large country and a global marketplace, where there may always be someone hungry and willing to work for less, unbridled wage competition leads to misery. Our religious values are rooted in the fundamental worth of all humans and the notion of a fair day's wage for a fair day's work. Workers should earn at least a "living wage," enough to have a decent life and support a flourishing family life. A family should not have to work seventy to a hundred hours a week in the paid labor force to survive. Rather, work should enable families to rise out of poverty.

As labor's clout has declined, so have the laws and regulations establishing minimum wage standards. While efforts to change the minimum wage at the federal level have been stalled in recent years, there are growing state and local movements pressing to raise state and local minimum wages.[11] Across the United States religious and community coalitions have formed to press for local "living wage" ordinances. Journalist Robert Kuttner calls living wage struggles "the most interesting

THE FAMILY BUDGET CALCULATOR

The federal poverty level has been the traditional measure of whether a family has an adequate income to lift them out of poverty. Yet this "poverty line" is largely inadequate in measuring the real costs of supporting a working family.

The Economic Policy Institute has an interesting tool to measure the real cost of living in different regions of the country. On the Internet, you can input your family size and region into a "Family Budget Calculator" that looks at the real costs of housing, transportation, food, child care and other expenses in over four hundred sub-regions of the United States.[12]

A family with two parents and three children living in Hattiesburg, Mississippi, needs an income of $43,476 to sustain a decent life. Yet almost 30 percent of Mississippi families fall below the "family budget line." The same size family would need an income closer to $60,000 in Seattle, Washington, where 27 percent fall below the "family budget line."

As the designers of the Family Budget Calculator observe, this family budget is very basic. "It comprises only the amounts a family needs to spend to feed, shelter, and clothe itself, get to work and school, and subsist in twenty-first-century America. Hence, it includes no savings, no restaurant meals, no funds for emergencies — not even renters' insurance to protect against fire, flood or theft."[13]

(and under-reported) grassroots enterprise to emerge since the civil rights movement."[14]

In 1995, the city of Baltimore passed the country's first living wage ordinance. The effort was led by a coalition of religious groups with strong leadership and funding from Catholic institutions and the Catholic Campaign for Human Development. As of August 2006, over 140 cities, counties, and universities have passed living wage ordinances.[15] These include Los Angeles, Oakland, St. Louis, San Antonio, Boston, Chicago, and Milwaukee. In addition, there are currently 115 active campaigns pressing for living wages. These laws typically require companies that do business with a state or city government to pay a living wage, usually pegged to the amount that would lift a family of three or four above the region's poverty level. In other words, cities are declaring that if you want to do business with them, your company must pay better than poverty wages. Most ordinances apply to private vendors, building contractors, and other organizations that receive substantial government subsidies, including real estate developers who get housing development subsidies.

In July 2004, the city of Sonoma, California, passed a living wage ordinance that covered private companies with city contracts worth at least $10,000 and nonprofits with city contracts of at least $75,000. Workers in these businesses get an hourly wage of $11.70 if they have health benefits or $13.20 if they don't. Covered employers must also provide a minimum of twelve days a year of paid vacation and ten days of uncompensated days off. Smaller businesses are exempt from the law.

In Durham, North Carolina, a grassroots group, Durham Congregations, Associations and Neighborhoods, organized for a living wage law. In June 2004, the Durham Board of County Commissioners passed an ordinance fixing the county's living wage at 7.5 percent above the federal poverty level. For a family of four in Durham County that was $9.00 per hour at the time the law passed. It applies to all county workers and those with private business contracts with the county.[16]

The debate over whether or not to raise the minimum wage has largely been consumed by the question of whether boosting the wage will cause job losses. This concern persists despite the fact that most research shows that the job loss effects of raising the minimum wage are minimal or nonexistent.[17]

One moral dimension to the minimum wage question is who actually benefits from minimum wage and living wage laws. Any negative effect of raising the minimum wage is offset by the enormous benefits to individuals and low-income communities. Research shows that beneficiaries of an increased minimum wage are exclusively those most in need, adult workers in low-income families.[18]

There is also a public benefit in that if employers pay a living wage, taxpayers don't have to subsidize low-wage companies by supplementing their low wages with food stamps, housing subsidies, and emergency room health care for their uninsured workers. Wal-Mart is one of the most profitable corporations and the largest employer in the United States, with over 1.3 million employees. But only 47 percent of Wal-Mart workers have any sort of health coverage. As a result, Wal-Mart employees are among the largest users of state Medicaid programs in the United States.[19] As taxpayers, we pick up the tab for Wal-Mart.

Even businesses benefit from increased morale and efficiency, more incentives to train employees, and reduced employee turnover. Living wage ordinances can contribute to a "high road" development strategy as communities discontinue the practice of subsidizing employers with tax breaks and grants without asking for any community benefits in return.

Figure 5.3

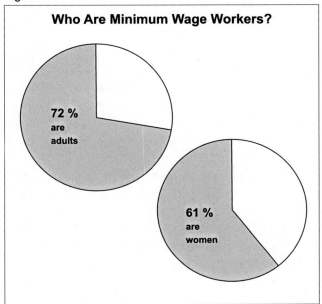

Who Are Minimum Wage Workers?

72 %
are
adults

61 %
are
women

Source: Economic Policy Institute, "Minimum Wage Frequently Asked Questions," updated January 2006.

Many communities now require good "living wage jobs" in exchange for any development assistance.[20]

One group of principled business leaders argues that paying a decent living wage is good for business. In 2000, several hundred employers and top managers formed Business Leaders for a Living Wage and took a pledge to pay a living wage, while investors pledged to scrutinize companies for their practices related to wages and wage disparities. These business leaders make the case that paying workers a decent wage encourages loyalty, reduces employee turnover, and boosts morale and productivity. High road businesses find it difficult to compete with businesses that pay a poverty-wage. By raising the minimum wage, they argue, businesses can compete in terms of other qualities such as innovation, quality of services, and efficiency, not on the basis of who can pay their workers less.[21]

Judy Wicks is a Philadelphia restaurant owner who believes the restaurant industry can do much better in terms of wages and quality of work. "The traditional value system in the restaurant business of running people

ALABAMA'S REGRESSIVE TAX SYSTEM
AND THE BIBLE

In 2003, Alabama law professor Susan Pace Hamill stirred things up in her state when she wrote an article arguing that the Alabama state tax system failed to conform to Christian principles. Alabama has the distinction of having the most regressive state tax system in the country because it harshly overtaxes the working poor and undertaxes wealthy timber companies.

In Alabama, income taxes are taken out of paychecks starting at the very low income of $4,600. The property tax rate is extremely low, which is good for timber companies that, according to Hamill, own 71 percent of the land but pay less than 2 percent of the property tax. Regressive sales taxes are extremely high, including taxation of basic needs and food. "The least among us are suffering the worst," observed Hamill.

"We're living in the Bible Belt here," Hamill told *Sojourners* magazine. "This tax inequity is a product of our laws, and our laws are a product of our voting, which is a product of our people. So we're talking about a bunch of voting Christians tolerating this."

Hamill has written several law review articles looking at state and federal tax systems from the perspective of Christian ethics.[22] Like all Christian teachings, the biblical perspective on taxes is rooted in the dignity and worth of all humans. "We're talking about human beings made in the image of God. Whether or not the recipient (of government programs)

into the ground needs to change in order to create a more fulfilling workplace for everyone," said Wicks. Her restaurant employs over a hundred workers who are paid Philadelphia's "living wage" standard.

Her employees experience a greater sense of professionalism and self-respect from earning a living wage, which ultimately improves morale and eases the job of restaurant managers. One employee, Oliver Collins, remarked, "It made a big difference in my life. First I paid off a credit loan I had been worrying about. I have three children and now I can afford to buy them some things they have always wanted. But the best thing is that I'm talking with a realtor about buying a house so I can move my kids to a safer neighborhood."[23]

ALABAMA'S REGRESSIVE TAX SYSTEM
AND THE BIBLE (continued)

deserves it is irrelevant. This is very important. People have said, 'Why should I be concerned with people who are lazy?' My response is that if . . . you're Christian, you must be." "We are all in the image, and what does that mean? It means that your faith in God and your relationship is not a one-way street; it's a triangle situation. You've got God, and you, and the others in the image. And they're connected to God. It is a triangle you can't break. So to disregard others, to treat them as something less than the image, is a sin directly against the Maker. You cannot divorce the connection.

"When you start talking about community, taxes are an important element, because you're not going to run an infrastructure from charitable contributions; we're too greedy for that! You've got to run it through the arm of the law, and that brings in justice. Justice in the community means a minimum chance of improving one's lot if you're at the bottom. No matter how despicable you think they are, Jesus says you have to love them anyway, and that's the minimum bar.

"This is according to an orthodox, Judeo-Christian, biblically based, evangelical, divine command, ethical approach — and you cannot get more conservative than that. It's not about class. It's about the standard that we will not dip below with regard to any human being. If that standard is set by mammon and the market, you're not operating under any godly principles."[24]

Growing Hostility
toward Government and Taxation

Do church teachings have anything to say about Uncle Sam and the Internal Revenue Service? Indeed they do. But we should first reflect on current signs of the times.

There is a lot of anti-government grumbling in the air. Each of us can think of an irritating example of government waste or a way we wish government didn't spend our money. There are, however, no institutions free of human sin, whether governments, businesses, or religious or non-profit organizations. The key is to foster systems of participation and accountability that keep human-governed institutions healthy. Some of these attacks on government are part of a selfish political program rooted in a philosophy that is "anti-solidarity," a belief that "I am not responsible for anyone else." This may be popular, but it is not in accordance with Christian teachings.

Our feelings about government emerge from our disappointment with the limitations of human institutions, the examples of inefficiency, and periodic corruption. But is important not to dismiss the important role that government plays. The U.S. bishops note that "government has a moral function: protecting human rights and securing basic justice for all members of the commonwealth."[25] We are called as faithful citizens not to withdraw from the governing institutions of society but to deepen our involvement, participation, and influence to advance justice. We want to struggle for a government that is robust, responsive, and efficient, and that strengthens the common good.

Many people believe that the problems of poverty and economic security should be addressed through charitable giving. They are suspicious of government and would rather see such duties carried out by the independent nonprofit sector and faith-based organizations. But anyone who reasonably considers the scale and depth of needed response understands the necessity for a strong partnership between different levels of government and community-based private service organizations. The charitable sector does not have the capacity to fund and operate programs such as food stamps, affordable housing, and services for the mentally ill without government support.

One of the strategies to attack and weaken government is to undermine the system of taxation. How did our nation reach the point where raising sufficient revenue for basic services is political suicide for elected officials and increasing taxes is the ultimate political sin? Why do we allow state tax systems to remain regressive, with disproportionate responsibilities falling on lower-income taxpayers?

The cause is rooted in changing power, rules, and values. There is a powerful movement of organizations advocating limited government and reduced taxes. They have established national lobbying organizations and state-level advocacy groups to advance their long-term program of changing tax rules and attitudes toward government. They have articulated a set of extremely individualistic values that reject social responsibility toward the needy and oppose societal solutions to common problems ("It's your money").

INEQUALITY OF SACRIFICE

There is something unseemly about Congress's push over the years to permanently cut taxes for the very wealthy during a time of war. Never in the history of U.S. warfare has Congress pushed tax cuts for the very wealthy. Historically, the opposite has been true: wealth has been "conscripted," in the form of progressive income and estate taxes, to at least symbolize that everyone is sacrificing in some way.

During World War II, President Franklin D. Roosevelt understood that national domestic unity against Hitler depended on a sense of shared sacrifice by both Rockefeller and Rosie the Riveter. Top income tax rates were boosted, and the estate tax was increased so that fortunes exceeding $50 million would be taxed at 70 percent. FDR spoke out boldly against war profiteering, saying, "I don't want to see a single war millionaire created in the United States as a result of this world disaster."

"During World War II, every town had tire drives and rationing," said Charlie Richardson of Military Families Speak Out. "Right now it's the opposite. They are trying to isolate as many people as possible from the impact of the war. During the Civil War, rich people could buy their way out of the draft. Now the wealthy don't have to pay anything to avoid the draft and they get tax cuts on top."

Veterans' organizations point to the injustice of President Bush's 2004 budget that included a $6.2 billion budget cut in veterans' services. Changes since 2003 have included a new $250 fee for veterans wishing to use health services, the elimination of thousands of VA hospital beds, and a tripling of co-payments for prescription drugs.[26] Cutting veterans' services, for present and future veterans, to pay for tax cuts for the wealthy is a sin. As Catholics, we need to point out the grotesque inequality of sacrifice that is occurring in U.S. society and the ways in which these tax cuts for the wealthy reinforce this inequality.

These anti-tax organizations have been successful in reframing the terms of public debate and fostering a political climate that is reflexively anti-government. State governments now routinely cut basic lifeline social programs for the poor before they consider raising taxes to cover budget deficits caused by tax loopholes, corporate welfare, and antiquated tax systems. Nor has the federal government significantly assisted states with budget shortfalls, as they did in the past.

The stated goal of many of these anti-tax advocates is to "starve" the government "beast" through tax cuts. "You'll have a tax cut each year," declared one of their leaders, Grover Norquist of the Americans for Tax Reform. "Our goal is to shrink government to the size where we can drown it in a bathtub."[27] Their values of extreme individualism are anti-Christian and deeply out of step with the vast majority of religious people of all traditions. Most people believe that government should work to create a level playing field, ensure equality of opportunity, and assist those who are most vulnerable.

Gospel teachings suggest several principles in relation to the tax system, including ensuring an adequacy of revenue and progressivity in who pays. The tax system should raise adequate revenues to pay for the public needs of society, especially the minimum required to address poverty. The tax system should be progressive, meaning "those with relatively greater financial resources pay a higher rate of taxation." The tax system should be one of the remedies for reducing "the severe inequalities of income and wealth in the nation."[28]

In the parable of the widow's mite (Mark 12:41–44), Jesus watches as people contribute to the treasury. He observes that the widow "put in more than all the contributors to the treasury; for they all put in out of their surplus, but she, out of her poverty, put in all she owned, all she had to live on." She reached into her sustenance to contribute, whereas the others gave substantially less of their capacity.

This distinction illustrates the moral basis for a progressive tax system: those with the greatest capacity to pay should pay a higher percentage. Ten percent of the income of a family with a $10,000 income cuts into their basic sustenance. Ten percent of the income of a family with a $1 million income does not. In other words, a very simple unadorned "flat tax" is not consistent with Catholic teachings. Simply taxing everyone at the same rate is not fair because it imposes a greater burden on lower-income households.

Judged accordingly, our federal tax system and most of our state tax systems are found wanting. Federal tax cuts have contributed to massive budget deficits and blocked possibilities for spending on human needs. Between 2000 and 2003, almost every state in the union faced terrible budget gaps. These budget shortfalls forced localities to lay off teachers, firefighters, police officers, and social workers; close libraries and health clinics; and cut childcare, mental health services, public transit, and pollution control. This reduces the capacity for subsidiarity and the solving of problems at the local level.

In most states, the tax systems regressively put a greater burden on the poor and lower-income taxpayers. In Washington, Tennessee, and

Florida, for example, the lowest 20 percent of income-tax payers pay as much as 14 percent of their income in state and local taxes, whereas the wealthiest 1 percent of income earners pay less than 5 percent.

Their political program of *rule changes* can be characterized as "shrink and shift."

Shrink. To advance the goal of shrinking or limiting government, anti-government activists are targeting government programs developed over the last seventy years to level the economic playing field, including college tuition grants and loans, health insurance, programs for first-time home-buyers, retirement pensions, and programs that assist people to move out of poverty.

In practice, these anti-government crusaders don't aim to shrink the entire government. They are primarily opposed to the "Opportunity State," the government functions that foster social justice and broaden wealth and opportunity for all Americans. They also aim to eliminate or weaken the role of state and local government in regulating corporations to protect workers, the environment, and community interests. They don't vigorously oppose "corporate welfare" subsidies for needy corporations. "Corporate welfare" refers to the billions of direct subsidies and tax breaks that governments give to corporations, such as $42 million in tax breaks the state of Maryland gave to Marriott Hotels to remain in their state or money given to privately owned sports teams to build stadiums. So while they advocate shrinking government, they don't oppose tax subsidies and breaks for corporations.

Shift. A key strategy in the "starve the beast" program is to weaken the progressive tax system by shifting the tax burden off of wealth and onto wages and consumption. For several decades, tax-cutters have advocated incremental rule changes to reduce taxes on capital gains, dividends, inherited estates, and higher incomes. This has left other taxes, primarily on lower incomes, consumption, sales, and property ownership, to fill the gap of paying for our common expenses.

Under the federal tax cuts passed between 2001 and 2004, many lower- and middle-income taxpayers received a modest tax cut from the federal government. But they sometimes ended up paying more because of these largely invisible tax shifts, often in the form of increased local property taxes, state sales taxes, and dozens of nitpicky fee increases.

Nilda Garcia of New Bedford, Massachusetts, was pleased in 2003 when she received her $400 federal tax cut in an envelope with a letter from the president. But then she started to notice that while the federal government was feeling mighty generous, her state and city were taxing her more. Her driver's license fee went up, along with her property taxes. On the family vacation, they had to pay entrance fees to national and state parks that used to be free. Meanwhile, the public school that her children attended had to make a 10 percent cutback; the special education reading teacher who taught one of her children was laid off. "They just took up a collection from parents to buy new chairs, because they can't afford new ones," said Nilda Garcia.

"I slowly began to connect the dots," said Garcia. "The feds are giving massive tax cuts, mostly to the rich. I'm getting something, but the reality is I'm spending my tax cut to cover the cuts in services." Garcia's tax burden was being shifted onto other taxes and fees. And because the federal government was borrowing money at the same time it was taxing, they were shifting the tax burden onto her children as well. "The tax cut looks like a pretty package," observed Garcia. "But in the long run, working people like me and my children are going to end up paying more."

Other rule changes have shifted tax responsibilities off of large corporations and onto small businesses. One example is that Congress has placed a moratorium on states being able to levy sales taxes on Internet purchases. The biggest tax haven is now in cyberspace where on-line merchants can sell their goods tax free, while the local business down the street has to charge sales tax.

Another major shift has transferred the tax and spending burden off the federal government, with its comparatively more progressive system, to state and local governments, which have more regressive tax systems that are structured around property and consumption taxes.

The shrink and shift program results in budget cuts and tax shifts that erode the quality of life for all people. This shrink and shift program is actively underway and will take many forms in the coming years. Current debates over "tax reform" must be monitored closely for their fairness (i.e., who will be picking up additional tax duties) and the system's adequacy in meeting our shared responsibilities.

In the coming years, there will be a major debate over whether the 2001–2003 tax cuts for the very wealthy should be made "permanent." The costs of doing this should be weighed carefully. The price tag for making these tax cuts permanent over the next seventy-five years will be $11.7 trillion, $2.9 trillion of which are tax cuts for the richest 1 percent of households, those with annual incomes over $337,000 and average wealth of $5.8 million.[29] The priority of these tax cuts should be weighed against deficits, the costs of war, and the social needs that have been neglected in the current political environment. They should also be measured according to whether they will exacerbate or reduce inequality of income and wealth.

The rules governing the tax system have been changed dramatically in the last few decades. At the federal level, they have lessened the fairness of the tax system. The key step is to stop the erosion of fairness and defend our country's most progressive taxes, such as the estate tax. The moral justification for taxing great wealth at higher rates, and imposing estate or inheritance taxes, is that the wealthy have benefited disproportionately from the defense of property and the fertile ground created by public investment for private wealth. In the words of Bill Gates Sr., it is a "payback to society, the price of building and protecting wealth in the United States."

There are always tax reform proposals being debated, many of which are complicated to understand. The key is to apply what we know through Catholic social teachings to an assessment of any tax proposal:

- Who will pay more?
- Who will pay less?
- Will the tax proposal increase the tax burden on the poor, making it more difficult to live with dignity?
- Will it reduce the resources available for maintaining a vital commonwealth and minimal basic needs for the poor?

Tax cut mania is the result of our failure to recognize our interdependence and the necessity of solidarity for our survival and flourishing. Taxation is not only the "price we pay for civilization," as noted by Oliver Wendell Holmes; it is the price of solidarity. At stake is the question of what kind of society we want to become. Do we want to dismantle the ladder of opportunity we have attempted to build over the last half century? Do we want to further polarize our country along the lines of wealth and power?

The resentment toward taxation is an understandable response to the periodic examples we encounter of government waste and corruption. We need to accept that human institutions have flaws and that our democratic participation and vigilance is the only way to lessen waste and corruption and ensure that government serves the greater good.

Ultimately, defense of a fair revenue system must be linked to a broader moral framework and vision of what kind of communities and society we want to have. This is something that religious voices — your voices — can uniquely add to this debate.

Chapter Six

Root Causes, Part II
Global Trade and the Power of Corporations

The challenge is to ensure a globalization in solidarity, a globalization without marginalization.
— Pope John Paul II[1]

Solidarity in the Global Economy

For twenty-six years, Joylyn Billy rode a bus from her home in Cleveland, Ohio, to the Mr. Coffee plant in suburban Glenwillow. While former baseball great Joe DiMaggio pitched the Mr. Coffee appliances to consumers on television commercials, Joylyn Billy made them.

She reported to work on an assembly line that turned out as many as fifty-eight hundred coffee makers a day. She went to work through both her pregnancies and jokingly refers to two sons as "Mr. Coffee babies."

In 2000, she earned $10 an hour because of her seniority, while many workers earned closer to $8.00 an hour. She had health care benefits but no retirement pension. Her $20,000 a year income, combined with her husband's modest salary, still didn't give them much money to spare. Their house was small, they took no vacations, but they sent both their sons to college. "I live under my means," she says. "My husband and I chose education."

In the late 1990s, the Mr. Coffee plant took on a second shift and hired over one hundred workers who were transitioning off of welfare. Most of these workers were African American single mothers and grandmothers with children to care for. For many years, Joylyn Billy served as a team leader, teaching new recruits the fine points of their assembly line jobs.

In 1998, the Sunbeam Corporation bought Mr. Coffee. Two years later, they announced their plan to close the Glenwillow facility and move production to Matamoros, Mexico. Sunbeam said the closing would eliminate 380 jobs and save $7.5 million in its first year. That year Sunbeam CEO Jerry Levin was paid $2.7 million.[2]

Workers like Joylyn Billy were stunned, and it was a severe blow for many of the single-parent employees. "We did an excellent job all along," Billy said upon hearing the news. "People were proud of their work. People are not happy that they've lost their jobs."

In 2000, Billy traveled to the Sunbeam shareholders' meeting in Boca Raton, Florida, to express her alarm over the plant closing. "We were told how profitable we were," said Billy. "Jerry Levin told us last year that there was no reason to move us to Mexico."[3] At the time, she was still hopeful that the plant would stay open. "I'm a person who believes strongly in prayer, because it changes things," she told a reporter. "I believe when the hammer comes down, we'll still be here."

But at the end of May 2000, Mr. Coffee permanently closed its Ohio facilities. "Right now it's happening to us," said Billy, reflecting on job losses as a result of the globalizing economy. "But this is not Mr. Coffee alone. It's a national shame."[4]

When Mr. Coffee relocated its facilities to Matamoros, Mexico, along the U.S. border, María de Jesús Vásquez Rodríguez got a job. Vásquez Rodríguez was twenty-five when she started working as an inspector in the Mr. Coffee *maquiladora,* or assembly factory. She earned 700 pesos a week, the equivalent of $60. She lives with her parents, husband, and two sons in a housing development run by her Mexican union.

Vásquez Rodríguez and other workers were concerned from the beginning about Mr. Coffee's commitment to Matamoros. "We are worried about the plant's closing," said Vásquez Rodríguez. "Matamoros is based on industry. If the companies leave, we don't know where the work will come from." While Ohio workers earned $8 to $10 an hour, the Mexican workers earned $5.93 to $7.78 *per day.* But apparently that was not low enough, and Sunbeam's loyalty to Mexico was even more fleeting. In 2003, Sunbeam closed the Matamoros facility and moved Mr. Coffee manufacturing to China. After the plant closing, Vásquez Rodríguez looked for other work and her husband took a second job in order to support the family.[5]

Chinese workers at Mr. Coffee are paid between 25 and 41 cents an hour and have no labor protections. Many international factories in China have poor working conditions and violate human and worker rights. U.S. inspectors observe that "some Chinese factories make employees work 20-hour days without paying overtime, and that they live in overcrowded dormitories and use dangerous chemicals without safety equipment."[6]

Who is to blame for these changes? One Mr. Coffee manager said they started to explore overseas production after Wal-Mart demanded a $1.00 reduction in the wholesale price for coffeemakers. But Wal-Mart spokesman Bill Wertz says the company is just seeking better value for their customers. "We're a seller of goods, not a producer of goods," Wertz says. "Customers make the choice."

"We have little power in the global economy," said Virginia Green, a former coworker of Joylyn Billy at the Glenwillow, Ohio, plant. Green has been laid off from two other jobs since losing her job at Mr. Coffee. Companies are moving jobs to lower-wage countries because those companies are required to maximize profits for their shareholders, and currently there is no countervailing influence, no rule or regulation, and no organization that can stop them from doing so.[7]

This is one of a thousand stories that illustrate the dramatic changes occurring in the complex global economy we live in. It is hard to observe these multifaceted trends except through the analysis and reporting of others. Yet they are vital in explaining our economic lives today. As the U.S. bishops observed in 1996, "The preeminent role of the United States in an increasingly interdependent global economy is a central sign of our times."[8]

There are many marvelous books and resources to assist us to learn more about the global economy and how it works (see the resources section). In this discussion, we will consider the impact of the global economy on our communities and on our global neighbors as well as the meaning of solidarity across borders.

"Globalization" has been a highly charged buzzword in the last few years. Yet the United States has been part of a global economy for several centuries. Colonial ships plied trade routes to Europe, Africa, and Asia as the colonists traded rum, sugar, silk, spices, tea, and enslaved humans. What has changed is the nature, scale, and pace of globalization. Our own economic life is now integrated into the global economy in ways that our parents could never have envisioned.

"Globalization" describes the system of global trade in goods and services. "Free trade" refers to the lowering or removal of national barriers such as import restrictions, tariffs, and internal subsidies. Globalization also refers to the governing institutions of the global economy that shape the rules and results. These include the World Bank, the International Monetary Fund, and the World Trade Organization.

The Catholic Church itself is a transnational institution, which enables it to play a unique role in exploring the ethical implications of the global economy. The questions that concern us as Christians are: How does globalization affect human dignity, economic security for families, and social and environmental health? Does it strengthen human communities, family life, and participation in decision making? As Pope John Paul II observed, "There is an economic globalization which brings some positive consequences.... However, if globalization is ruled merely by the laws of the market applied to suit the powerful, the consequences cannot but be negative."[9] Understanding the role of the United States in the global economy is important. Our leaders have disproportionate power over the shape of the global economy and whether we as a human community come together to solve the enormous problems facing our planet.

There are those who enthusiastically embrace "free trade" as though it *pitting people out of poverty* were a new religion. Few if any politicians are truly free traders, as most support the preservation of trade rules that protect the jobs and salaries of their favored constituencies. On the other hand, there are those who appear to be "against globalization" because of its impact on U.S. jobs, global poverty, and immigration. The debate, however, is not *whether* we globalize, but *how* we integrate into the global economy.

The current brand of corporate-driven free trade globalization has fostered enormous inequalities. Understanding this type of globalization helps explain the competitive pressures that have led to the restructuring of work in our economy and why wages in the United States have stayed flat. It explains the flood of inexpensive consumer items in our marketplace and the tensions that underlie our relationships with other countries in the world.

Our first challenge is simply to open our hearts to the reality of human suffering around the world. To recognize that we are "one body" at the global level is part of our calling as U.S. Christians. Our job is to discern what this means. It is staggering to grasp the overwhelming impact of AIDS in Africa and the reality that thirty thousand children a day die from disease and malnutrition. One in six African children dies before the age of five. Two billion of the earth's inhabitants live on less than $2 a day and a billion live in "extreme poverty" without the most basic of necessities.[10] In truth, there is no way to fully grasp the magnitude of the situation without God's help.

To be born or to live in the United States is as if we were given a gift, received an inheritance, or won the lottery at birth! If we don't recognize this gift — and the obligations that come with it — then the world as we know it will perish. God willing, we will answer this call!

Once we understand our unique position and calling, then it becomes clear that we have some power and responsibility to shape the future of the global economy. As Jeffrey Sachs writes in *The End of Poverty*, "Currently, more than eight million people around the world die each year because they are too poor to stay alive. Our generation can choose to end that extreme poverty by the year 2025."[11] People of faith, putting their values into action, can lead this shift.

What Is New
in the Global Economy?

The global economy is perhaps the most powerful engine in our economic lives. Some believe that globalization is an inevitable, nature-like force that cannot be stopped or directed. But our Gospel perspective is very important here: The global economy is shaped by power, values, and human-created rules.

We are in a "constitutional moment" where the framework and rules that will shape the global economy for the next several generations are being decided. The alphabet soup of free trade treaties — NAFTA, FTAA, and CAFTA — are part of this rule-writing process. These treaties urgently call out for a moral vision rooted in Gospel teachings and values. What is new about the global economy?

Pace of Technological Change. Thanks to the Internet and other forms of advanced technology, the whole pace of globalization has accelerated. U.S. corporations can rapidly outsource assembly operations and activities like call centers to other countries.

Rapid Movement of Capital. Money moves much faster than it once did throughout the global economy, with the accompanying potential for instability. In 1980, over $336 billion a day (in 2004 dollars) circulated around the planet through the Clearing House Interbank Payments System (CHIPS), the single largest processor of U.S. dollar transactions. By 2004, the amount of funds transferred through the CHIPS system had quadrupled to $1.3 trillion a day.[12] This is five times the amount that all national central banks have on hand. Less than 2 percent of these transactions are related to trade or foreign investment. The remainder is, according to researchers John Cavanagh and Sarah Anderson, "for speculation and short-term investments that are subject to rapid flight when investors' perceptions change."[13]

Corporate Power. What's also new is the relative size and power of transnational corporations and their clout in shaping the rules of the global market. The two hundred largest companies are the most powerful, with annual sales exceeding the annual Gross Domestic Products of many nation states.[14] While some of these companies have created useful products and efficient economies of scale, the problem lies in their enormous size and power to shape laws, global trade rules, and markets.

The Impact of Globalization on People

We are now more interconnected with the rest of the world. The way the global economy is currently organized has some benefits to workers and consumers in different parts of the world. But it is also causing enormous problems and suffering. These problems include environmental degradation, an increase in extreme poverty, and the pitting of workers from different countries against one another.

Although there are ways that globalization has hurt people in the United States, we've also benefited at the expense of other countries. The United States has more power in the negotiating process and has used this power to its advantage. For example, we've urged other countries to open up their markets while we've continued to protect and subsidize some U.S. producers. And U.S.-based companies have benefited from pitting countries against each other, for example, countries that produce basic staples like coffee. Ordinary U.S. residents might benefit from low prices, but the huge beneficiaries are transnational corporations that profit by paying poverty wages in the Global South.

The "Race to the Bottom" Dynamic. Ever since the advent of the global economy, nation states concerned about protecting jobs and other national interests have erected barriers to free trade. The United States, for instance, has historically protected our agricultural, textile, and steel industries by barring some imports or imposing steep tax tariffs on imported products to ensure they won't undercut domestic markets.

To improve the quality of life in the United States, social movements have pressed for minimum wage and workplace safety rules, environmental protections, product safety regulations, and other standards. These standards also can raise barriers to imports that don't meet our requirements.

Part of the treaty-writing process of globalization is for countries to agree, in consort, to lower barriers to free trade and adopt uniform rules. It makes sense, in the language of trade agreements, to "harmonize standards," so that an electric blender made in South Korea can meet commonly agreed upon product safety rules and be sold in fifty other countries.

Where this gets tricky is in the struggle over who has to *lower* their standards and who has to *raise* their standards. And what if these "standards" are rules to protect the natural environment or maintain minimal worker protections. What happens, for instance, when a soccer ball made by child laborers in Pakistan competes against a Canadian soccer ball made by a unionized workforce with health insurance? It is obvious which soccer ball is going to be cheaper to purchase. But who should alter their standards and which is fairer from a moral perspective? Or what about a jacket made in a Seattle manufacturing plant that has strong worker safety rules and conforms to local environmental standards not to pollute the community. Can the Seattle company compete against a Chinese jacket manufacturer that pays its employees less than $1 a day and dumps pollutants into a stream? This is not a level playing field.

So the term "race to the bottom" has emerged to describe the process whereby countries with higher standards are forced to lower their standards as part of the globalization process. As the United States competes under these new rules, we experience tremendous pressure to lower our wage, worker safety and environmental standards. Global corporations, ironically, benefit from this race to the bottom. They can pit one community against another in deciding where to locate a manufacturing plant or service center. Whoever agrees to have the lowest wages, weakest safety rules, and lowest environmental standards wins!

Instead of lifting worker or environmental standards, most of the modern global trade debate has focused on issues such as protecting intellectual property. For example, the powerful Disney Corporation wants to ensure that *The Lion King* DVDs won't be illegally copied and sold in China. By comparison, there is very little focus on protecting environmental and labor standards.

Economic Insecurity and Poverty. The impact of "race to the bottom" policies on the economic security of U.S. families is significant. Wages have remained flat or fallen because many U.S. employers, like Mr. Coffee, are either moving plants or outsourcing work to other countries. Manufacturers have used the threat of relocation to force employees to take wage cuts and face reductions or eliminations of benefits. One U.S. company intimidated its employees during a labor negotiation by putting stickers on factory equipment saying, "Ship to Mexico."[15]

U.S. and Chinese workers should not be forced to compete against one another. In China, wages are depressed, workers are denied the right to form unions, and human rights organizations report the use of forced prison labor. Nor should U.S. workers be forced to compete to produce products at low cost with countries that employ child labor. A number of U.S.-based corporations have manufacturing plants in Nepal and Kenya, where over 40 percent of children between the ages of ten and fourteen are full-time workers.[16] The lesson is not to become anti-Chinese or anti-Kenyan, as these are humans struggling for dignity just like everyone else. Instead, our challenge is to be pro-human rights and encourage workers everywhere to achieve a minimum level of respect, dignity, and standards.

Advocates of unrestricted free trade argue that globalization will reduce poverty and bring better paying jobs to extremely poor regions of the world. There are certainly examples where trade has improved economic prospects for disenfranchised and poor people (see the case study "Guacamole and Corn" on p. 112). But without a moral vision and commitment to broadening wealth and opportunity, globalization will contribute to even greater inequalities. A clothing assembly factory in Honduras may pay higher wages than other jobs in the community, and this may lead to real improvements in the quality of life for some families. But the driving logic of unrestrained globalization is to keep searching for the lowest wages and the least-demanding communities to do business. As soon as the workers in Honduras come together, for example, and ask for bathroom breaks or a day off for a religious holiday or better wages — the assembly plant will pick up and relocate to the next low-wage haven. The plant in Honduras closes and another opens in Malaysia. When employees in Malaysia want to improve their lives, the corporation is off to China. Like the Mr. Coffee plants in Ohio and Mexico, Sunbeam Corporation has no national or regional loyalty and moved to China for lower wages.

The most serious problem is extreme global poverty, which has been exacerbated by some globalization policies. According to the United Nations Development Program, over one-third of the world's population — 2.7 billion people — live on less than $2 dollar per day. China accounts for almost 600 million of these people. Global trade practices have worsened these problems by devastating local agricultural sectors and forcing cuts in subsidies for basic food staples. The promise that global trade would actually lift up the poor has been largely unrealized. But there are encouraging examples of regions of the Global South that have taken steps toward expanding economic prosperity and harnessing control over the future of their economies.[17]

Defending the Environment. In the last several decades, we in the United States have made a lot of progress toward becoming better stewards of God's creation. There is broad support for laws protecting the environment, outlawing pollution of water, air, and land, and protecting endangered species. Individuals have become more aware of their own individual consumption of resources and are choosing to consume less electricity and drive more efficient cars. Children are taught the three Rs in school: Reduce, Reuse, and Recycle.

But new global treaties may have the effect of weakening U.S. environmental laws. For example, a 1996 ruling of the World Trade Organization challenged the U.S. Clean Air Act. This forced the United

GUACAMOLE AND CORN
MEXICO AND OPEN MARKETS

There are some positive stories for Mexicans about the impact of the opening of U.S. markets, including the story of avocado exports from Mexico. At the same time, many Mexicans have become poorer as a result of the North American Free Trade Agreement (NAFTA), the 1994 treaty that opened up more free trade between Mexico, Canada, and the United States.

For eight decades, the United States imposed barriers on the import of avocados from Mexico. Even under the terms of NAFTA, the United States only allowed Mexican avocados to gradually enter the country. In 1997, Mexican growers were allowed to sell in eighteen states but only during four months of the year. But now restrictions are being lifted and the number of Mexican avocados entering the United States doubled in the last year and is expected to continue to boom. In 2007, the final impediment to Mexican exports will be gone, as Mexican avocados will be allowed into the major U.S. avocado-growing markets of California, Florida, and Hawaii.

Many Mexicans felt that the historical avocado restrictions were unfair and protectionist. U.S. grower associations alleged that Mexican avocados were inferior in terms of sanitary restrictions and used this to justify import restrictions. Mexican growers now pay to have USDA inspectors in their packing plants to certify avocados for the U.S. market. Between

States to weaken our regulations and allow gas imports that failed to meet our cleanliness standards.[18] Meanwhile, the United States is "outsourcing" a lot of our pollution as we shift our core manufacturing overseas.

Laws protecting the environment in countries in the Global South are often weak, as they were in the United States several decades ago. Global companies flee to these countries in order to avoid paying the costs of ecologically sustainable processes and technologies. They join other global companies that are consuming the ecological treasure of creation as fast as possible. As a result, precious water around the world is being consumed or contaminated at a startling rate. Forests are being leveled and factories belch pollution into the air. Biodiversity is being rapidly destroyed in order to meet the short-term economic needs of our planet's residents.

GUACAMOLE AND CORN
(continued)

1997 and 2005, the number of certified growers in the avocado-lush state of Michoacán increased from sixty to twenty-five hundred. This has brought tremendous prosperity to the region, as evidenced by new housing construction, consumer purchases, and the number of workers flooding into regions like Michoacán, where field wages have grown 25 to 33 percent in two years.

The good news is that U.S. growers didn't lose out thanks to the growing popularity of avocados for guacamole and its health benefits. Since 2000, U.S. avocado consumption increased 80 percent and is expected to grow 15 percent a year. There are also burgeoning markets for avocados in China and other Asian countries, which Mexican growers hope to take advantage of.[19]

Avocado trade is a positive example of the benefits of open markets and a win-win situation thanks to an expanding market. But there are many other ways that Mexicans have lost ground as the result of free trade.

People don't usually connect the dots between NAFTA and the surge in illegal immigration to the United States from Mexico. NAFTA was marketed to the legislatures of all three countries as "trade, not aid" and as a means to *reduce* immigration. Trade has indeed soared between Mexico, the United States, and Canada. But the benefits have not gone to the great mass of Mexicans.

(continued)

Undermining Democracy and Participation. Besides implementing local environmental laws, there are many things communities are doing to improve the quality of community life. Some use local land use laws to restrict certain kinds of development that they deem harmful to the community. In order to receive property tax breaks, some towns require companies to pay a living wage and provide health insurance to their employees.

But what if a global trade treaty, negotiated in Geneva, Switzerland, declares these local ordinances to be illegal because they are a "restraint on trade"? What does this do to people's sense of local control? If this sounds implausible, such possibilities are very much part of active trade negotiations. As mentioned earlier, such practices are in violation of Gospel principles of participation and self-governance.

GUACAMOLE AND CORN
(continued)

Real wages for most Mexicans are lower than when NAFTA took effect in 1994. Even though Mexican worker productivity rose by 60 percent between 1993 and 2002, real wages declined by 5 percent in the same period. Many communities in rural Mexico are now ghost towns after being devastated by the loss of 2 million agricultural jobs since NAFTA went into effect. Mexican farmers were unable to compete with the imports flowing in from subsidized U.S. farmers, particularly corn. In the 2004–5 growing season, the United States exported 8 million tons of corn to Mexico, a 22 percent increase over 1995. And barriers to U.S. corn exports to Mexico will be completely eliminated in 2008.[20]

Illegal migration, which was actually declining in the years before NAFTA, has surged to between five hundred thousand and 1 million Mexicans a year in search of a lifeline to survival. People don't uproot from their communities, families, and culture unless there are powerful forces both pushing and pulling.

As David Morris wrote, "Ironically, one could argue that illegal migration is the only thing saving Mexico from the ravages of NAFTA and preventing it from collapsing into economic and social chaos."[21] In 2005, Mexicans working legally and illegally in the United States sent home $20 billion in remittances, the second largest source of foreign income after petroleum sales. Depending on how global trade is organized, there may be many more losers.

The global treaty-writing process might disenfranchise communities in the United States, but many less developed countries feel even more excluded. Many people in the Global South already feel as though the decisions that affect their lives are made in New York, London, or Hong Kong. This has led to a deep backlash against this form of globalization and resentment toward the powerful role of the United States in shaping the new rules of the global economy.

To read the Bible in the context of the global economy can stimulate some powerful reflections. Like the enslavement of the Israelites in Egypt, the chains of debt impoverish and enslave billions of people. The sheer numbers of people who are living in extreme poverty and in marginalized communities call out for bold responses.

Debt Bondage. Many developing countries are trapped into paying enormous annual interest payments. Debt burdens in Asia, Africa, and Latin America have caused massive suffering. These nations are forced to choose between investing in internal development and making interest payments to private banks and the International Monetary Fund based in the northern industrialized countries.

Many of these debts date from the 1970s and 1980s when corrupt government regimes borrowed extravagantly to purchase military equipment and finance the profligate lifestyles of high government officials. For example, former Zairian President Mobutu Sese Seko looted an estimated $5 billion from his country's treasury for his personal use during his thirty-year dictatorship beginning in 1965. Most of these funds were borrowed from international lenders.[22] According to the International Monetary Fund, over 70 percent of the people of the Congo (formerly Zaire) live below the international poverty level of U.S.$1 a day. But while few benefited from these international loans, they are stuck paying back an estimated $9.2 billion.[23]

There are seventy-seven nations that are characterized as "heavily indebted countries," including fifty-nine countries whose debt is more than half their Gross Domestic Product. For example, the Philippines owes over $62.6 billion in accumulated debt, which is 72.4 percent of its annual Gross Domestic Product. At the same time, 47 percent of the population of the Philippines lives on less than $2 per day.

As a result of this debt crisis, the last thirty years have been "lost decades" in the countries of the Global South, as literacy rates have dropped, disease and infant mortality rates have risen, infrastructure has crumbled, and the quality of life has deteriorated.

These conditions are not only precarious for citizens of these nations but "boomerang" to have negative consequences on the affluent countries of the Global North. As Sarah Anderson wrote in her report *Debt Boomerang,* "Most Americans know intuitively that today's world is an interconnected place. . . . Canceling developing country debts is not only the moral and just thing to do. It is also in our interest."[24] Anderson points out several ways that global debt boomerangs back and hits us in the United States.

- ◆ **Lost jobs and markets.** International debt forces countries in the Global South to lower wages and export products for less, which in turn forces U.S. wages down in the "race to the bottom" described earlier. Debt burdened countries make weak trading partners, adding to the U.S. trade deficit.

- **International health undermined.** Communicable diseases such as AIDS, malaria, and Asian bird flu do not recognize borders. In an interconnected world, the United States is also put at risk when impoverished and indebted countries must pay interest on their loans rather than invest in public health.

- **Global warming.** Heavily indebted countries are more inclined, out of desperation, to cut down rainforests and exploit other natural resources such as oil to raise revenue in order to pay debts. This contributes to global climate change, which is already affecting the United States through decreased air quality, groundwater contamination, and weather fluctuations.

- **Global insecurity.** Debt burdens make it more difficult for countries to maintain stability and prevent and recover from wars and internal conflicts. Such instability leads to increased militarization and repression, as countries impose austerity measures to pay back external debts. All this contributes to global insecurity, terrorism, and war.

- **Immigration pressures.** As we saw in our discussion of Mexico, countries swimming in debt are unable to invest in their own economic development, driving millions of people to migrate to other lands to survive.

We are one world. And though we are called to take unselfish action in solidarity with others, in the case of international debt, we have a shared interest in alleviating suffering and indebtedness in the Global South.

Gospel Values in the Global Economy

A law of indiscriminate profit is being globalized, and by its application all too many corporations contribute to the abuse of human rights in poor countries.
— Ricardo Bangi, Coop Italia, one of the largest
commercial enterprises in Europe[25]

In order to understand the roots of economic problems, we must explore the values and powerful institutions that drive the global economy. The unquestioned faith in the marketplace is a central value in this process with its emphasis on individual self-interest and unlimited consumption.

The current values of the global economy are competition without regard for outcomes, disconnection across borders, and a view that everyone is "alone and on their own." Some of the anti-globalization groups have adopted similar values — to ignore our fundamental interdependence and build up national walls, a sort of "Fortress America" mentality that denies our interconnection with the rest of the world.

Applying our Gospel values, we must foster new values of global sol-idarity, remembering that we are "one body" and "one humanity." Our integration is human, economic, and ecological. Whether or not China develops its economy in an ecologically sustainable way is very impor-tant to those of us on the rest of the planet. We all live downstream now, though some of us live further downstream.

The powerful elites in different countries share more in common with each other than they do with the citizens of their own countries who sleep outside their doors. Jeff Faux refers to this interconnected global elite as the "Party of Davos," a reference to the annual gathering of corporate and government leaders in Davos, Switzerland. The Party of Davos is well organized, shares a worldview, and has built institutions such as the World Trade Organization to virtually bypass national governments and advance a corporate free trade agenda. As Vatican officials write, "The governments of individual countries find their actions in the economic and social spheres ever more strongly conditioned by the expectations of international capital markets."[26]

The power of the Party of Davos in the global economy strengthens the clout of international corporations and shrinks the power of nation states and civil societies in shaping the outcomes of globalization. Through aggressive advocacy of liberalized or free trade in goods and services and the removal of barriers to the flow of capital, corporations have fueled a race to the bottom. These corporations have pushed a new system of rules and influenced the global financial institutions set up after World War II to expand free market capitalism around the planet.

In the last three decades, corporations have aggressively promoted an economic values system that is described, in most of the world, as "neoliberalism," the belief that virtually any government involvement in an economy is bad and that unfettered or free markets are always superior. As we have discussed earlier, Gospel teachings reject this vision of unrestrained capitalism.

The rules of the global economy have gradually changed through the process of writing new trade treaties and implementing the policies of institutions that manage the global economy, such as the International Monetary Fund and the World Trade Organization. These rule changes have created new winners and losers, with the vast number of losers being the global poor.

A faithful response to corporate globalization involves building a new countervailing moral power to address the current brand of globalization. U.S. consumers have tremendous clout in pushing for "high road" solu-tions to trade practices. The "fair trade" movement has touched many of our churches as our coffee hours now serve coffee made under certified "fair trade" conditions of adequate returns for growers and ecological sustainability. But the fair trade movement is branching out to include other food products, clothing, and artisan crafts.[27]

Through our institutions, we must monitor the process of global rule writing, ensuring that religious and civic organizations have a seat at the table and a voice over the moral vision for the global economy. The U.S. Conference of Catholic Bishops plays an important role in coalitions that are monitoring these developments. The church also played a leadership role in Jubilee 2000, one of the most important religious movements focused on global debt. The Jubilee 2000 movement took its name from the biblical injunction to forgive debts and redistribute concentrations of land every fifty years. Pope John Paul II spoke of both the church's jubilee year as well as the importance of the international movement to cancel the debts strangling many impoverished countries around the world. Thanks to church activists, the biblical principles of jubilee became part of the international economic discussion at the World Bank and the International Monetary Fund. By 2001, the Jubilee movement had won allies from diverse quarters, including televangelist Pat Robertson, rock star Bono of U2, former senator Jesse Helms, and the presidents of Britain and the United States.

During the summer of 2005, the occasional summit of the "G-8," the wealthiest countries in the world, met to approve a radical debt reduction program for the most heavily indebted countries in the world. There is no question that this has dramatically improved the prospects of the global poor. But this is just a beginning.

A major focus of religious activists concerned about extreme poverty is to ensure that the members of the United Nations attain the Millennium Development Goals of reducing extreme poverty by half by the year 2015. Passed in 2000 by all 191 member nations, the eight Millennium Development Goals hold out one of the most important promises and economic possibilities.[28] Part of the promise is for wealthy nations to provide increased development assistance and fairer rules in the global economy.

The problems of injustice in the global economy are profound. Yet we continue to think in terms of borders, nation-states, and national interests. Faux writes that "as long as the people of Canada, Mexico, and the United States see their political interests as separate from one another, while the elites of these same nations see their interests as joined, the gap in wealth and opportunity between the Party of Davos and the rest of us will continue to grow in all three nations."[29]

Faux suggests that an alternative way to participate in the global economy is to start with the creation of a North American common market with Canada and Mexico. Such a common market, like the European Union, would remove trade barriers among the three countries and permit greater flow of goods and workers. Together, the three countries would create a customs union and a common tariff that would protect them from a competitive race to the bottom with emerging trade blocs in Asia, especially China with hourly wages of less than 50 cents. This would encourage other nations to form regional blocs, raise standards, trade among each other, and strengthen fair and free trade.

A North American market could include a development fund for Mexico, a continental bill of rights that would raise labor and environmental standards, and a North American Congress for citizen participation in governance. Today, such a common market would stretch from Chiapas, Mexico, to the Arctic North, include 430 million people, and have a Gross Domestic Product of $20 trillion a year. It would include the economies of the United States, Canada, and Mexico, the world's first, eleventh, and twelfth largest economies respectively. The three countries are already deeply intertwined, with 85–90 percent of exports from Canada and Mexico already going to the United States.

This North American common market would interact and trade with other regional trade blocs throughout the world. Gradually, such trade blocs would expand, not through a race to the bottom but by lifting up standards. While global governance seems elusive at the moment, the idea of greater regional government has some real possibilities. As the U.S. economy struggles with economic challenges in the coming years, there will be a practical question of how people left to live and work in the United States will participate in the global market and maintain a sustainable standard of living. Traditional protectionism ignores how bound together we are with ordinary citizens of Canada and Mexico.

Hope lies in the examples of citizens building alliances across borders around issues such as debt relief, labor rights, public access to water, environmental policy, and many others. As Jeffrey Sachs writes, "When the end of poverty arrives, as it can and should in our own generation, it will be citizens in a million communities in rich and poor countries alike, rather than a handful of political leaders, who will have turned the tide."[30] These movements and experiments in broadening prosperity will serve as a model of how to build a global economy with solidarity.

WELCOMING THE STRANGER:
CHRISTIAN PERSPECTIVES ON IMMIGRATION

I pray for those who remain in the shadows of our society, for those who are unable to defend their rights or give their full talents to their communities without fear. I pray for those who feel compelled to risk their lives in crossing the vast desert that soon their suffering may end.
— Cardinal Theodore McCarrick[31]

One of the most divisive current issues in the United States is over immigration, particularly the immigration of people from Mexico and Central America. Congressional debate on this issue consists of discussions about how tall the wall should be between United States and Mexico and whether the United States should grant "amnesty" to immigrants who are currently in the United States without legal status.

How people feel about the immigration issue cuts across many constituencies and ideologies. But everyone agrees that the system is broken and in need of repair. There are an estimated 11 million immigrants living in the United States without documentation. And an estimated three hundred thousand to five hundred thousand enter the country each year. Since 1993, the United States has invested over $25 billion in securing the U.S.–Mexican border, tripling the number of border patrol agents. Over the same years, over three thousand migrants have died attempting to cross the deserts of Texas, New Mexico, Arizona, and California.[32]

In some respects, the immigration issue is a test of the Gospel notion of global solidarity in a heated public debate. There are pragmatic opponents

Addressing Concentrated Corporate Power

One of the most dramatic signs of the times is the rapid consolidation of corporate power. The world's two hundred largest global corporations exercise tremendous clout in the process of writing the laws and rules of the U.S. and global economies. It is impossible to understand the changes in the economy without understanding the role of these colossal corporations.

WELCOMING THE STRANGER
(continued)

of expanded legal immigration who are doubtful about the capacity of our country to absorb and integrate newcomers. But the issue is also infused with coded and deep attitudes of national and racial superiority.

The Catholic Church is deeply involved in the immigration issue because of the Gospel mandate. The Old and New Testament are full of lessons about the treatment of migrants and travelers. Jesus calls on us "welcome the stranger," for "what you do to the least of my brethren, you do unto me" [Matthew 25:35, 40]. The other reality is that many in the Catholic community are recent immigrants who need the assistance and the supporting voice of the church. We are a nation of immigrants and a church of immigrants. Because of Christian respect for life, we are concerned about human suffering and the moral consequences of the broken immigration system. The current system, for example, forces families to separate and live in fear.

In January 2003, the U.S. and Mexican bishops joined together to issue a joint pastoral letter concerning migration, *Strangers No Longer: Together on the Journey of Hope*. The letter was the result of several years of listening and studying the matter from both sides of the border. Catholic and other Christian organizations have been at the forefront of lobbying for changes in U.S. immigration law. The letter advocates the creation of a temporary worker program with worker protections, a process for earning the right to citizenship, reductions in

(continued)

Corporate concentration is in part the result of mergers, as big fish swallow up smaller fish. In the last decade there have been more corporate mergers than any previous period in modern history. Most of these mergers are taking place in finance, technology, petroleum, and communications. In 2005, over $2.7 trillion in mergers were announced worldwide ($1.3 trillion in the United States), up from $464 billion worldwide ($195 billion in the United States) in 1990.[33]

As a culture, we have accepted this rise of corporate power without much critical questioning about what it means for our democracy,

WELCOMING THE STRANGER
(continued)

waiting times for separated families, and the restoration of due process for immigrants.[34]

Our Gospel values also call on us to look at the roots of the migration-immigration issue: Why are people coming to work in the United States? What conditions are they leaving behind?

Take the example of Sabina Bautista. When Sabina Bautista gives a tour of her village of Santa Ana de Valle in Mexico's southern state of Oaxaca, the words "ghost town" come to mind. A fifty-six-year-old restaurant owner, Bautista has seen her Zapotec Indian farming and rug-weaving village empty out over the last two decades. "The people who own that house are working in Los Angeles," she said, pointing at a boarded-up brick house. "The people next door are in Oregon. These people would like to stay here," Bautista observes, "but there is no work. Some day, they will come home to retire."[35]

Emigration, poverty, and the collapse of Mexico's rural economy help to explain the reason that almost half a million people a year migrate to the United States. There is a growing and troubling fault line between Mexico's northern and southern regions. Residents of the industrialized northern border states are more affluent. Residents of the agricultural southern states and Mexico City are among the majority of the 80 percent of Mexicans who make less than $500 U.S. per month. In southern Mexico, villages like Santa Ana de Valle are common. Farmers and farm workers in this region face the challenges described

economy, and culture. We take for granted the role that corporations play in different arenas of our lives, including media ownership, health care, energy policy, and advertising. We uncritically allow corporations to pay for political conventions, lobby our elected officials, and prepare draft environmental laws for legislators. How did this come to pass?

Perhaps we tolerate the presence of massive corporations because of the good we perceive they contribute to our society, as employers and the providers of useful products and services. We've seen a few bad eggs, in the

WELCOMING THE STRANGER
(continued)

earlier in this chapter (see "Guacamole and Corn" on pages 112–14). They have been devastated by free trade policies that have flooded local markets with cheap U.S. corn and beans, subsidized by U.S. taxpayers.

In Mexico, the gap between rich and poor is the largest of the thirty industrialized countries that are part of the Organization for Economic Cooperation and Development. Since 2000, according to the Center for Economic and Research Policy, Mexico's wages have been flat and growth has been a stagnant 2 percent.[36] These nationwide statistics fail to reflect the even worse conditions in the country's south.

If the United States wants Mexico to address the root causes of emigration, it needs to understand what life looks like in Santa Ana de Valle. The U.S. and Mexico must respond together to the deep distress facing Sabina Bautista and her neighbors with bold efforts to create opportunities for employment and sustainable agriculture. Mexico will need some real help from the United States, not just more sermons about "free trade, not aid" and calls to open up Mexico's national oil industry to U.S. investors.

The Catholic Church has played an important role in advocating sustainable development policies, fair trade, and economic policies that address the plight of agricultural and low-skilled workers in the global economy. Only actions that address deep economic inequalities at the global level will solve the problem of forced migration.

form of Enron and WorldCom, but we may consider them as exceptions to the rule. Gospel teachings affirm the importance of private enterprise and an acceptable level of profit. But the nature of private business and the amount of profit must be balanced by other moral measures and concerns, such as justice.

A key concern with corporate expansion lies in the concentration of power in the hands of a few. This power imbalance becomes most apparent in our relative powerlessness to stop corporate harm. The examples, unfortunately, could fill another book.

- Citigroup buys up smaller banks and private mortgage brokers that engage in predatory lending practices, bilking thousands of senior citizens out of their homes. How do we stop this practice?

- Corporations use their lobbyists and tax accountants to game the federal tax system in order to reduce their tax bills and receive billions in government subsidies. How do we ensure that corporations pay their fair share?

- Unocal wants to build an oil pipeline in Southeast Asia and formally collaborates with a repressive military regime in Myanmar, notorious for its blatant human rights abuses. Should we allow this to happen?

- Union Carbide overlooks plant safety requirements leading to an explosion that kills thousands of people and injures hundreds of thousands in Bhopal, India. None of the six back-up safety systems were operational. Should this company be allowed to continue to exist and make profits for its shareholders?

- Many companies violate pollution laws, but when they are caught, they view the paying of fines as a "cost of doing business." How can we ensure corporations obey the law and respect our ecological treasure?

It is reasonable to ask, in this context, "Who rules whom?" How did corporations get so much power in our society? Are "we the people" still the sovereign, and corporations subordinate to us? Or are corporations becoming the new sovereign, the new royalty, and we the subjects? Or to slightly modify a question discussed earlier: Do corporations serve people or do people serve corporations?

A number of scholars have grappled with the question of how corporations have evolved in our society and how they accumulated such power and influence. In theory, corporations are legal constructs, not people. We the sovereign citizens allow individuals to form corporations through our legal system. In the century following the American Revolution, state governments granted limited corporate charters for specific purposes, such as creating a flour mill or building a road. If a corporation failed to live up to its purpose or broke a law, its charter was revoked. Most corporations were chartered for a limited period of time, less than ten years, and were prohibited from owning other corporations. Owners were personally liable for the moral behavior and debts of their corporations — unlike today, where owners and managers hide behind a "corporate veil" of limited liability.[37]

In the last half of the nineteenth century, corporations gained new powers and protections. Through a series of legal decisions and state laws, the modern corporation gained certain rights associated with people or "personhood." They obtained the right of free speech, which has been used to influence elections and lobby on legislation and government policy. State corporate charters were altered to allow corporations to exist forever, to own other corporations, and to be protected by the right to privacy, thwarting citizen efforts for greater accountability.[38] Understanding this history helps inform our discussion on corporate ethical responsibility.

Gospel Values and Corporate Responsibility

An important question from a Christian perspective is whether corporations are ethical entities. We know there are ethical individuals serving on corporate boards, functioning as shareholders, and working as managers and employees within corporations. But the "hard-wiring" of most corporations is toward maximization of profit for shareholders and reducing any costs (labor, environmental, regulatory, taxation) that diminish this profitability. If profit is the ethical compass, are good individuals ethically constrained by the focus and values of the larger institution?

Many Christians, in their work for economic justice, find themselves face-to-face working to change corporate behavior or limit corporate harm. Here they encounter a values clash. Instead of embracing responsibility, many corporations are involved in the activity of shifting responsibility and costs. Workers are not responsible for the behavior of the corporation, we are told, because they must obey management or lose their jobs. Managers and chief executive officers (CEOs) are not responsible, because they are only responding to their corporate boards. Corporate board members have limited liability and claim to be representing "shareholder interests." But further investigation reveals that shareholders, try as they might, have very little clout to change corporate behavior.

In Gospel economics, there is no passing the buck on ethical responsibility. Simply put, we are *all* responsible. As one of the precepts of Catholic economic teaching states, "Workers, owners, managers, stockholders, and consumers are moral agents in economic life. By our choices, initiative, creativity, and investment, we enhance or diminish economic opportunity, community life, and social justice."

It appears there is something inherent in the structure of the modern corporation that limits accountability and constrains the ability of individuals to act ethically. Because the principal purpose of the corporation is the maximization of profits, the internal systems and values of corporations are focused on this goal, to the exclusion of other values. All choices and behaviors are measured against the "bottom line," including obedience to U.S. laws. Many corporations might explicitly state their fealty to the rule of law, but they spend enormous resources to rework these laws or to circumvent them by basing operations in other countries and jurisdictions.

Individuals can make a difference within corporations. In *Saving the Corporate Soul*, David Batstone chronicles many of the ethical decisions that corporate managers can and do make that influence the behavior of corporations. "Companies that lack integrity do not develop overnight," Batstone writes. "A series of small, subtle choices led them to their fate; each decision sets the stage for the next, more corrosive act.... The problem actually lies in the company's culture, and how it encourages individuals to consider deviant behavior as standard operating procedure."[39] Individuals and companies can change this culture, with powerful and meaningful positive outcomes.

Catholic teaching affirms the importance of private enterprise, business, and free markets. But the moral compass in large corporations seems to be aimed in a different direction. As Pope John Paul II said in an important speech in Canada: "The needs of the poor take priority over the desires of the rich; the rights of workers over the maximization of profits; the preservation of the environment over uncontrolled industrial expansion; production to meet social needs over production for military purposes."[40]

As we've stated, the problem is one of power imbalance. Concentrated corporate power has been one of the major *engines* of economic change. To alter this dynamic, we must not only build a countervailing set of values and interests, but we must also change the internal wiring of corporations as they are currently defined. Some of the ways to address unchecked corporate actions lie in consumer action, government rules, and using the power of ethical ownership to press for change.

For several years, corporate scandals such as Enron and WorldCom have drawn attention to the breakdown of accountability. Enron used its political power to rewrite government rules, weaken accounting standards, and lie about its financial soundness. These scandals prompted legislative changes in 2002, in the form of the Sarbanes-Oxley Public Company Accounting and Investor Protection Act.[41] These legal reforms addressed internal corporate governance matters but didn't tackle the fundamental problems of wider corporate accountability.

Many of the changes in corporations that our society needs are not anti-business and will actually strengthen healthy business activities. The economy benefits from the flourishing of a wide range of types and sizes of business entities. And as a society, we share the social good that comes from a robust marketplace without excessive government involvement and interference. But all businesses need a framework of fair rules to operate, and small businesses especially need fair rules that don't put them at a competitive disadvantage with large companies. Some of the following actions proposed to address corporate harms don't necessarily involve government involvement. But ultimately some government rule making is required to prevent the most blatant abuses.

Exercising Shareholder Power. In theory, shareholders can use their status as owners to influence corporate practices. Many shareholders have used this power to influence the moral vision of companies. Some of the earliest shareholder activists were religious orders of Catholic sisters. In the mid-1960s, the Sisters of Loreto were concerned about strip-mining practices surrounding the poor Appalachian communities where they worked and lived. They purchased stock in the Blue Diamond Coal Company and filed a series of shareholder resolutions calling on "their company" to improve their environmental practices. The prophetic sisters were persistent, showing up at shareholder meetings to press their case and garnering massive publicity and support for their position. The company, which called the sisters the "stinging nuns," eventually modified its mining practices.

For over forty years, socially concerned organizations have utilized the shareholder process to attempt to change corporate behavior. Over 275 religious organizations of all denominations have taken the lead through the Interfaith Center on Corporate Responsibility. Even if shareholder initiatives don't win a majority of shareholder votes, they raise public awareness and open up dialogues with corporate management. The most effective shareholder resolutions are introduced in tandem with larger organizing efforts to educate the public and press for change, such as the movement to pressure U.S. companies to stop doing business in South Africa during the apartheid era.

Socially Responsible Investing. Another way that owners can use their power is by avoiding investments in socially injurious corporations. A growing number of religious institutions and individuals are demanding that ethical criteria inform their investment portfolios, which has spawned a growth industry in "socially responsible investment." In 2005, over $2.29 trillion in investments were managed according to ethical criteria.[42] There is evidence that companies care about their reputations and will change their behavior to be included within such investment portfolios.

Consumer Action. Another important influence on corporate behavior is the consumer. In a business climate where "customer satisfaction" is supposedly king, organized consumers have real leverage to affect corporate behavior. During the 1970s, consumer boycotts of textile products manufactured by the J. P. Stevens Company drew national attention to the company's hardball anti-worker practices. From the boycott of the Nestlé Company because of its unethical marketing campaigns promoting infant formula in developing countries, to the grape boycotts called by the United Farm Workers, consumers have been effective in altering corporate practices.

In 2001, a group of tomato pickers in Florida launched a nationwide boycott of Taco Bell fast-food restaurants. The Coalition of Immokalee Workers pressed for higher pay and improved working conditions for the largely Central American immigrant pickers. The *Washington Post* reported that Taco Bell was the target because the company pressed growers for volume discounts. "Farmworkers today," the report said, "usually earn forty cents for each thirty-two-pound bucket of tomatoes they pick, the same rate as thirty years ago, and have to pick 2 tons of tomatoes to earn about $50." Hundreds of religious and community organizations participated in the boycott. In March 2005, they announced a victorious agreement with Taco Bell, which agreed to pay an additional penny per pound of tomatoes, the increase being directly passed onto the workers.[43]

There is a large constituency of religious and ethical consumers who will purchase products made by ethical companies and avoid products and services from companies that treat their workers and the environment poorly. Surveys and experience also show that many consumers will pay more for products that are certified as meeting higher ethical standards, for example, not being produced in sweatshops or with toxic chemicals.

There is a growing movement of "green" consumers who won't buy products that are bad for the environment. And as we discussed in the previous section, there is a significant movement of consumers who demand "fair trade" practices in their purchase of products such as coffee, tea, clothing, and crafts. In Bangor, Maine, a "clean clothing" campaign pressured clothing merchants to identify and sell clothing that was not made in global sweatshops. Conscientious consumers who apply ethical criteria to their shopping have changed corporate behaviors.

Laws That Could Strengthen Corporate Accountability. There are a number of rule changes that could strengthen the chain of responsibility within corporate governance and broaden accountability and clout for boards, shareholders, accountants, and other oversight officials. These include:

- **Board independence.** Many corporate boards still include board members with fundamental conflicts of interest, for example, board members who are also paid consultants or business partners with management. Public corporations should have independent boards free of insider connections so that they can hold management properly accountable.

- **Democratic reforms.** Corporations are not very democratic institutions. They rarely have contested elections for board members. Shareholders should be able to put forward candidates and slates in board elections. Some shareholder groups have proposed that candidates that fail to win 50 percent of shareholder votes should not be elected, giving shareholders the power of choosing "none of the above." The voting process should ensure "one share, one vote" policies and eliminate automatic proxy votes for management, which is the current procedure.

- **Shareholder power.** One of the few ways that shareholders can exercise power is by introducing shareholder resolutions. With minimal obstacles shareholders should be able to put forward resolutions that have a real impact on management. Rules and regulations governing shareholder resolutions and actions should be neutral, not biased in favor of management. Shareholder resolutions passed in two consecutive years should be binding on the corporation, not just advisory.

- **Community rights.** Communities have a right to know certain private information regarding corporate actions that have a direct impact on the health and financial solvency of the community. Communities should be able to require corporate disclosure about public subsidies received, labor practices, taxes paid, laws broken, and environmental practices, including use of toxic chemicals.

Rewiring the Corporation

We recognize that many reform efforts related to corporations fall short in changing corporate behavior and mitigating harm. We need to "rewire" the corporate accountability machinery, with a new legal and ethical framework, if we are going to address the root causes of the problem.

One important area of reform would redefine the governance system to expand the voice and power of other stakeholders. Presently, the absentee investor is the principal voice and stakeholder in the modern global corporation. One meaningful reform would be to expand the legal definition of the corporate governing board to include representation of other stakeholders, for example, workers, consumers, environmental stewards, and the communities where the business operates. The charters of many corporations in European countries already have these features of what they call "co-determination," which ensures that corporations have representation of workers and communities on their boards.

A more far-reaching change would be to fundamentally alter the legal framework within which corporations exist. This would mean expanding the public's power in relation to oversight of corporate practices and rethinking some of the rights and powers that corporations have usurped in our democracy. Important reforms include:

Federally Chartered Corporations. Those corporations that operate across state and international boundaries should be chartered at the federal level and include clearly spelled out rights and obligations. No longer should corporations pit states against one another in a race for the lowest standards and fewest social obligations. Over time, perhaps there will be internationally chartered corporations for global businesses. Such overarching charters could broaden the definition of corporations to make them responsible for including long-term sustainability as part of their fiduciary and financial responsibilities.

Corporate Charter Reform. A federal or state corporate charter reform effort could fundamentally shift some corporate dynamics. For instance, uniform corporate charters could curtail unlimited corporate powers, legislate real board independence, limit the lifespan of corporations without review, and more actively revoke charters of outlaw corporations. There is no reason, for example, that the Union Carbide Corporation should continue to exist after its extreme negligence in Bhopal, India.

Limiting Corporate Influence in Our Democracy. Corporations should be prohibited from participation in our democratic processes, including elections, funding of candidates, political parties, and advertising aimed at influencing the outcome of elections and legislation. To some, this may seem like a prohibition on free speech. We should vigorously defend personal free speech, but there is no constitutional right to free speech for legal constructs called corporations. And unfortunately corporate speech has drowned out other forms of human free speech.

This rewired corporation of the future will still be vibrant, innovative, and productive. Some corporations will have thousands of employees and high public profiles. But they will be much more accountable to shareholders, to the communities in which they operate, and to customers, employees, and the public interest. Their concentrations of economic power will not entail political power, undermining our democratic institutions. Their power in our society will be tempered by the common good and human rights.[44]

It is perhaps difficult to imagine that the actions of an individual or church social action group could make a dramatic difference in the behavior of powerful global corporations. And we shouldn't delude ourselves into thinking that powerful corporations will change easily. But the reality is that conscientious action and witness is making an impact every day of the year.

As Ralph Estes wrote in *Taking Back the Corporation*, "Nothing will be more effective in reforming corporations than millions of individual voices raised in many localities and through many means and media, creating a force that cannot be denied. Your voice, and your action is essential."[45]

The last two chapters have looked at the root causes of the economic trends that touch our daily lives. We know that the economy is a human created institution, shaped by human beings and our values. This creates a real responsibility for each of us to engage as faithful citizens to ensure that the rules are fair. The direction of wages, global trade, and tax policy all call for a recognition of Gospel values.

There have been dramatic challenges in our current economy, especially for the poor. The worship of the market, the invisibility of those in need, the powerful organized interests of greed and selfishness — all are formidable forces. The rules of the economy currently lean toward perpetuating injustice. And the dominant values reinforce these rules.

There is an empty space waiting for a moral dialogue about the economy. The overwhelming feeling is that "There Is No Alternative" (TINA) sometimes referred to as the "TINA Syndrome." It is very difficult to envision an alternative to the current economy that might be organized according to different values while still retaining the best aspects of a free market economy. But here is where Catholic social teaching and principles can have a major impact — not just in opposing the injustices in the economy, but in framing a vision for a just economy.

Chapter Seven

The Moral Measures
for Our Economy

In our discussion of economic life, we have mostly focused on the problems in our economy and the roots causes of economic injustice. Let us now turn toward a bolder and more affirmative expression of Christian economics.

While there are no economic systems free from human sin, we can identify the principles and practices that would be part of a more just economic system. There are emerging economic organizations that give us a glimpse of the possibilities for an economy governed by a more Christian moral vision. In chapter 8, we will explore some of the new institutions and organizations that are part of this alternative economy. Many of these alternatives — some which are not well known — embody Christian principles that we can learn from. In this chapter, we'll focus on some of the moral measures for evaluating economic development efforts and explore more deeply the notion of "common wealth."

Moral Measures

At the foundation of values underlying a Christian perspective on economic life is our respect for all life and our recognition of human interconnection and solidarity. Some of the principles of this new economic framework are completely rooted in the biblical teachings on economics that we discussed earlier. These include:

- **Work as a fundamental expression of human dignity.** Economic activity should affirm the fundamental worth and dignity of the individual and create opportunities for the expression of our humanness and creativity.

- **The importance of the private market.** Our principles affirm the importance of privately owned businesses and the private marketplace as a mechanism for exchange, trade, initiative, entrepreneurship, and livelihood.

132

- **Private property balanced with the common good.** Our tradition recognizes and affirms the right of private ownership of property, such as housing and capital. A cornerstone of a healthy economy is a broad ownership of private wealth and opportunity. But unlimited individual wealth is not an absolute right and must be balanced by considerations of the common good.

- **The vital role of government.** The role of government is to protect human rights and secure basic economic justice for all members of society.

- **Global-local interconnection.** We recognize the interconnection between the global economy and our local economic lives — as well as understanding that our local choices and economic activity have implications for the global economy.

- **A stakeholder economy.** Based on these principles, we are seeking economic models that recognize that there are a variety of stakeholders in the economy, not just absentee owners of investment capital. We seek models of corporate and public governance that represent the concerns and interests of workers, investment capital, consumers, managers, community residents, and the ecological world.

- **Social mortgage on capital.** A just economy recognizes that there is no absolute right to capital. As the pastoral letter observes: "Resources created by human industry are also held in trust. Owners and managers have not created this capital on their own. They have benefited from the work of many others and from the local communities that support their endeavors."[1] The bishops call this a "social mortgage" in order to underscore that society has a mortgage, a claim, on private capital.

- **A just allocation of value.** A moral economy allocates value based on its source. The sale of a product should, for instance, result in the allocation of value and profit to the various stakeholders: investors, managers, and workers.

- **Recognition of the commons and the commonwealth.** A healthy economy recognizes that economic life depends on the protection of the ecological and social commons — or "commonwealth."

There are three Christian economic concepts that we've already mentioned, but deserve a deeper exploration. These are the "preferential option for the poor," solidarity, and subsidiarity.

The Preferential Option for the Poor

Earlier we discussed the principle that the moral measure of the health of the economy is gauged by how the poor are faring. We mentioned the "preferential option for the poor," not as an invocation of class against class, but as part of the commitment of respect for life.

The church's love for the poor is inspired by the poverty of Jesus and by his attention and ministry to the poor and excluded. In the Gospel of Matthew, the Beatitudes are

- Blessed are the poor in spirit: for theirs is the kingdom of heaven.
- Blessed are the meek: for they shall possess the land.
- Blessed are they who mourn: for they shall be comforted.
- Blessed are they that hunger and thirst after justice: for they shall have their fill.
- Blessed are the merciful: for they shall obtain mercy.
- Blessed are the clean of heart: for they shall see God.
- Blessed are the peacemakers: for they shall be called the children of God.
- Blessed are they that suffer persecution for justice' sake, for theirs is the kingdom of heaven.

In Aramaic, the language of Jesus, the words "poor" and "meek" refer to those who are bent down, miserable, afflicted, impoverished — and also humbled. This reflects how love for the poor is concerned with both material poverty and social marginalization. It recognizes that we all have a claim on God's bounty. God gave the earth to everyone for sustenance, and each person has a claim on this gift for his or her full human development. The poor, by definition, lack what they need to flourish as humans; a "preferential love and option" for the poor hopes to ensure their fulfillment. Given the global dimensions of poverty, Pope John Paul II wrote, this "love of preference for the poor, and the decisions which it inspires in us, cannot but embrace the immense multitudes of the hungry, the needy, the homeless, those without health care and, above all, those without hope of a better future."[2]

Christian attitudes toward addressing poverty are a radical departure from the traditional notion of charity, service, and sharing. As the Pontifical Council for Justice and Peace observed, our perspective toward serving the poor is rooted in the Gospel injunction that "you have received without paying, give without pay" (Matthew 10:8). St. Gregory the Great said, "When we attend to the needs of the those in want, we give them what is theirs, not ours. More than performing works of mercy, we are paying a debt of justice."[3]

In practical terms the global and national economy should be focused on the elimination of poverty. Corporations, government, local businesses, and civic organizations should see this as central to their missions, not as an external factor they are not responsible for. Our society should hold as a central measure of success the progress toward ending extreme poverty at the global level and the elimination of poverty and marginalization in the United States.

Solidarity

As in the parable of the good Samaritan, the measure of solidarity is not only how we treat family members, people who live in our neighborhood, or fellow congregants at our church. The "neighbor" that we must treat as well as ourselves includes people we don't know, who may not look like us or live near us. They are the strangers, the poor, the "least of these" who are often invisible in our communities.

Our religious tradition reminds us that we are "one body," interconnected and interdependent. Every day of our lives, though we seldom realize it, we are completely dependent upon the kindness and good will of strangers. A thousand times a day we rely on others to faithfully do their work in the world — the bus driver, the teacher, the food inspector, the seamstress, the farmer, the counselor at the poison-control center, the police officer, the business manager, the sewage pump operator, and so on. Without these threads of human trust and solidarity, society as we know it would unravel.

We are responsible for one another. Not only do we have a duty to be responsible for ourselves, but our faith requires us to be responsible for others. Each of us has multiple roles in society: parent, child, worker, owner, tenant, landlord, shareholder, consumer, neighbor, manager. We may not own any shares of a corporation, but we are a member of a church that does, and so we have a responsibility of stewardship for investments. In each of these roles we have ethical rights and responsibilities toward others. One of our challenges is to reflect on all our various roles and the power we have to make a difference. As the pastoral letter on the economy reminds us, "By our choices, initiative, creativity, and investment, we enhance or diminish economic opportunity, community life, and social justice." Our actions *or inactions* are not neutral: we either contribute or detract from economic outcomes by our choices.

As John Paul II wrote in his encyclical letter *Sollicitudo Rei Socialis,*

> Solidarity is an authentic moral virtue, not a feeling of vague compassion or shallow distress at the misfortunes of so many people, both near and far. On the contrary, it is a firm and persevering determination to commit oneself to the common good. That is to say

to the good of all and of each individual, because we are all really responsible for all.[4]

The process of changing institutions — and the underlying economic and social structures — is the hardest work. The bishops' pastoral letter on the economy observes, "The transformation of social structures begins with and is always accompanied by a conversion of the heart."[5] But it also requires persistent witness and collaboration with others.

What does it mean, in particular, to stand in solidarity with the poor in today's global economy? The Canadian Catholic bishops made a significant contribution to reflecting on this topic in a five-step process that moves us from standing with the poor to taking action in solidarity:

1. Be present with and listen to the experiences of the poor, the marginalized, the oppressed of our society.

2. Develop a critical analysis of the economic, political, and social structures that cause human suffering.

3. Make judgments in the light of the Gospel principles concerning social values and priorities.

4. Stimulate creative thought and action regarding alternative models for social and economic development.

5. Act in solidarity with popular groups in their struggles to transform society.[6]

The Reverend James Forbes of New York City's treasured Riverside Church put it another way. "In order to get into heaven," he preaches, "you will need a letter of reference from the poor."

MAHATMA GANDHI'S CONCEPT OF SOLIDARITY

I will give you a talisman. Whenever you are in doubt, or when the self becomes too much with you, apply the following test. Recall the face of the poorest and the weakest person whom you may have seen, and ask yourself, if the step you contemplate is going to be of any use to him or her. Will this person gain anything by it? Will it restore them to a control over their own life and destiny? In other words, will it lead to swaraj [freedom] for the hungry and spiritually starving millions? Then you will find your doubts and your self melt away.

—Mahatma Gandhi, 1948[7]

Subsidiarity

An important question in a just economy is where power should reside and at what level of government. Catholic teaching argues that government and other institutions should operate by the principle of subsidiarity, which calls for a decentralization of decision making when appropriate. In essence, problems should be addressed as close to their source as possible. In his 1931 encyclical letter, *Quadragesimo Anno*, Pope Pius XI poetically describes the principle of subsidiarity:

> Just as it is gravely wrong to take from individuals what they can accomplish by their own initiative and industry and give it to the community, so also it is an injustice and at the same time a graver evil and disturbance of right order to assign to a greater and higher association what lesser and subordinate organizations can do. For every social activity ought of its very nature to furnish help (*subsidium*) to the members of the body social, and never destroy and absorb them.[8]

Decision making should be as close to those affected as possible, encouraging participation and discouraging distant and remote governance. Sometimes "subsidiarity" is misinterpreted to mean local control and devolution of responsibility, but this would be inaccurate. As a Vatican statement observes, "Subsidiarity without solidarity runs the risk of encouraging forms of self-centered localism."[9] There are some government responses to poverty, for instance, that might best be administered at the federal level to avoid local bias.

There is a qualification to the notion of subsidiarity. As Mary Jo Bane writes in *Lifting Up the Poor*, a book about Catholic theology and poverty, "higher levels of civil society and government must take responsibility when lower levels cannot and do not. Neighbors provide care when families fail; local governments assume responsibilities not exercised by neighborhood groups; the federal government acts when state action is inadequate or inequitable."[10] Subsidiarity is not a substitute for solidarity.

The Commonwealth Economy

In the summer of 1997, hundreds of summer camps run by the Girl Scouts and other charitable groups around the United States received a shocking letter. The letter informed them that in order to sing such campfire favorites as "Row, Row, Row," "Puff the Magic Dragon," or "This Land Is Your Land," they would have to pay a licensing fee to the American Society of Composers, Authors and Publishers (ASCAP).

ASCAP holds the legal copyright to many songs that most of us assumed could be sung for free, without permission. But in 1997 ASCAP decided it was time to collect some money for "public performances," including summer camps in their definition.

ASCAP began its negotiations with the American Camping Association with an offer of $1200 per season per camp, eventually agreeing on a lower fee. In his book *Brand Name Bullies,* David Bollier describes the reaction of Sharon Kosch, the director of the San Francisco Bay Girl Scout Councils programs, to an ASCAP letter demanding $591. Her first thought was "You guys have got to be kidding. They can't sing the songs?" If payment was not forthcoming, ASCAP would sue for legal recourse. "It's pretty threatening," said Kosch. "We were told the penalty can be $5,000 and six days in jail."[11]

After a storm cloud of adverse publicity, ASCAP backed off their threats against the Girl Scouts. But they did not concede any legal ground or grant any wider use rights to the music. This is just one of thousands of examples of how for-profit concerns are aggressively finding ways to charge money for songs and other forms of culture and knowledge that have historically been in the cultural commons.

The last half of this chapter will look at the ways that we need to rethink the organization of economic life. How do we protect the songs like "Happy Birthday" from becoming someone's property to rent to the rest of us? How do we defend our various forms of commonly owned wealth and culture? How do we deal with the lack of environmental sustainability of the current economy?

There are two future paths for the economy: the high road and the low road. The high road economy respects the importance and contribution of all stakeholders in the economy. It balances private enterprise with the common good. It justly rewards work and supports the flourishing of families and community life. It protects our ecological "commonwealth" and works as a proper steward for future generations of God's gift of nature's bounty. It honors the social commons, the institutions and societal wealth we build and share together.

The low road is an economy built on exploitation of human labor and natural wealth. It tries to "enclose" the remaining ecological and social commons and convert it into privately held wealth.[12] It has a very short-term private-gain outlook rather than a longer-term common-good perspective.

Traveling down the highway metaphor a bit further, we want to discourage low road activity and reward high road activity. We want to use our various sources of power (consumer, ownership, ethical witness, etc.) to encourage and *pave* the way to the high road and *block off* the low road. Paving the high road includes activities such as buying fair trade products, investing in companies that pay a living wage, and directing public purchases toward companies that use ecologically sustainable products.

Blocking off the low road includes activities such as raising legal standards like the minimum wage, banning the sale of products made in sweatshops, owning common resources. By raising the costs or outright banning of "low road" economic practices, we encourage more people to pull onto the "high road." High road doesn't mean high cost. But it usually requires us to look at the wide variety of social costs shifted off of private business and onto the community.

One thing that bears repeating from our discussion of the values that underlie our economy: extreme individualism is our cultural default position. We look at the world through an individual lens and with an individualist paradigm. We don't clearly see or acknowledge the ways in which our individual existence is wound together with community life. We are often oblivious to the various ways in which societal wealth and investments make our personal opportunities possible.

Because most social wealth — or what we call the "commonwealth" or "commons" — is largely invisible, we don't think about it or factor it into our theories about the economy. For instance, when we think about ownership, we immediately think of *individual* ownership: homeownership, real estate, and personal savings accounts. But we need to develop our "commonwealth" mind-set to ensure our ecological and social survival.

The "commons" is a new expression of a very old idea — that there are some forms of wealth that belong to all of us because they are either the result of shared human endeavor or they are gifts that God has entrusted to us. God's creation includes the gift of our existence, our natural bounty and the creations of our human hands.

The commons includes, in the words of Peter Barnes, "the gifts of nature, plus the gifts of society that we share and inherit together — and that we have an obligation to pass on to our heirs, undiminished and more or less equally." There are three basic forms of common wealth. The first is the *ecological commons* and includes the land, water, seeds, sky, oceans, wildlife, and wilderness. The second includes the *socially created commons,* those things that no one privately owns, such as our property law system, the broadcast spectrum, and the Internet. The third form of common wealth is the *knowledge and cultural commons,* including libraries, universities, museums, and all our accumulated scientific knowledge.[13] We are all citizens of a commonwealth, with obligations to defend this wealth we hold in common.

Big problems occur when we ignore the existence or rights of the commons or ignore its boundaries. There are two major problems we must understand in order to develop our commonwealth mind-set. The first has to do with *dumping* in the commons, and the second has to do with *looting* the commons.

As a society, we should not permit private actors, such as corporations, to shift their "costs" onto the commons. The examples related to the ecological commons are the easiest to grasp. A company, for example, has the choice of either illegally dumping polluted water into the stream (where we all pay the "costs"), or cleaning the water, returning it to the stream, and building the extra cost into its product or service. Economists make the distinction here between "externalizing" the cost — i.e., getting everyone else to pay — and "internalizing" the cost, by incorporating it into the cost of doing business.

In the current marketplace, a theoretical bug spray company has enormous incentive to "externalize" as many of its costs as possible. If the company buys chemicals to make its product and dumps the residue down the drain into the city sewers, the whole society pays the clean-up cost. If it pays its workers a minimum wage with no health insurance, society ends up paying for food stamps and emergency health care for the workers. If the company hires a big accounting firm to find or create tax loopholes, other taxpayers pick up the costs for the roads, education system, and national defense. The more a company externalizes, the less it has to pay the real costs of making its bug spray. The more it externalizes, the more profitable it is. The more profitable, the more its share prices go up and its investors are happy. But at what price?

Wal-Mart is a real-life example of a company that externalizes as many of its costs as possible, particularly the costs of sustaining its employees and opening new stores. Wal-Mart externalizes the costs of its 1.3 million employees by paying them less than a living wage and providing fewer than half of them with health insurance — while encouraging them to enroll in taxpayer-funded health programs. A 2004 congressional study estimated that taxpayers subsidize an average Wal-Mart store to the tune of over $420,000 a year, or more than $2,000 per employee.[14] This takes the form of government-funded food stamps, housing subsidies, and health insurance programs. Another study found that the state of California spent a total of $86 million a year on public assistance for Wal-Mart workers, or over $1,900 per worker. Wal-Mart employees were the largest users of state health care programs in eleven out of thirteen states that reported employer usage.

Wal-Mart externalizes the costs of developing their new stores and facilities by getting taxpayers to provide substantial subsidies to Wal-Mart stores in the form of real estate development funds and reduced property taxes. One study found that 90 percent of Wal-Mart distribution centers received tax breaks and other subsidies, valued at an average of $7.4 million per distribution center. Wal-Mart sought and received subsidies averaging about $2.8 million at eleven hundred of their locations, about one-third of its U.S. stores.[15]

Wal-Mart is not alone among retail businesses in shifting its costs off its balance sheets and onto taxpayers. Wal-Mart simply leads the way in a business model that includes other "big box" stores such as retailers Target and K-Mart. But such a choice is not inevitable. Costco, for example, has pursued a model of paying its workers higher wages and providing better benefits. They believe this leads to higher employee morale and retention and is good for their business.[16]

The second problem comes when individuals and businesses encroach upon or loot the environmental and socially created commons without compensation. Imagine going to the local public library to take out a book. As you enter, there is a small ticket booth with the name "Time Warner" or "Comcast" on it. In order to pass, you must pay $5. Most of us would feel outraged. After all, we've already paid our taxes to ensure that the library is free and open to the public. But this is effectively what is happening in dozens of areas of our economy, as private corporations and individuals encroach upon the commons in order to privatize part of it and make money. The Internet and World Wide Web are a form of "commons." No one owns it — it was built with taxpayer-funded research and knowledge gifts from thousands of individuals and organizations. It is an amazing creation that enables easy access to amazing amounts of information. But there are many private vendors who, if they could have their way, would put up tollbooths along the "information super highway" and charge you at many different points.

There are many institutions that we consider to be part of the commons that are experiencing encroachment. Public schools are under full commercial attack, as was mentioned in chapter 1. Public parks and bus stops are filled with commercial advertisements. Even at the beach, planes fly over trailing advertisements.

Corporations are now suing to protect words they claim to own. Apple computer claims the rights to the word "Pod." McDonalds sues businesses and websites that use the prefix "Mc." And as we have seen, the American Society of Composers, Authors and Publishers pursued the Girl Scouts of America to collect licensing fees for the right to sing campfire songs. The real question, writes David Bollier in *Brand Name Bullies,* is "whether free speech and culture belong to everyone or chiefly to commercial interests."[17] Instead of accepting this passively, our "commonwealth sensibilities" should be outraged.

There are sacred areas of creation that were once thought to be "off limits" to commercial activity. But that is changing. Imagine going to church and the priest beginning his homily by saying, "this homily is brought to you by Juicy Fruit gum. Double your pleasure, double your fun, with Doublemint, Doublemint, Doublemint Gum." Okay, things have not gotten that bad ... yet. But sacred and natural things that we once thought could not be bought and sold are now commodities, including babies, body organs, genes, sex, seeds, and sacred religious objects.

As Harvey Cox wrote in his essay called "The Market as God,"

> Lakes, meadows, and church buildings — everything carries a sticker price. But this practice itself exacts a cost. As everything in what used to be called creation becomes a commodity, human beings begin to look at one another, and at themselves, in a funny way, and they see colored price tags. There was a time when people spoke, at least occasionally, of "inherent worth" — if not of things, then at least of persons.[18]

The good news is that the church, as an organized and public institution, often defends the sacred commons and upholds boundaries against encroachment. But a big problem in our economy is the shortage of strong institutions or organizations able to defend all the different parts of the commons and give them legal standing, power, and voice. Who is hurt when our fictional bug spray company or Wal-Mart passes on its costs to society? Who defends the ecology, the workers, and the taxpayers from their clever cost-shifting activities? Almost everyone in society has to pick up the costs of Wal-Mart or the bug spray company, but who will defend the public interest?

We mostly look to government to defend the commons. And it is true that local, state, and federal forms of government have an enormous responsibility vested in them to defend our common wealth. But government has its limits, often because it is short on resources to defend the commons.

Government might be able to pass laws and impose fines on an encroacher, but the commons needs a more aggressive defender. Otherwise, the incentive to shift and externalize costs continues. There are institutions that can play an important "trustee" role in regard to the commons. One simple example is the nature land conservancy movement. Most conservation land trusts are private corporations, formed to uphold a public purpose.

All across the country people are coming together to defend common wealth and assets.[19] In many communities, these movements take the form of protecting natural wealth by starting land conservancies, establishing environmental organizations, and searching for local and renewable sources of energy. These groups are protecting farmland, restoring rivers and fisheries, saving forests, and ensuring the quality of public water supplies.

In urban and suburban communities, there are active efforts to expand public space, build and maintain parks, and guard against commercial encroachment on these spaces. People are establishing farmers markets, community gardens, and public sports facilities.

The Internet is like the sidewalk of the twenty-first century, so we should be concerned if someone wants to build a tollbooth on the sidewalk. There are movements to make high-speed Internet access a free and public service. As of 2006, nearly 150 U.S. cities were using or developing public wi-fi networks.

There is a strong movement in the emerging field of technology to defend the intellectual property commons against encroaching by money-makers. An interesting example is the Free Software Foundation. Creative software designers donate their "intellectual property" creations to the Free Software Foundation, ensuring common ownership and wide public access. Who will defend knowledge that is out in the public domain against encroachment?

The challenge for us is to see and name these various forms of common wealth. Once we see the commons, we should claim it, protect it, and grow it. It is up to all of us to be good stewards of this common wealth.

The new economic paradigm is rooted in some old biblical teachings. It recognizes that there is wealth that is created not exclusively by individuals but also through the blessing of creation and the commonwealth built by others. It defends this commons and rewires the corporation as an economic entity to be more accountable to the common good. It puts the quality of human dignity and life as primary, not subordinate, in the organization of the economy. So what institutions can we look to that embody this new paradigm? What can we learn from those who have experimented before us?

Chapter Eight

Solidarity in Action

Alternatives for a Just Economy

A New Economy in the Shell of the Old

One of the challenges of Catholic social teaching is to begin building a more just economy while at the same time working to prevent economic injustice. It is possible, as many are proving, to build new institutions for economic life that attempt to embody the principles we discussed in the previous chapter. These institutions are far from perfect, as they are products of human endeavor. But they can begin to meet real human needs for food, housing, and secure livelihood while reducing the worst aspects of economic injustice.

Dorothy Day and the Catholic Worker movement spoke about the importance of building a "new economy in the shell of the old." This is the process of incorporating our faith tradition into the existing institutions we are part of as well as participating in the development of new institutions.

There is a burgeoning field of experimentation in the building of alternative economic institutions. This activity has a number of rubrics including "sustainable development," "socially responsible development," and "community economics." Gar Alperovitz, who writes a lot about local community development innovations, observes that there are

> ...various ways in which communities build up ownership of wealth themselves — in order to gain power, in order to begin even to fund some social programs, but most important, to begin to lay down the outlines of a new paradigm for larger state and national programs and policies.[1]

Christians have been integrally involved in these activities, as initiators, funders, and participants. The Catholic Campaign for Human Development has an entire program devoted to supporting economic alternatives.[2]

144

This new paradigm is driven in part by several urgent needs. The "shrink and shift" trends that we are seeing in the area of taxation are leading many communities to look at creative ways to generate revenue to pay for basic services. Communities are also struggling, in the new global economy, to find ways to anchor jobs and build the locally controlled aspects of their economies. Fortunately, a large part of our economy remains rooted at the local level. Global conglomerates might own hardware stores, coffee shops, and pest-removal businesses, but a lot of the jobs at these enterprises still remain at the local level.

There are compelling examples of homegrown "high road" economic alternatives that are both an inspiration and an invitation to all of us to envision a fairer economy. These are mostly efforts to gain greater control over a local economy and ensure that the benefits of economic development flow fairly to local workers, residents, and enterprises. The challenge for community development is to gain control and ownership of the traditional factors of production, including the ecological commons of a locality in the form of land and other natural wealth, labor (workers), and capital (credit, finance, accumulated labor value in the form of money).

An unsustainable aspect of modern capitalism has been its focus on taking wealth from the natural commons and human labor to provide reward and profits to the owners of capital. Great accumulations of wealth and capital come from successfully getting more work value out of people than they are paid for and consuming more of the earth's common resources than one pays back through environmental stewardship. Both of these violate fundamental Christian principles of human dignity and stewardship of the earth and, taken to extreme levels, lead to human degradation and ecological disaster.

In terms of ecological stewardship, we need to practice the "compost theory" of sustainable economic development. Like wise farmers who know they cannot just take from the earth but need to give something back, we need to return crop residue, compost, and manure to rebuild the soil that provides our food. Gone are the days when we thought we could exploit without limit the forests, the waterways, and the air. Now we more fully understand the real limits of our high-energy consumption: nothing comes without an ecological cost.

Sometimes it is useful to think of a community's local economy as a bucket full of holes. A community that does not own or control its natural resources, the flow of capital, or the sources of employment is like a leaky bucket. Investment flows in and out, but because of absentee-ownership, very little water stays in the bucket. You can witness this in very low income urban and rural communities where there is tremendous natural wealth and human capacity, but the residents are impoverished. This is because absentee landlords or corporations that control the natural resources of the community own the land and housing. When the owners and lenders of capital don't reside in the community, they often withdraw the community's capital and invest it elsewhere. A local community becomes essentially a colony, owned and controlled by forces outside its control. All this leads to impoverishment. If economic development doesn't address these fundamental ownership and control issues, it won't truly benefit a locality.

The residents of one section of East St. Louis, Illinois, did an analysis of their neighborhood's money flow. They found that 75 percent of the land and housing were absentee-owned, so income from rents flowed out of the community. There were few locally owned businesses and a large number of national chain stores, also absentee owned. And while there were several bank branches in the neighborhood, for every dollar deposited by a resident of the neighborhood, only ten cents returned to the neighborhood in the form of loans. This is the experience of low-income neighborhoods and rural communities all across the country.[3]

For several decades, there has been a thoughtful and constructive "community economic development" movement working to empower local communities and gain greater control over their development. In a growing number of communities there are community development corporations, worker-owned cooperatives, community land trusts, community development credit unions, reinvestment corporations, nonprofit housing corporations, small business development centers, consumer cooperatives, and much more. Each strategy is trying to bring greater community control and participation to the economy, while limiting exploitation from the outside.

Land, Housing, and Natural Resources

Affordable Housing. There is a highly evolved new paradigm emerging in the area of housing. This includes efforts to provide affordable housing and homeownership through new models such as community land trusts, housing cooperatives, mutual housing associations, and other institutional forms. There are over four thousand nonprofit community development corporations in operation around the country that develop an estimated 37,500 units of affordable housing each year. These include homeownership, nonprofit-owned rental housing, and cooperatives.[4]

This nonprofit housing sector has dramatically grown in the last two decades to become a vital "third sector" in the housing market, an alternative to the "first sector" private market and the "second sector" of government-owned public housing. The nonprofit sector is also providing a spectrum of housing options different from rental housing in the private market and out-of-reach homeownership.

The community land trust movement, for example, now includes over one hundred locally based organizations working to remove land and housing from the speculative real estate market and increase access to affordable homeownership. They are concerned not only with providing initial affordability, but ensuring the long-term affordability of housing for future generations. They embody the Christian principle of "a just allocation of value" because individual homeowners build wealth based on their investment of time and money. But the community recaptures its investment in order to enable future low-income people to buy into the community land trust.

As of 2005, community land trust organizations had developed approximately seventy-five hundred units of housing.[5] In Albuquerque, New Mexico, one land trust is rising from the wood chips on the land of a former sawmill.

Charlie and Josie Pflieger had rented their housing for over sixteen years and had dreamed of owning a larger home for their growing family of three young daughters. Yet the cost of housing in their Albuquerque, New Mexico, neighborhood was out of reach, especially in the neighborhood where they rented near the city's historic Old Town. Development pressures and gentrification had pushed up housing costs.

Then they heard about the newly formed Sawmill Community Land Trust and the twenty-three new permanently affordable homes it was building in their "Arbolera de Vida," or Orchard of Life, community. The Pfliegers applied and were approved for a four-bedroom, two-story house. "It's a freeing experience," said Josie Pflieger. "We wanted to be able to stand on our own feet."

In 1997, area residents organized to get the city to purchase twenty-seven acres of land previously occupied by lumberyards and sawmills near Old Town. They advocated a comprehensive redevelopment plan to build not only housing, but also a central plaza, a park, and a community center. The first phase has been completed, and Phase II is underway with the construction of sixty-eight additional ownership homes, twenty-two senior apartments, and a trail system with park and orchard.

The focus is not just houses. "A neighborhood is more than just buildings," said Ken Balizer, the executive director of the Sawmill Community Land Trust. "A neighborhood is about people getting to know each other." The land trust organizes holiday events and fiestas — which strengthen relationships and overall care for the community. "People aren't apathetic," observed Balizer, pointing to the high involvement of neighborhood residents. "They're just tired of being ignored. Here, people aren't ignored."

The long-time residents of the adjoining neighborhood are thrilled to have new life nearby. Max Ramirez is seventy-two and has lived in his family house next to the new Arbolera de Vida community all his life. When he was growing up, his house didn't have electricity. He remembers pushing a wheelbarrow to the old sawmill and lumberyards to pick up scraps of wood for heat. "I've lived here all my life, and I've never had any problems."

Ramirez recalls that when he was a boy he used to walk with his family to San Felipe de Neri Catholic Church on Old Town Plaza. The land trust has helped keep the congregation together in the face of growing real estate pressures that displaced many members. Because the land trust prioritizes selling homes to former residents of the neighborhood, some of the parish's long-time families were able to buy homes back in the community. "We pray. We laugh. We do everything together," Ramirez said. "We take care of each other."

For new families like the Pfliegers, it is a joy to have community elders like Max Ramirez nearby in the newly active Sawmill community. "Since we're all in this together, we want to make it a family-friendly neighborhood," said Josie Pflieger.[6]

Good Food through Community Supported Farms. In the area of food production, there is a new form of organization that forges an interesting partnership between individual farmers and urban consumers. These institutions, called "Community Supported Agriculture" (CSAs), have emerged since 1986 in a number of regions of the country. Food consumers purchase shares in advance of the harvest season, which provides up-front capital to farmers. It also allows farmers to share the risks and rewards of farming with their customers. CSA shareholders get a weekly share allocation of produce every week. During good harvests, it can be a bumper crop that includes surplus food for canning or storage.

There are an estimated seventeen hundred CSAs operating in the United States and Canada, providing produce to over a hundred thousand households.[7] CSAs are not only an excellent source of high quality food, but a much more sustainable model of food production and food security. Most food products travel an average of thirteen hundred miles to reach consumers, and most states are dependent on other states for over 80 percent of their food. CSAs keep food production local and enable food dollars to circulate in the local economy.

For Cheryl McCormick of Sylvania Township outside Toledo, Ohio, participating in the CSA is a great way to get healthy food for her family of four. It is also affordable; she paid $330 for her annual share. Each week from May until October, she receives the delivery of her share in a large basket from the TenMile Creek Farm, just a few miles from her home. She admits she sometimes needs to be creative with what arrives each week. "I had to be ready to do the cooking and not let it waste," she said. "I felt better about eating it knowing I was eating organic."

It works for the farmer too. "We were looking for a way to save the family farm," said Robin Ford-Parker of TenMile Creek Farm. "It's only 300 acres, so cash-crop farming isn't profitable anymore, especially with the cost of gas." Starting the CSA has kept them in business, and each year the number of shareholder members keeps growing.[8]

Jobs with Ownership

Worker Ownership. One of the new paradigms aimed at increasing local control over business opportunities and job creation is worker-owned businesses. Worker ownership can take a variety of forms, including Employee Stock Option Plans (ESOPs), which give workers an ownership stake in the company, though not always management control. There are now over ten thousand ESOPs with over 8 million worker-owner members. Together these workers own over $300 billion in equity in their businesses. Worker-owners have a greater stake in their companies, and the productivity of ESOP-owned firms is 4–5 percent higher than comparable for-profit firms.[9] Wages are also 5–12 percent higher for employees in worker-owned firms compared to wages in a comparable non-ESOP company.[10] A highly advanced example of worker ownership from Spain, the Mondragón cooperatives, has been an inspiration to groups across the United States. (See "A Vision of a Cooperative Future" on the following two pages.)

Enterprising Cities

Other strategies for retaining jobs and business wealth in communities include new forms of business ownership with large stakes owned by local municipalities and community development corporations. Such ownership allows these municipalities to raise revenue for public services without raising taxes.

There are a variety of creative ownership arrangements that increase community benefits and accountability. A number of "enterprising cities" have retained ownership of land and prime real estate when making substantial investments in their communities.

A VISION OF A COOPERATIVE FUTURE
THE MONDRAGÓN COOPERATIVES

After the Spanish Civil War, the Basque region of Spain was devastated with high unemployment. A twenty-six-year-old priest, Father José María Arizmendiarrieta, arrived in 1941 and saw part of his pastoral duties as encouraging the economic development of the region along the line of Catholic economic principles. There had been a history of economic self-help organizations and cooperatives in the region prior to the war, but most had been destroyed.

Arizmendiarrieta, who was co-pastor for the region of Mondragón, in 1943 founded a technical school that helped to train many of the individuals who later became business leaders of the Mondragón cooperatives. The first cooperative business was founded in 1955 and manufactured heating and cooking appliances. In 1959, they formed a credit union called the "Caja Laboral Popular" ("People's Worker Bank"), which served the credit needs of individual families and workers, but also provided start-up financing for new cooperative business ventures. During the 1960s, dozens of other cooperative businesses were formed after careful planning, market research, and worker-owner training.

The Mondragón cooperatives celebrated their fiftieth anniversary on October 20, 2005. There are now 150 cooperative companies linked together through the larger Mondragón Cooperative Corporation, embodying the important cooperative principle of "cooperation among cooperatives." During the 1980s, this helped the companies make the transition into the new global economy. Instead of shedding jobs, employment in the Mondragón cooperatives grew from twenty-five thousand employees in 1992 to over sixty-eight thousand in 2003.

The cooperative businesses operate in three sectors — industrial, financial, and distribution. The industrial sector includes cooperatives in seven divisions focused on the production of goods and services. The financial group includes banking, insurance, and social welfare. The distribution division is made up of a range of food and commercial distribution enterprises, including a trucking company and Spain's largest supermarket chain. There is integration between these cooperatives and a preference for doing business with one another. Worker-owned trucking companies distribute products made by the industrial cooperatives to cooperatively

A VISION OF A COOPERATIVE FUTURE
(continued)

owned stores. Workers in these firms typically would get their health insurance, pension programs, and banking services through cooperative financial institutions.

New businesses benefit from the Mondragón system's commitment to reinvestment in the local cooperative sector and their unique capital allocation system. A start-up business can write up a business plan and submit it to the cooperative bank. If accepted, it will get a loan plus the technical assistance services they need to succeed. Their initial financing will be at lower rates than the successful existing businesses that can afford higher interest. This is the opposite of the experience of most start-ups in the United States, which must pay higher interest rates, while larger established borrowers pay less.

Underpinning the entire infrastructure is a cooperative education system that includes Mondragón University and special technical schools. These institutes emphasize education to prepare workers to be part of cooperative enterprises.

The principles governing the Mondragón cooperatives come directly from Catholic social teachings on economic life. Capital is subordinate to labor in these cooperatives, meaning that the cooperative exists for the worker, not absentee investors from outside the community. And in the case of Mondragón, the capital is "worker's capital," invested in service of the cooperative sector. There is a high level of worker participation in the governance of the company, not to mention a broad sharing of the company's wealth.

These principles have served the cooperatives well in a competitive global economy. In a statement about their production system, the MCC states, "we have developed a way of making companies more human and participatory." They believe their approach has the added benefit of "fitting-in" well with the latest and most advanced management models, which tend to place more value on workers themselves as the principal asset and source of competitive advantage of modern companies."[11]

Within the region where Mondragón cooperatives are most concentrated, there is a high standard of living and a fair distribution of wealth. The cooperatives use the word "solidarity" to describe their relationship to the community, their employees, and their various stakeholders.

In Washington, D.C., the city's transit authority retained ownership of key properties around newly constructed "Metro" subway stations, leasing the property and recapturing rents. They now have fifty-six revenue-generating development projects, earning $14 million in 2002. This is an example of communities recapturing value that comes from public investment by remaining landlords or land-leasers. Other cities like Cincinnati, San Antonio, and Louisville have functioned as partners in business and commercial developments, reaping revenue from the operations of hotels, sports teams, and civic centers. A number of municipalities are getting into the technological infrastructure business, owning Internet providers and selling low-cost access. These municipalities are turning the traditional development model of giving away public assets on its head. They are protecting the public's investment and reducing the need for future taxes.[12]

Community Control over Capital

Communities that cannot retain or control the flow of capital are likely to be impoverished. Many low-income communities have large flows of income and spending, but because of absentee ownership, the money flows out. Something must be done to keep the bucket from leaking.

Many communities have used the Community Reinvestment Act, legislation passed in the late 1970s, to require banks to increase local lending in the communities from which they draw deposits. Others have formed their own financial institutions, such as credit unions, cooperative and community-oriented banks and other financial institutions.

One of the best examples of a community-oriented bank is ShoreBank, formerly the South Shore Bank of Chicago. In the early 1970s, when a bank was threatening to relocate out of the disinvested South Side neighborhood, neighborhood residents protested and forced federal bank regulators to deny the bank's request to relocate. The bank was put up for sale and was purchased by a group interested in reorienting the bank to be a powerful force for reinvestment in the community.

ShoreBank began operations in August 1973, working closely with a number of community development organizations to purchase and rehabilitate rental housing, expand homeownership, and encourage minority-owned business development. The bank's goal was to demonstrate that a regulated bank could be an instrument in revitalizing communities that were being denied credit by other financial institutions. In 1978, ShoreBank formed three affiliates to advance these goals: a real estate development company, a nonprofit community development corporation, and a minority venture capital fund.

ShoreBank has been nationally recognized for its incredible impact on the revitalization of the South Shore Neighborhood. ShoreBank has created similar companies in Chicago, Cleveland, Detroit, the Upper Peninsula of Michigan, and the Pacific Northwest. Among the bank's values are to seek a "triple bottom line," instead of the single "bottom line" of maximizing profits. They strive to simultaneously meet the three objectives of building wealth for all in economically integrated communities, promoting environmental health, and operating profitably.[13]

The first credit unions were formed by working people to pool capital for purchases of consumer goods like cars and even homes. In 2005, there were over nine thousand credit unions, with 87 million members and assets of $700 billion.[14] Of these, there are 225 that consider themselves "community development credit unions," with an even stronger mission of meeting the credit needs of low-income urban and rural communities. Some have created youth lending branches, overseen by boards composed of young people. These community-oriented credit unions manage over $2 billion in funds and fill the gap where traditional banks are absent.[15]

Since the 1980s, the community development finance sector has expanded to include community development loan funds and programs that draw investments from individuals, religious organizations, and foundations to provide financing to locally controlled community development projects such as worker-owned businesses, affordable housing, and consumer cooperatives. This was important because as ownership in the banking sector became more concentrated, many of the banks didn't want to be involved in financing small or unusual projects.

Founded in 1985 as the Delaware Valley Community Reinvestment Fund, TRF (The Reinvestment Fund) has provided almost half a billion dollars in financing to over 1,600 community projects in Philadelphia and western New Jersey and facilitated the development of more than 13,800 housing units and 29,100 jobs.[16] The fund now manages over $6 billion in funds.[17]

Many of these innovative examples of community-based economic development are small in scale. But they give us a vision of what an ethical economy might look like on a larger scale. For several decades, the Catholic Church has been a major partner in helping build these new institutions, many of which have emerged as a result of Catholic social action organizations.

As we reflect on our religious teachings and the economy, it is clear there is a lot of work to be done and many different places to make a difference. There are social action campaigns to engage government and corporations to advance social justice. And there are opportunities to build new institutions that better embody our faith values and directly meet human needs in our communities. Where can we best devote our time and skills?

Signs of Solidarity

The remainder of this chapter includes a number of stories about individuals and organizations working to gain control over their local economies. Many of these are institutions searching for volunteers, leaders, and partners. These "signs of solidarity" stories feature a number of inspiring organizations funded by the Catholic Campaign for Human Development.

Building Something New from the Ashes

On September 11, 2001, when terrorists attacked New York's World Trade Center, one of the casualties was the famous Windows on the World restaurant at the top of the North Tower. Some 73 employees were killed and another 250 lost their jobs.

Banquet cook Sekou Siby had the day off on September 11, but he suffered in the aftermath. "I couldn't find work and wasn't prepared to work because of the many friends I lost," he said. In the months after the attack he drove a cab, but he soon joined many of his former co-workers to start a new restaurant.

On September 12, 2005, four years later, a new restaurant named Colors opened to rave reviews. Television personality Al Roker hosted a gala event called "Food for Thought," attended by over three hundred people. Colors is New York City's first worker-owned cooperative restaurant. An upscale restaurant in Lower Manhattan, it seats over 120 and employs thirty former Windows employees.

The restaurant start-up got help from the Restaurant Opportunities Center of New York (ROC-NY), which works to help improve conditions for the 160,000 mostly low-income and immigrant restaurant workers in the city. Restaurant workers have a median income of less than $15,000 a year and are vulnerable to exploitation and unsafe working conditions. Most work multiple jobs to survive economically.

The new restaurant will raise the bar in terms of how workers are treated and paid. Dishwashers will earn a starting hourly wage of $13.50, which is more than double New York State's minimum wage. In addition to being owners and sharing in the business's profits, workers will have health coverage, workmen's compensation, and overtime pay. Sekou Siby was excited as the opening gala for Colors approached. "Since we too will be owners, we want to show other restaurant owners how workers should be treated," he said.

For more information, see *www.rocny.org*. There are worker centers and affiliates of the National Interfaith Center on Worker Justice in many regions of the country. See *www.workerjustice.org* for the location of affiliates. These organizations provide opportunities to be directly engaged in efforts to defend worker dignity and rights.

Holding Ground: Getting Control of Wealth and Assets

In 1988, tenants of the Spring Meadow apartment complex in Springfield, Massachusetts, learned that the federal subsidies that kept their 270-unit apartment building affordable were going to expire in eighteen months. This would give the development's owners the opportunity to convert the housing to market rate apartments or condos, while evicting those who could not afford higher rents.

With help from a group of religious leaders and community members, the tenants formed the Anti-Displacement Project (ADP). A few years later, the Spring Meadow tenants took ownership of their apartment building, forming a resident-controlled cooperative. The ADP approach has been not just to secure the housing, but also to gain ownership control of wealth and assets — ensuring institutional stability and financial independence.[18]

"In more traditional tenant organizing, we would have been fighting with the owner over repairs," said lead organizer Caroline Murray. "Now instead, the tenants of that building control a major asset and make day-to-day decisions about rents, repairs, etc. They're thinking strategically, making sure all bank accounts are in local banks, for example. These tenants are more than tenants; they're major land holders in the city."

Today, ADP includes five large tenant-owned housing cooperatives with 1,350 apartments, four tenant associations representing 1,600 residents, one neighborhood association, and a for-profit worker-owned business. The ADP represents over 10,000 families led by a core group of 300 leaders who have been trained in community organizing and leadership skills.

The project has gone well beyond its original mission of preserving affordable housing. ADP is now a full-fledged leadership development organization whose mission is to "organize and empower low-income families in Western Massachusetts in order to build political and economic power, achieve resident control of affordable housing, promote cooperative economic development, and create lasting social and economic change."

Many of these housing communities contract out for substantial services. In June 2001, ADP helped create United Landscaping and Painting, LLC, a for-profit worker-owned cooperative business employing thirteen employee-owners earning living wages with benefits and profit sharing. Their first year sales were over $500,000. "Now that we're controlling this money, we can keep it flowing in the community," says Murray.[19]

There are many encouraging efforts like the Anti-Displacement Project (*www.a-dp.org*) that need community involvement and energy. Many of them can be found through networks such as the Center for Community Change (*www.communitychange.org*).

Holy Anger in San Antonio

In 1993, Christina Castro was doing a parish census of community needs for her church, St. Henry's in San Antonio, Texas. She met a needy ninety-year-old man who was living in extreme poverty. A few months later, he was burned to death while cooking a meal outdoors, the result of his utilities having been turned off. A "holy anger" stirred Christina to action. After attending a social justice class at the chancery office, she got connected to an organization called Communities Organized for Public Service (COPS).

For Christina, COPS was "a mini-university, letting people know their true worth." Christina became a leader in COPS work on affordable housing, something that was not easy for her. "I only have a high school education," she said. "My husband abandoned me when I was pregnant with our third child. I had a very low self-image. COPS selects people like myself, who have potential, but nothing to offer except sweat, and educates us. It made me grow."

COPS was founded in 1974 to organize churches and community organizations and to build leaders like Christina Castro. They formed a powerful coalition in neglected neighborhoods in San Antonio. "We help organize neighbors and connect people to existing institutions, like churches, so they act on their own behalf and find solutions to their problems," says Ramón Durán, an organizer with COPS. Today, COPS has over seventy member churches, schools, and labor unions.

In over three decades of work, COPS has dramatically increased the power of disenfranchised neighborhoods and improved public services, schools, housing, and living-wage jobs. It worked with parishioners from the south side parish of St. Leo the Great to organize against a bad smell in their neighborhood. After researching the problem, community residents learned that the city sewer pumping station had not been properly buried. They pressed the city to agree to make an $800,000 improvement and eliminate the smell.

Hundreds of organizing efforts like that addressing the sewer problem built COPS. Residents can draw on "local wisdom," according to Durán, to solve problems. "They need to have enough power to make the people in charge pay attention to them and give them what they need," says Ramón. "Government looks mysterious until people poke around and see that the people in government aren't much different than they are."

Christina Castro now co-chairs the housing committee for COPS. "You feel good belonging to something like this where your collective holy anger can be directed," says Castro. "The Lord *does* hear the cry of the poor."[20]

For an inspirational book about COPS and its faith-based approach to organizing, see Mary Beth Rogers, *Cold Anger: A Story of Faith and Power Politics* (University of North Texas Press, 1990).

Prospering on the Family Farm

The agricultural heartland of the United States has seen a lot of change in the last three generations as the number of family farmers continues to decrease. Those who continue have found that to stay competitive, they must enlarge their operations, make expensive investments in equipment, and utilize capital and labor-intensive farming techniques. But there is another path that a growing number of farmers are taking: sustainable agriculture.

Dan and Muriel French are third-generation Minnesota dairy farmers who have shifted to farming techniques that are profitable, are better for the environment, and promote stable rural communities. Instead of a large dairy barn facility with hundreds of cows hooked up to computerized milking machines, the Frenches now let their cows graze freely, staying outside all year around and coming inside only for milking and calving. Instead of eating expensive grain-based feed, the cows roam and graze on grass. "God gave them feet to walk and made grass with roots, so it stays put," says Dan French "That's the way it should be." As a result of their outdoor living, the Frenches' cows are healthier, are more disease resistant, and don't need the massive amount of antibiotics and hormone injections that modern dairy farms require.

To strengthen the economic viability of their farm, the Frenches have joined with four other dairy farm families to establish a dairy producer cooperative called Pastureland. The coop produces and sells butter and cheese made with the milk of grass-fed cows. These products, which are aimed at a growing health-conscious consumer market interested in organic foods, increase profits for the coop members.

"I expect to do this for a long time," says Dan French. "While there are policy issues and large companies that would like to make sure we don't survive, consumers are willing to help farmers make a living. The food has to taste good, be good, be good for you, and be fairly priced."[21]

Supporting local agriculture and family farms is important for promoting ecologically and economically sustainable rural communities. The food is better too. For more information, see the National Family Farm Coalition (*www.nffc.net*) and the National Catholic Rural Life Conference (*www.ncrlc.com*).

Mobile Home Owners: Hostages No More

"To know you have your own home, that's fine," reflects mobile home owner Richard Doherty. "But knowing that you don't own the land that it's on top of, it doesn't feel right."

Doherty is like many mobile home owners who feel the insecurity of knowing that the land in their mobile home community could be sold out from under them. Doherty lives with seventy-three other families in the Barrington Estates community in Barrington, New Hampshire. He works the 6:00 p.m. to 6:00 a.m. shift in a local factory, while his wife works daylight hours. As is the case for many low-income people in rural communities, a mobile home was the only affordable homeownership option available to them.

Many people haven't given a second thought to mobile homes, but they represent one of the fastest growing segments of the affordable housing market. Over 9 million Americans live in mobile or manufactured housing, mostly in parks owned by nonresidents. Twenty percent of new housing construction is in such communities.

Mobile home residents feel the sting of insults ("trailer trash") directed toward them by neighbors and zoning boards attempting to bar their existence. But thanks to some creative organizing, many mobile home residents are taking control of their lives.

Doherty and his neighbors have turned to the New Hampshire Community Loan Fund for help. Since 1984, the loan fund has worked with residents in seventy-one communities to help them purchase their parks as resident-owned cooperatives. They helped establish a state law giving mobile home park tenants the first right of refusal to buy a park when it comes up for sale. As a result, they have been able to anchor over 15 percent of the state's mobile home residents in secure owner-occupied residential communities.

These new communities not only build pride of ownership and human dignity; they also preserve the value of the individual homes, which dramatically lose value in absentee-owned parks. Homes in New Hampshire cooperative parks appreciate and there are long waiting lists of future interested buyers.[22]

In Athens, Georgia, residents of the Garden Springs Mobile Home Park found themselves with nowhere to go after their park was sold to a developer of luxury homes. All 109 resident families were evicted, and many of their homes were legally demolished because their occupants were unable to move them.

They banded together to form "People of Hope" with the goal of developing their own cooperative mobile home community. The largely Hispanic membership has worked hard to purchase land and begin the process of site development, including the building of roads, the installation of utilities, and the construction of storm-water retention ponds. Over thirty families have stayed together with the intention of moving together to the finished community.

"I know we'll make it to the new park, even though it won't be soon," said Moises Casales, a resident. "To people who say it's taking too long, I say it's not just a single house; it's a big park and it will be a good one if we keep on working."[23]

Across the country, there are community development organizations and efforts like these to prevent displacement and increase home-ownership opportunities. Many of them would welcome volunteers and donations of time and money.

Chapter Nine

Preparing for Discipleship

Jesus called us to "love one another." Our Lord's example and words demand care for the "least of these" from each of us. Yet they also require action on a broader scale. Faithful citizenship is about more than elections. It requires ongoing participation."

—U.S. Conference of Catholic Bishops, *Faithful Citizenship: A Catholic Call to Political Responsibility,* 2004

What Can I Do?

There is a natural human response to the information we've discussed so far: What can I do? Most of us don't have a lot of extra time in our lives to spend with our loved ones, let alone become part-time disciples for justice.

There are a few axioms to remember in this context:

+ No one can accomplish much completely alone. We need to be part of an organized group to make a difference.

+ At the same time, individual choices do make a difference.

+ The impact of a small group of committed people should never be underestimated, as anthropologist Margaret Mead once said.

+ Faith is remembering that our actions do add up to change.

To adhere to Jesus' admonition to "Come follow me" requires us to reflect, find others, and encourage one another to take meaningful action. Fortunately, many of us are members of parishes and faith communities that will support the formation of study action groups. And within the church, the JustFaith movement, which we will discuss below, provides a very concrete model for us.

When the U.S. bishops were reflecting on the possible impact of the 1986 pastoral letter on the economy, they observed that its greatest contribution "was to remind us that the pursuit of economic justice is a work of

160

faith and an imperative of the Gospel." Working for justice, they under-scored, is not part of a political program or theological choice, but a "response to the Scriptures and a requirement of Catholic teaching."

Discipleship is to faithfully reject the dominant secular values of individualism, consumerism, and minimal obligation to one another. Disciples are called to live by Gospel values of solidarity and acts of justice. Our faith calls us to maximize justice, a call that sometimes puts us into conflict with the profit maximization commandment of the marketplace. There is even a biblical injunction against passivity in the face of injustice.

What's a faithful but busy person to do? There is an understandable desire to leap into works of charity and social action. For some, there is an urge to quickly write a check to a justice organization, sort of like plucking out a thorn to relieve the short-term suffering. But as Father Daniel Berrigan once joked to a group of urgent social activists: "Don't Just Do Something, Sit There!" To really be of use requires us to reflect on our own lives, attitudes, and choices. In other words, the first meaningful action we can take involves prayer and reflection. We need to prepare for discipleship, not to postpone action, but to inform it and to be more effective.

Recognizing the Gifts That We Have Received

The principle of solidarity requires that men and women of our day cultivate a greater awareness that they are debtors of the society of which they have become part. They are debtors because of those conditions that make human existence livable, and because of the invisible and indispensable legacy constituted by culture, scientific and technical knowledge, material and immaterial goods and by all that the human condition has produced. A similar debt must be recognized in the various forms of social interaction, so that humanity's journey will not be interrupted but remain open to present and future generations, all of them called together to share in the same gift of solidarity.

— Pontifical Council for Justice and Peace,
"Compendium of the Social Doctrine of the Church,"
no. 195

What would it be like to always remember the gift of Creation? In his book *Doing Faithjustice,* Jesuit priest Fred Kammer describes the common process of moving from an awareness of our "original blessing" to a self-identity that considers us as owners and creators of wealth. This original blessing is the gift of our lives, of our innate qualities, and the wonder of God's creation in the form of this amazing planet. The first great disconnect is when we move from "God made it" to "I made it."[1]

In his description of the "Cycle of Baal," Kammer describes the process whereby we forget the original blessing of God's creation, including our stewardship duties and the command to live in community and share this blessing. As people become "owners" and accumulate wealth, they forget the poor, which is synonymous in the Bible with forgetting Yahweh. Instead of worshipping God, we develop new gods and idols. Individual wealth replaces God. We worship at the altar of The Market.[2]

Our contemporary culture is full of examples of those who have forgotten God's blessing and built idols to their own achievement. The United States has always celebrated individual achievement, but the rapid accumulation of wealth in the last two decades, thanks in part to changing technology, has amplified these voices and stories.

There is a revealing new version of the personal wealth creation story that forgets about God's grace and society's contribution to individual wealth and opportunity. Stories enshrining individual success fill the pages of business publications and echo over the public talk radio forums. This is the "great man" story of wealth creation, the person who owes nothing to anyone else. "I did it all myself." "I'm a self-made man." "I built this fortune myself." "I never got any help from anyone."

In 1999, co-author Chuck Collins introduced a shareholder resolution at General Electric calling on the company to reduce the dizzying disparity between top management compensation and average worker pay within the company. The CEO at the time, Jack Welch, was paid about $75 million a year plus options. During the public discussion about the resolution, Welch stated that he had "created hundreds of billions in shareholder value over his tenure at GE." In other words, "I'm priceless."[3]

In a similar vein, "Chainsaw" Al Dunlap, when he was CEO at Scott Paper, was asked on *PBS News Hour* to justify his $100 million annual pay package. "I created six and a half billion dollars of value," retorted Dunlap. "I received less than 2 percent of the value I created."[4] Dennis Kozlowski, the former CEO of Tyco International, was asked to justify his $170 million pay package in 1999, which was second on the annual *Business Week* executive compensation list. He responded, "I created about $37 billion in shareholder value." There was no mention of the share of wealth created by the company's other 180,000 employees.[5]

In each of these examples, the important word is "I." All of these men truly believe that they are the principal actors on the economic stage.

In the Book of Deuteronomy, God warns against being overly comfortable and forgetting the original blessing:

> When you have eaten your fill and have built fine houses and live in them, and when your herds and flocks have multiplied, and your silver and gold is multiplied, and all that you have is multiplied, then do not exalt yourself, forgetting the LORD your God, who brought you out of the land of Egypt, out of the house of slavery, who led you through the great and terrible wilderness. (Deuteronomy 8:12–15)

In several places in both the Old and New Testaments, God reminds us who is the real "landlord." He rails against those who would look at their accumulated wealth and say "I built this wealth myself" or "I'm a self-made man."

> Do not say to yourself, "My power and might of my own hand have gotten me this wealth." But remember the LORD your God, for it is he who gives you power to get wealth, so that he may confirm his covenant that he swore to your ancestors, as he is doing today. (Deuteronomy 8:17–18)

The penalty for this form of "self-idolatry" is clear and severe:

> If you do forget the LORD your God and follow other gods to serve and worship them, I solemnly warn you today that you shall surely perish. Like the nations that the LORD is destroying before you, so shall you perish, because you would not obey the voice of the LORD your God. (Deuteronomy 8:19–20)

There is a real danger of forgetting that we are all essentially "passing through," that we have serious obligations as stewards of creation and duties to the community. We are thankful that there are individuals who take initiative and assume the responsibilities of leadership for large business corporations and governmental organizations. But let us not forget the original blessing. To think otherwise is human hubris, which is a sin.

To remember the gifts of creation and community is to be thankful, to live with a feeling of gratitude in our hearts, to be humbled by the perfection and beauty of creation. We are minor bit players in this program, and we should not forget it. To remember is to live with a constant prayer of thankfulness.

Justice: What Belongs to God, to Me, and to Us

To define justice in our time requires us to reflect on the questions: What belongs to God? What is mine? What is ours together? In other words: What is a part of divine creation that none of us can claim as belonging to us as individuals? What are the products of my own labor that I can rightfully claim as my own property? What belongs to the commons — that which we built or inherit together as a society and belongs to all of us — and should not be claimed by any individual?

These are important questions that many historians, economists, and theologians have grappled with. But they are also personal questions, with deeply personal implications for each of us.

In the Catholic tradition, there is a clear affirmative support for private property. The right to private property is essential in a just economy, and widespread ownership has the benefit of avoiding excessive concentrations of political power. But this notion of "what is mine" is tempered by the larger knowledge that we really don't "own" anything. We are tenants on the earth. Or as Yahweh reminds us in the Book of Leviticus, we are strangers in the land. "The land is mine saith the Lord." Don't abuse it.

We have to confess that often our imagination is limited when it comes to envisioning what this actually means, that God is the real owner of creation. Some of us gird ourselves for an imaginary invasion. We envision the police showing up to force us to open up our carefully built patio and garden to a horde of unruly neighbors who trample on our flowers. For others, it might bring to mind images of totalitarian communism, with Stalin's police knocking on your door to arrest you for "anti-social thinking" including "incorrect attitudes" toward property.

It is helpful to imagine God as a more compassionate landlord who is willing to give us a very long-term lease, as long as we keep some basic promises. The first promise is, of course, not to forget who the real owner is. The other promises have to do with not using the property in a way that hurts our neighbors. With our growing understanding of the interconnectedness of all creation, we are not allowed to dump our garbage in the river that flows through our property. Another promise is that we cannot hoard to such an extent that we deny others access to a piece of creation for their sustenance and livelihood.

This is the basis of what Catholic social teaching calls the "social mortgage" on private property. "Social mortgage" refers to society's moral claim on privately owned property and wealth.[6] In the papal encyclical letter *On the Development of Peoples*, Pope Paul VI affirmed, "Private property does not constitute for anyone an absolute or unconditional right. No one is justified in keeping for his exclusive use what he does not need, when others lack necessities."[7] There is no right to unlimited accumulation of wealth.

Seeing Society's Wealth. We have another significant blind spot in the area of "what is ours together?" We have discussed the notion of "commons" and "commonwealth" and the importance of developing a mind-set and an array of economic institutions that protect the commons and give it economic standing.

Because of our enshrinement of individual achievement, we often overlook society's enormous role in individual wealth creation and success. The United States, in particular, has a remarkably fertile soil for the creation of wealth. It is part of the inheritance that most of us receive in the form of public and social investments that have been made over hundreds of years. After forgetting God's original blessing, this is perhaps our country's most misunderstood and ignored part of the individual success narrative.

The United States has a dynamic and robust economy because we have order, stability, a predictable system of rules for investing, and mechanisms to resolve disputes. We can function with the confidence that the rules today will more or less be the same next year and the year after. And we have an educated and skilled work force thanks to our nation's substantial investment in public education and infrastructure.

What follows are a few more examples of the commonwealth that we have built together:

- **Public infrastructure.** We have an incredible public infrastructure of roads, power, ports, rail, and communications.

- **Charitable institutions.** We have a remarkable infrastructure of charitable and cultural institutions, including universities, hospitals, research institutions, humanitarian organizations, museums, and civic and cultural institutions. Our tax system encourages people to direct wealth to these institutions.

- **Public investment in productivity-increasing technology.** Our society commits substantial resources to public investment in research and technology. This accounts for an enormous percentage of the productivity gains in our economy.[8] Our government, funded by our tax dollars, is the biggest venture capitalist in the world. Government-funded research investments have created the Internet, life-saving drugs and medical research, and other innovations that create the bedrock for wealth creation and the quality of life we enjoy.

- **Property rights law.** Our society has a highly developed framework of property law that enables individuals to own and sell many different types of property. Without these mechanisms, there would be less private investment and risk-taking.

- **Patent system and intellectual property.** In our society, you can claim ownership of ideas, recipes, inventions, formulas, dance steps, computer programs, and much more. A great deal of modern wealth comes from this system of private ownership of knowledge.

- **Public subsidies to individuals.** Through our government we've made public commitments to tuition assistance for higher education, mortgage assistance for first-time homebuyers, and flexible financing for business startups.

- **Public subsidies to corporations.** Corporations often benefit from a variety of direct and indirect subsidies such as free research, tax abatements, free or low-cost use of natural resources, and direct cash payments.[9]

When we reflect on these and other factors, it helps us to better see "What is ours together" is quite significant. Without this vital "social commons," very little individual wealth would exist. As is the case with remembering the "original blessing" of creation, we often forget the invisible societal investments and inheritance that we have received.

What Is Mine? After identifying what is God's and what is ours together, what is left for us as individuals to claim? Well, not much . . . but so much. To live in awareness of God's love and the gift of creation is to be deeply enriched. Indeed, one of the implications of this is cultivating an attitude of gratitude. To see the gifts we receive in each moment is a walking devotion.

A revised understanding of what is mine, what is ours together, and what is a gift of creation fosters certain duties and obligations. As in the case of the "commons mind-set," we need to think about how to pass on, undiminished, the gifts of creation to the next generation. Our duties include protecting the environment and reducing our "footprint" on the planet. If we have had more fortune than misfortune, we have an obligation to give back to the society that created the conditions for our good lives. This includes giving our time, making charitable gifts and paying taxes. Ways we can contribute to a just economy are the subject of the remainder of this chapter and the next.

Reflecting on Privilege

One of the hardest discussions to have in our culture is about the nature and workings of privilege. We each like to believe we've earned our way in the world. We are attached to the notion that "I got what I have because of my effort, by merit." In a culture that prides itself on hard work, pulling yourself up by your bootstraps, and rugged individualism, confessing to having privileged advantages is a rare occurrence.

But from our earlier discussion, we know that we have each received an enormous gift — an original blessing. And we have been graced by God's presence and continuing gifts. We live in a society that has enormous societal wealth that our ancestors and elders built and for which we can personally claim very little credit. Consider our "technological inheritance," including the advent of computers, medical innovation, and advances in travel. No living person can claim credit for building the technological foundation that we all benefit from today. As Gar Alperovitz writes, "What we accomplish stands atop a Gibraltar of technological inheritance. Seemingly contemporary transformations inevitably build on knowledge accumulated over generations." Contemporary technological achievements in the field of computers are a good example of this. "Thousands of links in a chain of development — our shared inheritance," observes Alperovitz, "were in fact required before Bill Gates could add his contribution." Yet the benefits of our common inheritance are not widely shared. "Our technological legacy is distributed unequally also because it is largely bestowed on the heirs of the privileged few," writes Alperovitz.[10]

It is also important to reflect on the "original sin" underlying the wealth of the United States — wealth built on land stolen from indigenous peoples and wealth built with slave labor and underpaid immigrant toil. Consider how much wealth Africans involuntarily brought to these shores during the 246 years of slavery — with no compensation and little acknowledgment. As Randall Robinson observes in his book *The Debt,* this wealth is "now ossified. It is structural. Its framing beams are disguised." White Americans take it for granted as part of their invisible inheritance. In addition, we greatly benefit from the global rules that are tilted in our favor, as discussed in chapter 6.

We could work our whole lives, but the reality is that the vast amount of wealth around us existed before we arrived. We are essentially born graced and privileged, having inherited the social wealth created by the labors and technological advances of others. And if we are from the United States, we inherit a unique commonwealth that enhances our opportunities, health, and quality of life. Anyone who has traveled outside of the United States and to countries of the Global South can appreciate how fantastically wealthy we are as a society in relation to the rest of the world. And anyone who has made friendships across the borders can attest to the absurdity in the disparity between people's earnings. When you meet hardworking individuals it is impossible to believe that such disparities in earnings are the result of individual merit and not societal differences. As the U.S. bishops observe, "the concentration of privilege that exists today results far more from institutional relationships that distribute power and wealth inequitably than from differences in talent or lack of desire to work."[11]

In addition, we may have additional privileges that are a result of our family of origin. We may have won, in the words of business leader Warren Buffett, the "ovarian roulette" and been born with some advantages. These include the social privileges of white skin color, which unfortunately still confers many advantages in our society. Or it could be the advantages of being born or adopted into a family with social networks, business experience, or inherited wealth. We may have had a head start by virtue of sacrifices our parents or grandparents made. These advantages are sometimes invisible head starts. Research shows that even modest parental gifts or inheritances to pay for higher education, purchase a home, or start a business can transform a person's options and change that person's life trajectory.

We may feel uneasy or bristle at this discussion. This may be because life is rarely easy for any of us. And each of us can think about personal struggles, extra efforts, timely action, or smart decisions that may have contributed to any good fortune we have. None of what we are talking about diminishes the importance of individual action. We must find a way to celebrate and acknowledge the important role of individual choice, free will, ethical decisions, basic hard work, and sacrifice in our discussions of economic life. But understanding the nature of structural privilege has everything to do with being faithful followers of Gospel teachings and working for economic justice.

There is a powerful cultural credo that "people get what they deserve in our society, based on individual merit." If we believe this, then we inadvertently accept the corollary that people who are poor or disadvantaged are getting what they deserve because of lack of merit, the result of their individual actions or inactions.

Indeed, someone may be economically poor and marginalized because of individual poor choices, lack of effort, bad educational opportunities, immoral conduct, etc. We have affirmed that in our Catholic social teaching individual choices, as well as economic structural forces, explain outcomes. Individual choices and moral conduct *do* matter. We celebrate individual hard work, postponement of gratification, sacrifices made for children, and resistance to unhealthy temptations. In discussions of merit versus privilege, however, we often overlook the less visible structural advantages that many of us have. They are the hardest to see, especially for the beneficiaries, as they are often "hard-wired" into our lives.

There are obvious examples among the very wealthy of the ways that inherited wealth is a catapult to a privileged life. Almost a third of those listed on the Forbes 400 list of richest Americans were born onto the list. Others inherited a substantial head start — an existing business, ownership stake, or multi-million-dollar inheritance — and built upon that to accumulate even greater wealth. For example, Kenneth Field inherited the Ringling Brothers Circus in 1920 when it was worth tens of millions. He is now worth $650 million on the Forbes 400.[12]

Donald Trump sometimes derides people who inherit their wealth as members of the "lucky sperm club." But he personally inherited a real estate business from his father that was valued at more than $150 million.[13] In 2005, the Forbes 400 listed Philip Anschutz (net worth $7.2 billion) as "self-made" even though he inherited an oil and gas field worth $500 million.[14] Not a bad head start in life! Each of these individuals contributed something unique, but they had a significant boost compared to someone born into poverty or even a middle-class household. In the words of Seagram's heir Edgar Bronfman, "To turn $100 into $110 is work. To turn $100 million into $110 million is inevitable."[15]

These are quite obvious examples of unearned privilege. But many forms of privilege are not quite so visible or obvious. Sometimes people who inherit small amounts of wealth in the form of family help to buy a house or to pay college tuition, don't think of themselves as advantaged. Sociologist Tom Shapiro spent many years interviewing families for a study about the differences in wealth accumulation. He observed that modest inheritances of $10,000 or $15,000 could be transformative for middle-class families because of ways they can open up wealth-building opportunities. Yet he found that many families forget these inheritances and prefer to think of themselves as "self-made." Shapiro writes,

> I spoke to many families...who see no paradox in using inherited wealth to leverage advantages and opportunities unavailable to others. Their insistence upon how hard they work and how much they deserve their station in life seems to trump any recognition that unearned successes and benefits come at a price for others. This insistence upon wrapping advantage in the American Dream blurs the difference between thinking you are self-made and being self-made. Coming from families living in homes and communities they can afford only because of inherited wealth, the constant admonitions to the poor to take responsibility betrays and distorts the dream.[16]

In a similar way, after World War II, millions of families received substantial government assistance to purchase their first home. The government provided massive mortgage subsidies through the Federal Housing Administration, Farmers Home, and the Veterans Administration that enabled almost one-fifth of the population to get on the wealth-building train. Some of the beneficiaries were veterans of military service who might claim that their Veterans Administration low-interest mortgage was a form of compensation for the sacrifices of military services. But millions of others who did not serve in the military also benefited from these substantial housing subsidies.

The home ownership and college grant programs in the two decades after World War II were one of our country's biggest investments in broadening wealth and opportunity. It was a once-in-a-century investment that helped broaden our middle class and propel millions of people into higher paying jobs, increased home equity, and improved opportunity. Many of the children in these families also benefited by going to college and purchasing homes, as parents utilized the increased value of their homes to help their children purchase homes and pay for schooling. But how many of these families think of themselves as recipients of government subsidies? And how many consider that they are beneficiaries of white privilege? Ironically, many of them and their descendants don't think of themselves as beneficiaries of government subsidies and might even oppose such programs if they were helping others today.

As part of our reflection on privilege, let's reexamine the disparities in wealth along racial lines, using the experience of African American and white households as an illustration. As we discussed in the earlier section on wealth inequality, in 2004 the median net worth of white families was $140,700 while the equivalent for nonwhite or Hispanic families was $24,800.[17] Much of this disparity is explained by the different rates of homeownership between whites and people of color, but also by the disparity in incomes. These disparities cannot be explained solely in terms of a "merit-based" story. We are called to explore the structural forces at work.

The building of wealth is deeply shaped by multi-generational factors. A parent's wealth situation can greatly impact the next generation. There were deep racial biases built into these otherwise fabulous wealth-building programs we described above. Returning African American war veterans were not able to take advantage of the same GI Bill college opportunities in the Jim Crow South educational system. And there was overt racial discrimination in the home mortgage programs that propelled many families of European ancestry forward. As a result, many white families got on a multi-generational wealth-building train, while many people of color were left standing at the station. The percentage of white families that owned their own home rose dramatically in the decades after World War II so that in 2005, 72.7 percent of white families own their own home. By comparison, homeownership for blacks remained stalled at 48.2 percent.[18]

White families who own homes rarely consider that we are beneficiaries of a structural system of white privilege. It's just the way the system works. Even if we eliminate all present-day discrimination, the generational inequalities are "hard-wired" into the system.

Advantages have a way of piling up, sort of like sediment or compounding interest. Disadvantages also have a similar way of accumulating, sort of like compounding debt! For some people, the structural forces in the economy are working like an upward escalator as accumulated advantages increase or multiply. For others, the hole is getting deeper as the deficits pile up. Individual choices and actions obviously matter in this picture. And there are examples of people rising above the disadvantages — as well as squandering their advantages. But structural economic forces that are larger than any individual shape the overall thrust.

Imagine a five-hundred-meter running race where some contestants start the race a hundred meters from the finish line; and others stand at the starting line wearing thirty-pound leg weights. Clearly the effort of the individual runner will have an impact on the outcome of the race, but it is not a fair or level playing field.

Our society has done important things to eliminate barriers to equal opportunity. Fair housing and equal employment laws reduce discrimination. Investment in education and scholarships for higher education strengthen the ladder of opportunity. But we would be hard-pressed to claim that the playing field is now level. And there is still a legacy of discrimination that shapes people's opportunities.[19]

Economic privileges have real material benefits, just as disadvantages have real costs. Tom Shapiro describes how the "hidden cost of being African American" in our society translates into a substantially lower income and fewer assets. If you are born with a darker skin color, there is a greater likelihood your economic prospects will be limited. In the same way, being white has economic perks that directly translate into more money in the bank.

Privileges also have costs, though not as easily measurable. To accept unearned privileges is to ignore a bit of our personal humanity and our interconnection with others. For example, it injures us morally and psychologically to accept an extreme wage differential between ourselves and someone else when we know there is no just basis for it. There may be some rationale for a differential in pay based on effort, efficiency, experience, expertise, or training. But there is no economic principle or moral justification for someone being paid fifty times more than another person for an hour's labor, let alone five hundred times more, as some chief executive officers are compensated.

Anyone who has traveled or lived in the Global South has confronted this absurdity across borders. Someone might spend a day making a craft or working as a hotel maid. Yet that person's time is essentially worth twenty or fifty or one hundred times less than our time. Is there a way to morally explain this difference? We wouldn't be human if we didn't feel the emotional tug of unfairness in these arrangements.

We may have elaborate justifications for these inequalities. You will often hear "life is not fair," particularly from those who are the beneficiaries of an unfair system. Or we adopt a set of myths that attempt to explain or justify such inequalities or unearned privileges. But simplistic myths start to unravel the closer we get to people. The more we are in real relationships with people who are poor, impoverished, disadvantaged, or on the other side of the privilege equation, the more emotionally difficult it becomes to sustain these rationalizations. We might witness personal problems or limitations. But we also see how hard people work, the sacrifices they make for their children, the qualities of people's communities, and the structural barriers they run up against.

These experiences can be painful, and one of the ways we co-exist with our unearned privilege is by avoiding meaningful contact with those who are disadvantaged by the system. Another strategy is not to see poverty, so that it becomes invisible. Out of sight, out of mind, and out of heart. This partly explains the widening spatial gaps between different groups of people in our society. Living with such inequalities comes with a personal cost, though not a cost we can measure in dollars. It leads many privileged people to isolate themselves, form enclaves of privilege and "comfort zones" where they don't have to confront the pain of inequality and unearned privilege. And they miss out on the piece of humanity, spiritual aliveness, and life skills that other people have to offer. In *Nickel and Dimed*, Barbara Ehrenreich tells the stories of the invisible workers in our economy. Many religious people read these books and felt as if their blinders had been removed to reveal thousands of invisible servants making their existence possible.

Mindfulness of Privilege. The first step in developing mindfulness about privilege is to consider the possibility that the deck might be stacked in our favor. It means reflecting on questions such as:

- What are disadvantages, obstacles, and structural impediments that you have experienced in life?
- What are ways in which you may be privileged?
- What does disadvantage look and feel like?
- What does privilege look like? Feel like?

There is no simple mathematical equation that allows us to distinguish our individual merit from God's original blessing or society's structural privileges. Rather, we have to approach the question with a high level of humility and a self-reflective assessment of God's grace, our individual egos, and a better understanding of societal forces that contribute to health and well-being.

We certainly don't want to organize a society around the mistaken notion that individuals don't matter. Many societies are still healing from the wounds of the tyrannical Stalinist notion that the individual does not matter, only service to the community as represented by the state. On the other hand, our society needs to heal from the wounds of extreme individualism. We seek a healthy balance.

Acknowledging Help. Acknowledging when we've gotten help is more important than we think. Because if we don't admit to the times we've gotten help, then we perpetuate the myth of false self-sufficiency. It denies the basic truth that we are all interdependent and quite dependent on God and other people for whatever good fortune comes our way. It deepens our appreciation for the gifts of creation and reminds us that "gratitude is the attitude."

A New York–based software designer named Martin Rothenberg described all the ways he got help from people and society in the building of his $30 million company.

> My wealth is not only a product of my own hard work. It also resulted from a strong economy and lots of public investment in others and me.
>
> I received a good public school education and used free libraries and museums paid for by others. I went to college under the GI Bill. I went to graduate school to study computers and language on a complete government scholarship, paid for by others. While teaching at Syracuse University for 25 years, my research was supported by numerous government grants — again, paid for by others.
>
> My university research provided the basis for Syracuse Language Systems, a company I formed in 1991 with some graduate students and my son, Larry. I sold the company in 1998 and then started a

new company, Glottal Enterprises. These companies have benefited from the technology-driven economic expansion — a boom fueled by continual public and private investment.[20]

Rothenberg's story is an "I didn't do it alone" story. And the implication of getting help is that Rothenberg believes he has an obligation to give back to the society through charitable giving and paying his fair share of taxes. His family foundation addresses issues of poverty in his region of New York, and he anticipates paying estate taxes.

> I hope taxes on my estate will help fund the kind of programs that benefited others and me from humble backgrounds — a good education, money for research, and targeted investments in poor communities — to help bring opportunity to all Americans.[21]

This is an unusual statement, but as people recognize the gifts around them and acknowledge the real help they've received along the way, the implications and obligations become clearer. To the extent we have received gifts, it is our duty to pass them on.

Getting My Own House in Order

In moving toward social action and solidarity, there is a risk that we might leave our humility behind. We are a danger to others and ourselves in our potential for thoughtlessness and arrogance, especially if our attitude is "let's fix these other people" or "let's help them to be more like us." Such attitudes of paternalism and arrogance cut across race, gender, and ethnicity. The Gospel has several clear injunctions on the matter of judging others and preparing ourselves to be in solidarity with others.

The Gospel of Matthew asks why we see the faults in others before reflecting on our own lives: "Why do you see the speck in your neighbor's eye, but do not notice the log in your own eye? Or how can you say to your neighbor, 'Let me take the speck out of your eye,' while the log is in your own eye."

The Gospel's advice is to avoid being a hypocrite by first taking "the log out of your own eye, and then you will see clearly to take the speck out of your neighbor's eye" (Matthew 7:1–6). For those who want to make a difference in the world, this commandment calls us to "get our own house in order" as an essential part of engaging in solidarity. This includes seeing the gifts and blessings in our lives and wrestling with our own personal experience of oppression and privilege. Other activities include looking at our own levels of consumption and the ecological footprint that each of us leaves behind. It includes thinking about how we use our time, treasures, and talents.

Consumption

People often joke that the real national religion in the United States is shopping. If the market is God, then shopping is a form of worship. Today, a child in a Christian family under the age of ten is more likely to associate the Christmas holiday with trees, presents, and shopping malls than the birth of the baby Jesus in a manger.

The pressure to acquire more than we need is reinforced in advertising messages that bombard us everywhere in our lives.[22] It is countercultural in the United States to reflect on several simple questions: What are my true needs? How much is enough? What do I think I need because of advertising or pressures from neighbors?

Volume of Stuff. Do I need this thing? How much do we need? How much packaging comes with the product? Often the pleasurable sensation of buying something dissipates after it comes home and is out of the bag or box. How long will it be until this item breaks, is donated to a rummage sale, is thrown away, or is sold at a yard sale?

Materials and Environmental Impact. What natural resources were consumed in making or transporting the product? Who bears the brunt of the pollution?

Workplace Conditions of Products. What were the conditions like for workers who made these products? Were they paid a living wage? Do they have the freedom to associate and join unions? Are the products made in sweatshops or with child labor? Going out of our way to purchase "fair trade" food products and "union-made" clothing is one of the ways that we recognize the complex web of interconnections between physical products and their origins.

As the U.S. bishops noted, "All of us could well ask ourselves whether as Christian prophetic witness we are not called to adopt a simpler lifestyle, in the face of the excessive accumulation of material goods that characterizes an affluent society."[23]

Environmental Footprint

One of our biggest challenges as North Americans is to reduce the ecological impact of our lifestyles. The United States has 6 percent of the world's population but consumes more than half of its natural resources.

Certainly the rest of the world cannot develop along the same model of energy and material consumption. To do so would require six planet earths. We therefore must dramatically reduce our impact on the environment.

The standard middle-class U.S. lifestyle consumes massive amounts of petroleum products, water, electricity, wood, and coal. Each of our homes is a complex energy system. Many of us have employed preliminary common sense tactics to reduce energy consumption, such as turning off lights, taking shorter showers, weatherizing windows in the winter, or car-pooling. Some of our communities have recycling programs that we participate in.

Our personal choices and decisions clearly have global implications. Current wars over oil dramatize the need to reduce our international energy dependence. And many historians believe that future wars will be over the declining supply of potable water. Many parts of the United States already have insufficient water to sustain the communities that live there.

What is our fair share? What is an ecologically sustainable lifestyle? What can we do to make a difference? The choice to lead a more ecologically sustainable lifestyle doesn't have to feel like a daily harangue. Rather it can be an exercise in mindfulness, a walking prayer of respect and gratitude for our ecological inheritance.

Harangue — *Verb:* to criticize or question somebody or try to persuade somebody to do something in a forceful, angry way.
Noun: a loud, forceful, and angry speech criticizing somebody or trying to persuade somebody to do something.

Gratitude — *Noun:* a feeling of being thankful to somebody for doing something.

A fascinating first step in a deeper understanding of our ecological impact is to measure what is called an "ecological footprint." Imagine your footprint on a sandy beach. It displaces a bit of sand or soil. The bigger one's footprint, the more earth is pressed down. Our ecological footprint is our annual share of the earth's bounty, an estimate of the amount of productive land, water, and natural resources each of us uses and throws away. Ecological footprints can be calculated for individuals, families, communities, and even countries. Our challenge is to reduce our personal and collective footprints.

There are several terrific quizzes on the Internet that pose a series of questions, calculate an estimated footprint, and suggest ways to reduce your ecological impact. One site, sponsored by the organization Redefining Progress, also has a footprint exercise for young people. Their "Bobbie Bigfoot" curriculum could be used in school settings, but also with church youth groups and religious education classes.[24]

Redefining Progress reports that the average ecological footprint in the United States is 24 acres per person. Yet worldwide, there are only 4.5 biologically productive acres per person. Certainly population growth has an impact on the planet's sustainability. But most of the high-consumption countries are those with the least population growth. So the solution lies more in the problem of *how* we live, rather than how many of us live.

In this area of reducing our impact on the environment, there are a number of very concrete, measurable, and achievable things we can do. There are several organizations that have lesson plans, study guides, personal action programs, progress charts, and tools to help us to reduce our personal and community "footprint" on the earth. They include actions with our food, home energy use, and transportation choices, as well as ways to reduce the waste stream that flows through our homes and communities.

All of us have work to do as we prepare for discipleship — and the work is ongoing. We need to step forward with humility, an openness to learning, and a willingness to forgive others and ourselves as we make mistakes. The Beatitudes remind us, "Blessed are the merciful: for they shall obtain mercy." And we need to be merciful and forgiving as we step forward.

While it is important to strive to have our own "house in order" before engaging in social action, it is an elusive goal. Learning to live more ecologically and mindfully, for example, is a long-term commitment and God isn't finished with any of us yet. It is ultimately through the process of engaging with others and learning from social action that we will be transformed.

Chapter 10

Making a Difference

Politics . . . should be about an old idea with new power — the common good. The central question should not be, "Are you better off than you were four years ago?" It should be, "How can 'we' — all of us, especially the weak and vulnerable — be better off in the years ahead? How can we protect and promote human life and dignity? How can we pursue greater justice and peace?"

— U.S. Conference of Catholic Bishops, *Faithful Citizenship: A Catholic Call to Political Responsibility*, 2004

Faithful Citizenship for the Common Good

Catholic social teaching states that everyone has a duty and a right to participate in society and its organizational institutions. Justice requires minimum levels of participation by all people. The institutions through which we participate include government, civic organizations, churches, and religious and secular social action groups. This duty includes participating in the different levels of government and the public sector that touch our lives, including local, state, and federal politics. These responsibilities include being an informed voter, following public affairs, paying our taxes, and supporting the "commonwealth" functions of government.

At first, this may seem odd, as "government" often seems distant and the butt of many jokes. Recent polling and in-depth interviews reveal that people have an initial "rhetorical mode" when they are first asked about government, full of commonly repeated notions about government corruption, ineptness, and irrelevance. For many people, the word "government" initially has negative connotations: bitter elections, partisanship, corruption, waste, regulations, and taxes. But after reflection, people shift to a "reasonable mode," where they can reflect more thoughtfully about the complex roles that government plays.[1] One of our challenges is to go beyond reflexive complaining about government to recognize the important function that government plays in defending the common good and promoting justice.

The U.S. Conference of Catholic Bishops writes, "At this time, some Catholics may feel politically homeless, sensing that no political party and too few candidates share a consistent concern for human life and dignity. However, this is not a time for retreat or discouragement. We need more, not less engagement in political life." People of faith need to be more involved in our community and government institutions.

Government is a complex organism that is multi-leveled and many-layered. What other entity in our society would be capable of long-term planning, infrastructure development, and large complex responsibilities such as rebuilding the Gulf Coast after Hurricanes Katrina and Rita? What other entities can manage the divergent interests in our society, build consensus, or enforce compromises between groups of people?

Should government be run like a for-profit business? Yes and no. There are quality practices in the private sector that should be brought into government, such as the setting of clear measures of success and an orientation toward customers. Anyone who has stood in line waiting for an hour only to encounter a rude bureaucrat can appreciate the idea of taxpayers being treated like customers, with respect and attentiveness.

There are a number of "reinventing government" initiatives that have improved public sector services. And there are public-private partnerships that combine the best of private business sector culture with the social accountability of the public sector. There are certain government functions, however, that shouldn't be run like a for-profit corporation. Building and maintaining roads, feeding the hungry, or providing social insurance will never be profitable functions.

Government, for all we bellyache, fulfills an important *protector* function that is not appropriate for the private sector to play. For example, government must defend the rights of minorities, defend the environmental commons, and make investments in the institutions that move our society toward equality of opportunity. Subjects of in-depth interviews on their attitudes about government recognized "that government has a constraining, conscience-like function that is missing in the realm of business. In this respect government was cast as the collective moral conscience of the country — a role and characteristic that would be absent if the country were run by businesses alone."[2] It may be hard to think of government as playing a "moral" role, especially when it must play the role of mediator and compromiser between competing interest groups. But an engaged and accountable government serves a protector function that is fundamentally moral.

There are unfortunate examples where government has been "hijacked" by narrow and immoral special interests, but this is the result of a power imbalance or a breakdown in accountability. When we see things go wrong in society or observe inefficiency in government, it is our religious and civic duty to respond and hold these public and private institutions accountable. One important remedy is sunshine — transparency and accountability to improve the functioning of these institutions. Complaining about government but not participating in changing it is unconstructive. And attacking and withdrawing support from government is antisocial and un-Christian.

There are some who bemoan what they perceive to be a decline in civic values and community responsibility among the next generation. At the same time, these same people complain endlessly about government. What is the lesson communicated here? Do we want the next generation to withdraw or engage? Do we want to encourage national service or individual advancement?

Pope John Paul II believed that civic participation and social interaction are an expression of our human dignity: "It will be especially necessary to nurture the growing awareness in society of the dignity of every person and therefore to promote in the community a sense of the duty to participate in the political life in harmony with the Gospel. Involvement in the political field is clearly part of the vocation and activity of the lay faithful."[3]

In the end, things will work best when we each accept responsibility for government and recognize that as citizens we are part of the organism that *is* government. Government is an instrument, a tool, for accomplishing together what none of us can accomplish alone. The answer to our problems with government is not withdrawal, but engagement. Acting on our religious teachings for public life will hold government accountable to play its important roles as defender of the common good and promoter of justice.

Sharing Money and Time

Do not lay up for yourselves treasures on earth, where moth and rust consume and where thieves break in and steal, but lay up for yourselves treasures in heaven.... For where your treasure is, there will your heart be also.   —Matthew 6:19–21

Social Change Giving. Giving money to social change organizations — whether $15 or $5 million — is a powerful and meaningful way to make a difference. To be truly effective, however, we need to be smart and strategic givers and incorporate the principles of Christian economics into our donations.

There is a large element of charitable and philanthropic activity that does little to alleviate suffering or find solutions to social problems. Some types of philanthropic giving have more to do with flattering and reinforcing the privileged status of the giver than of making a difference with the money. As Pope Pius IX noted, "Let no one attempt with small gifts of charity to exempt himself from the great duties imposed by justice."[4] Our discussion is not concerned about country club charity events where people organize a party first and then go in search of a proper use for charitable donations.

But even among the areas of giving that are concerned with addressing social problems, there is an important distinction between giving to charity and contributing toward social action for justice. Both are necessary. Just as our analysis of social problems must go beyond looking only at individual factors and personal stories, so our faithful giving must work to address the structural causes of problems.

Traditional charity is sometimes characterized as "giving out Band-Aids." But as any parent or nurse can tell you, giving out Band-Aids is very important work. The problem occurs when our giving is limited to addressing only the symptoms.

At its best, traditional charity responds to immediate and urgent needs: feeding the hungry, clothing the naked, and sheltering the homeless. Traditional charities respond to mitigate short-term suffering, for example, with relief donations after an earthquake or hurricane. Or they may be concerned with ongoing service provisions, such as soup kitchens or shelters for homeless families.

Giving to social change organizations complements traditional charitable giving by attempting to address the root causes of problems. Such giving aims to change the sinful structures that create the need for traditional charity. It is concerned with longer-term institutional and structural change.

A Parable: Two Types of Giving. There is a simple parable that illustrates the distinction between traditional charitable responses and social change giving. The story takes place in a small village by a river. One day, a villager is fishing by the river and sees a cooing baby float by in a basket. She wades into the river and rescues the infant. She brings the baby back to the village, feeds it, and finds a family for the child.

The next day, two villagers are down by the river washing clothes when they see two baskets with babies float by. The two laundrymen run alongside the stream and intercept the baskets. Note the unusual gender division of work in this village. That night, the village meets to discuss the problem of caring for the infants. Two families step forward and volunteer to raise the children. A committee is formed to set up around-the-clock vigilance at the riverbank.

Within a few days, the villagers have rescued over twenty babies. They form several committees to care for the children, find them homes, monitor the riverbank, and develop improved nets and tools for intercepting floating baskets.

At a tense village meeting, one young woman stands up and proposes that the community form an expedition to travel upstream and determine why the children are ending up in the river. Several of the elders dismiss her idea, pointing out that they cannot spare any people because of the enormous work involved in intercepting children and caring for them. So weeks go by and the flow of infants in baskets continues unabated.

In this parable, the traditional charity response is to fund the urgent services in the village to care for children. Traditional charity might even contribute to improved research and technology for intercepting babies, including new nets. No one can dismiss the immediate and compassionate need to do this. At the same time, social changing givers would fund the expedition upstream to find out the source of the problem.

Traditional charity might address the problems of poverty by providing services and advocacy on behalf of the poor. Social change giving would aim at changing the rules and institutions that contribute to poverty and involve poor people in finding a solution to their own situations.

The Catholic Campaign for Human Development, the social change funding arm of the U.S. Conference of Catholic Bishops, has carefully thought through criteria for their giving. There is a strong focus on both addressing the root causes of problems and increasing participation and human development of those affected by problems. The criteria for receiving grants through their community organizing or economic development program include:

- The activity for which funding is requested must conform to the moral and social teachings of the Catholic Church.

- An applicant organization must demonstrate both the intention and capacity to effectively work toward the elimination of the root causes of poverty and to enact institutional change. CCHD defines institutional change as the modification of existing laws and/or policies, and the establishment of participatory and just social structures, and/or redistribution of decision-making powers so that people living in poverty can be involved in policymaking that affects their lives.

- Eligible organizations will build an economic development institution that will create income or assets for low-income people and communities.

- The organization should demonstrate ongoing leadership development because it is considered essential to the strength, depth, and sustainability of the organization.

These criteria are an example of stretching beyond traditional charity to address the deeper causes of social problems. As the Rev. Martin Luther King Jr. once said, "Philanthropy is no doubt commendable, but it must not cause the philanthropist to overlook the circumstances of economic injustice that make philanthropy necessary." Our faith teachings inspire us to develop a critical perspective on giving.

What is the difference between charity and change?

- **Charity:** Donating to a "Toys for Tots" campaign to buy Christmas presents for low-income workers unable to purchase gifts for their children.

- **Change:** Donating to the "living wage campaign" in your city, organizing to raise the minimum wage and enabling families to earn enough to buy toys for their own children.

- **Charity:** Contributing to a shelter for homeless families.

- **Change:** Contributing to the state affordable housing alliance, organizing to ensure the expansion of affordable housing opportunities for poor and low-income families.

- **Charity:** Donating to a health clinic in a low-income neighborhood to help with emergency care for children.

- **Change:** Donating to an advocacy organizing effort to expand state children's health care programs, covering millions of children.

Sharing Time and Talents. Some of us have the ability to give of our time and experience. But where can we make a difference? In many ways, choosing where to donate your volunteer time may not be that different from choosing where to give money. One has to consider whether to focus on direct service work that helps meet immediate needs or on organizing efforts aimed at changing institutions and structures. There is tremendous need in both areas.

Our criteria might be both where can we make a difference and where we might learn something about people from different circumstances. If part of our work is to change ourselves or broaden our own experiences, then work that enables us to build deep and real relationships with very low-income people is very important. This might lend itself toward volunteering in a more direct service setting. At the same time, there are now a growing number of exciting faith-based organizing coalitions and networks that we could plug into. These groups are working for more structural and systemic change.

Quality of Life Organizing

One struggle that would dramatically shift every other dimension is over the issue of time. With more time to devote to the things that matter, the possibilities for human and institutional change are limitless. Discipleship requires time to rest, recreate, participate, and serve.

One of the biggest changes resulting from industrialization of the 1800s was the transformation of our sense of work and time. Since then there has been a constant struggle for reduced work hours. When Pope Leo XIII wrote *Rerum Novarum* in 1873, the Catholic encyclical on the dignity of work, people were fighting and dying for the fifty-hour workweek. Organized labor led the charge for reduced work hours during the 1900s, so that today we have the bumper sticker: "The Labor Movement: The People Who Brought You the Weekend." In October 2005, the United States observed the sixty-fifth anniversary of the forty-hour workweek. One labor observer quipped: "We hope it doesn't retire!"

After a century of progress toward reducing work hours, there has been a reversal of gains, as the amount of time people spend laboring steadily increases. The productivity gains of the last three decades have not gone toward increased wages or reduced work hours, but instead have led to increased corporate profits. The engine behind declining leisure time is the expansion of mandatory overtime pay as many businesses find it less costly to pay overtime than to hire more employees, with their additional benefit costs and overhead. Obviously, many people choose to work overtime as a means to maintain a higher standard of living. But a big part of the problem lies in the "rules" in the United States that fail to protect family and personal time against the encroachments of work. This explains why the average European works nine weeks fewer on the job each year than people in the United States. The United States has no minimum paid vacation law, while Australia and the European countries have four or five weeks.

One solution is to reduce the hours of the workweek while maintaining a constant wage level. This would accomplish multiple social and economic goals, such as reducing unemployment and reducing job-related stresses. In 1998, France initiated the thirty-five-hour workweek, commenting that "productivity gains should be earmarked for a shorter working week rather than for wages." The French government provides a social security allowance designed to reduce the cost of labor. Italy also legislated a reduction of the workweek in March 1998.

A shorter workweek could immediately translate into expanded jobs for underemployed people. While some reduction in work hours is the result of technology, several studies estimate that 50 to 80 percent of reduced work hours translate into new jobs. The Canadian Auto Workers estimate that five thousand jobs were created or saved as a result of their 1993 contract shortening work time at "Big Three" auto plants.[5]

The "Take Back Your Time" coalition advocates a public policy agenda that would make a real difference in the amount of increased time people have to care for one another and their communities.[6] The program includes:

- Guaranteeing paid leave for all parents for the birth or adoption of a child. Today, only 40 percent of Americans are able to take advantage of the twelve weeks of unpaid leave provided by the Family and Medical Leave Act of 1993.

- Guaranteeing at least one week of paid sick leave for all workers. Many Americans work while sick, lowering productivity and endangering other workers.

- Guaranteeing at least three weeks of paid annual vacation leave for all workers. Studies show that 28 percent of all female employees and 37 percent of women earning less than $40,000 a year receive no paid vacation at all.

- Placing a limit on the amount of compulsory overtime work that an employer can impose, with the goal being to give employees the right to accept or refuse overtime work.

- Making Election Day a holiday, with the understanding that Americans need time for civic and political participation.

- Making it easier for Americans to choose part-time work through hourly wage parity and protection of promotions and pro-rated benefits for part-time workers.

Such provisions might actually increase productivity in the workplace. Studies show that those businesses that have good paid leave policies actually have higher productivity, employee morale, and profits. Reducing stress in the workplace and encouraging greater balance in our lives will result in improved health and wellness and reduce the estimated $300 billion a year that job stress–related illnesses cost U.S. businesses.

More free time would have other benefits. As we discussed at the outset of this book, without free time, people are less able to care for themselves, for prayer and renewal. They have less time to care for other people and God's creation. More free time is a precondition for faithful citizenship.

Solidarity and Social Action

What transforms us? What transforms the world? Usually a book is not what transforms people, though certain books and the written word have made enormous changes in people's lives. And a book or film experienced together with others can be powerful. Even the Bible is best read in a community of faith.

It is interesting to ask people involved in justice work what moved them into actions of solidarity and social action. For most, it was relationships with other people and finding a community of others to engage with. Isolated individuals cannot undertake things alone, but small groups of people committed to one another and meaningful action can accomplish a great deal.

Kim Bobo, the founder of Interfaith Worker Justice, finds that the transformative experience for many middle-class people of faith is when they engage in a witness or action of solidarity with a low-wage worker. People are deeply changed when they witness the indignity that low-wage workers suffer. Standing in solidarity with a low-wage worker at a vigil or picket line exposes an ally to the experience of isolation, insecurity, and possible mistreatment at the hands of employers and police. It is unforgettable. Instead of books, workshops, and reflection it is the process of taking action that really makes an impression.

For Kevin Cashman, executive director of Ministry of Money, the experience of taking people out of their context can be transforming. Ministry of Money leads "reverse mission" trips to Haiti, where participants get a first-hand experience of poverty in the global economy. The reverse mission concept refers to the way in which a North American citizen is transformed by an experience in another country. The mission is here in the United States, not somewhere else. Sometimes for us to see poverty and injustice in our own midst, it is helpful to see the global picture. These reverse mission trips are like pilgrimages that deepen one's commitment to social and economic justice.

Study and Reflection. What transforms many people is a combination of personal relationships, engagement in action, reflection, prayer, and study. The area of study should not be neglected, especially if it can be done as part of a discussion group with others. In the resources section of this book, there are a number of excellent books, articles, and resources for study and reflection.

Finding Others. It is important to find or found a group to sustain our personal solidarity and social action work over the long term. For many, it helps if the organization has a religious culture where we can draw on our faith and worship together. Shared prayer, music, and reflection has been the glue that has sustained many social action movements. What follows are a few places to find others, and there are more in the resources section.

JustFaith Ministries. Within the Catholic Church, the JustFaith network has been an inspiration to many and a home base for personal and social action. JustFaith is a thirty-week adult education and action program that is organized at the parish level. Together, participants explore Catholic social teachings and their personal faith. A weekly gathering employs books, videos, lectures, discussions, prayer and reflection, retreats and experiences where people cross the borders of their experience. The intent is "to provide a tapestry of learning opportunities that emphasize and enliven the remarkable justice tradition of the Church." It is an individual experience of study and growth, but also a community-building experience as participants share "a journey of faith and compassion that is both life-giving and challenging."

Over ten thousand people have participated in JustFaith programs in almost five hundred parishes in eighty-five dioceses throughout the United States. They have officially partnered with Catholic Relief Services, Catholic Charities USA, and the Catholic Campaign for Human Development. There are now highly developed resources and tools for organizing a JustFaith group in your parish at *www.justfaith.org*. Forming a JustFaith group might be a concrete personal action step coming out of reading this book.

Sojourners and Call to Renewal. The mission of Sojourners and Call to Renewal is to articulate the biblical call to social justice, inspiring hope and building a movement to transform individuals, communities, the church, and the world. *Sojourners* is a magazine for Christians that has been published since 1972. Call to Renewal, which recently merged with Sojourners, is a faith-based movement working to overcome poverty. Both organizations organize events, including an annual Pentecost gathering. "Sojomail" is one of the best online newsletters for Christians interested in culture, politics, and society.[7]

Sojourners and Call to Renewal have recently launched "A Covenant for a New America," a bold initiative to overcome poverty with religious commitment and political leadership. The covenant describes a program to move from poverty to opportunity. They argue that our society should make three fundamental commitments as a promise to those in poverty:

- Employment must work and provide family economic success and security.

- Children should not be poor.

- Extreme global poverty must end.

To make this vision possible, the signers to the covenant have articulated a policy strategy that includes both social and government responsibility and personal and community responsibility.[8]

Interfaith Worker Justice. In the mid-1990s, Interfaith Worker Justice was founded to help connect religious people, moved by their faith traditions, to efforts to improve the wages, benefits, and working conditions for low-wage workers. There are now over sixty local affiliates of IWJ throughout the country engaged in education, organizing, and mobilization.

The national and local organizations have engaged in direct efforts to protect and promote the dignity of workers. They have developed liturgical and educational resources for religious congregations on worker rights, living wage efforts, and the right to organize. They have worked to engage seminarians, rabbinical students, and novices in labor solidarity efforts. They have worked with religiously affiliated employers, such as hospitals and nursing homes, to model the highest standards of employer-employee relations.

IWJ played a leadership role in a national effort to support more than two hundred thousand poultry workers working in processing plants in small rural communities throughout the country. They have received consistent financial support for this work from the Catholic Campaign for Human Development and other Catholic organizations and individual churches. These low-wage workers, who are primarily Latino and African American, toil in some of the most dangerous working conditions in the country. IWJ organized religious leaders and lay people in communities to support poultry workers, formed fact-finding delegations to meet with workers and plant owners, and promoted ethical standards for workers in this industry.

For more information about Interfaith Worker Justice and to find the closest affiliate to you, see *www.iwj.org* or see the contact information at the back of the book.

Social Action Partnerships. As part of our commitment to solidarity, a key action might be to find a local social action organization that we can devote our time, talents, and treasure to. In every region, there are grassroots organizations of people coming together to make changes. They need volunteer energy, leaders, and allies. There are several groups profiled that embody the wide variety of activities and action that are consistent with Catholic social teaching. Though diverse, they generally demonstrate the following characteristics:

• They are involved in meeting both immediate needs and attempting to change institutional structures.

• They are committed to increasing the participation of all kinds of people in the changing of institutions, but especially the poor and the marginalized.

• They are locally or regionally based, allowing for face-to-face relationships and democratic participation to occur.

There are hundreds of congregation-based organizing efforts all over the country. Citizens Organized for Public Service (COPS) in San Antonio, Texas, discussed in chapter 8, is one example. There are now several networks of affiliated faith-based organizing groups around the country. You can probably find information about local congregation-based organizing efforts through your diocesan social action or Catholic Charities office. The networks include

• the Industrial Areas Foundation
(*www.industrialareasfoundation.org*)

• the Gamaliel Foundation
(*www.gamaliel.org*)

• the PICO Network
(*www.piconetwork.org*)

• Direct Action and Research Training (DART) Network
(*www.thedartcenter.org*)

• the Intervalley Project
(*www.intervalleyproject.org*)

These are a sample of the kinds of organizations that people of faith are actively working with. Contact your local diocesan social action office or Catholic Campaign for Human Development coordinator for information about groups that are active in your region.

Conclusion

For the Grace of God

"There but for the Grace of God go I."

When was the last time you heard someone say that phrase? Sometimes it pops up in a conversation in a colloquial way — or in the lyrics of an Irish ballad. Other cultures and religions have other ways of describing this fundamental human interconnection.

We remember hearing it among our elders when they learned of human tragedy or loss. They might have just read the news of a horrible accident or learned that a healthy friend had been struck down by an illness. This would bring forth the utterance, "There but for the Grace of God go I."

"There but ... " is a mini-prayer. It is an acknowledgment of the gift of life and our fundamental vulnerability. It reminds us that our lives, our health and what good fortune we may have are a gift from God. And it is an awareness that misfortune could happen to any of us at any time. So in gratitude for the moment, saying "there but for the Grace of God go I" is an exercise in mindfulness.

On any given day, reading the newspaper could be an exercise in such mindfulness. Children are shot at a school in Vermont. An earthquake hits a city in Turkey. A car bombing in Iraq kills twenty, including four children. There but for the Grace of God go I.

It seems that in contemporary culture and our economy, "There but for the Grace of God go I" has been replaced by "Too bad for them" or "glad it wasn't me." And it is not uncommon on talk radio to hear a more mean-spirited response: "They probably deserved it" or "Too bad their country is so messed up."

For most in the United States, the response to tragedy is a more benign "out of sight, out of mind." Or "it's so far away." After all, with news of human tragedy coming in twenty-four hours a day, seven days a week, there is only so much that any of us can take in. But a possible prayer in response to the news bombardment is "there but for the Grace of God go I."

It seems the way we respond to contemporary economic life is more akin to "as long as it doesn't touch my immediate family, it is not my problem." Such attitudes are diametrically the opposite of our Gospel tradition.

This book has been about how we organize the U.S. economy to recognize the gift of life and the vulnerabilities that all of us face. A "there but" economy minimizes human suffering and promotes human dignity.

The fundamental Gospel lesson and its implications for our economic and ecological life is that "we are all in this together." An injury to one is an injury to all. Love thy neighbor. Welcome the stranger for "what you do to the least of my brethren, you do unto me." Remember that "there but for the Grace of God go I" and organize the institutions and policies of the society as if it were you who were the suffering, marginalized, or impoverished person standing on the street corner. That is the simple meaning of solidarity.

In today's popular culture, there is tremendous focus on the outrageous newsmaker, the extremist politician, the glamorous celebrity, the iconic sports figure, or the colorful and racy individual.

But the most radical and countercultural people in our society rarely are in the news. They are simply practicing "solidarity." They remember, "We are all in this together" and praying, "there but for the Grace of God go I." They are living values quite distinct from the values of the secular marketplace.

Our challenge as Christians is to faithfully and courageously push beyond the "gospel of the market." This does not mean to be ignorant of the market, nor fail to recognize its important role and value in our society. It means bringing Gospel values into the marketplace and preventing market values from trumping our religious values.

As the U.S. bishops wrote, "Unless we teach our children basic values of honestly, compassion, and initiative they will not be equipped to deal with the 'counter values' of selfishness, consumerism, and materialism so prevalent in our society."[1] Our Gospel teachings are like a set of new glasses, enabling us to reexamine and read the signs of the times that are around us.

The signs of the times today are not pretty. Between growing inequality in the United States and the persistence of extreme poverty around the planet, we can't ignore the warning signs of a human race at risk. The call to discipleship is to deeply internalize the "good news" of Jesus' teachings and biblical values to guide our actions in the world.

Change does happen. But it requires messengers of hope and agents of change. We can each decide to play this role. As Jim Wallis notes, "Hope is believing, in spite of the evidence, that change is possible — and then watching the evidence change."

Discipleship is choosing to believe in one's self as a change maker. And this requires courage. With prayer, reflection, community, and God's help, each of us will summon this courage and discern the role we are called to play on the path toward justice for all.

Notes

Introduction

1. Peter J. Henriot, Edward P. DeBerri, and Michael J. Schultheis, *Catholic Social Teaching: Our Best Kept Secret* (Maryknoll, N.Y.: Orbis Books, and Washington, D.C.: Center of Concern, 1995).

2. National Conference of Catholic Bishops, *Economic Justice for All: Pastoral Letter on Catholic Social Teaching and the U.S. Economy,* tenth anniversary ed. (Washington, D.C.: U.S. Catholic Conference, 1997), 9.

3. Ibid., 23, no. 8.

4. Ibid., 14, no. 6.

5. Ibid., 19, no. 25.

1. Economics As If People Mattered

1. U.S. Department of Commerce, Bureau of Economic Analysis, National Income and Product Accounts Table 2.1: "Personal Income and Its Disposition, September 2006."

2. Center on Budget and Policy Priorities, "Poverty Remains Higher" (Washington, D.C., September 1, 2006). Historical data from U.S. Census Bureau, Historical Poverty Tables, Table 2, "Poverty Status of People by Family Relationship, Race, and Hispanic Origin: 1959 to 2004," *www.census.gov/hhes/www/poverty/histpov/ hstpov2.html,* accessed May 2006.

3. U.S. Census Bureau, Historical Health Insurance Tables, Table HI-1, "Health Insurance Coverage Status and Type of Coverage by Sex, Race and Hispanic Origin: 1987 to 2004." See *www.census.gov/hhes/www/hlthins/historic/hihi stt1.html,* accessed May 2006.

4. Average CEO pay in 1985 was $1.2 million, according to John A. Byrne, "Executive Pay: How the Boss Did in '85," *Business Week,* May 5, 1986. In 1985, average worker pay was $15,843, according to data found in Bureau of Labor Statistics, Employment, Hours and Earnings from the Current Employment Statistics Survey, Table B-2, *ftp://ftp.bls.gov/pub/suppl/empsit.ceseeb2.txt,* accessed May 2006.

5. Larry Mishel, Jared Bernstein, and Sylvia Allegretto, *State of Working America, 2006–2007* (Ithaca, N.Y.: Cornell University Press, 2007), 247–77.

6. U.S. Census Bureau, Historical Income Tables — Families, Table F-3, "Mean Income Received by Each Fifth and Top 5 Percent of Families, All Races: 1966 to 2004." See *www.census.gov/hhes/www/income/histinc/f03ar. html,* accessed May 2006.

7. Forbes 400: The Richest People in America, October 9, 2006, at *www.forbes .com/lists/2006/54/biz_06rich400_The-400-Richest-Americans_land.html.*

8. Center on Budget and Policy Priorities, "Poverty Remains Higher" (Washington, D.C.: September 1, 2006). U.S. Census Bureau, Historical Poverty Tables, Table 3, "Poverty Status of People, by Age, Race, and Hispanic Origin, 1959 to 2004." See *www.census.gov/hhes/www/poverty/histpov/hstpov3.html,* accessed May 2006.

On the racial breakdown of poverty data: In 1985, the number of white, non-Hispanic people in poverty was 18 million, or 9.7 percent of the white population. In 2004, the number of white, non-Hispanic people in poverty was 17 million, or 8.6 percent of the white population. In 1985, the number of African American people in poverty was 9 million, or 31.3 percent of the African American population. In 2004, the number of African American people in poverty was 9 million, or 24.7 percent of the African American population. In 1985, the number of Hispanic people in poverty was 5 million, or 29.0 percent of the Hispanic population. In 2004, the number of Hispanic people in poverty was 9 million, or 21.9 percent of the Hispanic population.

2. Our Best Kept Secret

1. National Conference of Catholic Bishops, *Economic Justice for All: Pastoral Letter on Catholic Social Teaching and the U.S. Economy,* tenth anniversary ed. (Washington, D.C.: U.S. Catholic Conference, 1997), 5.

2. Jim Wallis, *God's Politics: Why the Right Gets It Wrong and the Left Doesn't Get It* (San Francisco: HarperSanFrancisco, 2005), 212.

3. Peter J. Henriot, Edward P. DeBerri, and Michael J. Schultheis, *Catholic Social Teaching: Our Best Kept Secret* (Maryknoll, N.Y.: Orbis Books, and Washington, D.C.: Center of Concern, 1995).

4. National Conference of Catholic Bishops, *Economic Justice for All,* 31, no. 28.

5. Ibid., 32, nos. 31–34.

6. Ibid., 32 no. 32. Genesis 4–11.

7. Ibid., 32. See Isaiah 40:12–20; 44:1–20; Wisdom 13:1–14:31; Colossians 3:5, "the greed that is idolatry."

8. Ibid., 41, no. 66.

9. Ibid., 38, no. 38.

10. Matthew 4:1–11. In Luke Jesus is offered authority over all the kingdoms. Luke 4:1–12.

11. National Conference of Catholic Bishops, *Economic Justice for All,* 36, no. 44.

12. Ibid., 42, no. 68–76.

13. Ibid., 11.

14. Ibid.

15. Pontifical Council for Justice and Peace, *Compendium of the Social Doctrine of the Church,* English ed. (Washington, D.C.: U.S. Conference of Catholic Bishops, 2005), no. 167.

16. National Conference of Catholic Bishops, *Economic Justice for All,* 53, no. 112.

17. Pontifical Council for Justice and Peace, *Compendium of the Social Doctrine of the Church,* no. 321.

18. The authors wish to thank Scott Klinger for his work on developing educational resources on Catholic social teaching and his framing as of "Gospel values" and "market values."

19. Harvey Cox, "The Market Is My Shepherd, and I Shall Want and Want and Want," *U.S. Catholic,* February 1, 2000. See also Cox, "The Market as God," *Atlantic Monthly,* March 1, 1999.

3. Signs of the Times #1

1. Mary Leonard, "Stressed Families Feeling Left Out," *Boston Globe,* October 17, 2000.

2. Juliet B. Schor, *Born to Buy* (New York: Scribner, 2004), 10.

3. National Conference of Catholic Bishops, *Economic Justice for All: Pastoral Letter on Catholic Social Teaching and the U.S. Economy,* tenth anniversary ed. (Washington, D.C.: U.S. Catholic Conference, 1997), 128, no. 337.

4. For more on leisure and Sabbath, see ibid., 128, no. 338.

5. As the bishops queried in their pastoral letter, "Why is it one hears so little today about shortening the work week, especially if both parents are working?" See ibid., 128, no. 337.

6. Larry Mishel, Jared Bernstein, and Sylvia Allegretto, *State of Working America, 2006–2007* (Washington, D.C.: Economy Policy Institute, 2006). Fact sheet on "Work Hours."

7. See *www.globalworkingfamilies.org.*

8. Tamara Draut, *Strapped: Why America's 20- and 30-Somethings Can't Get Ahead* (New York: Doubleday, 2005), 2–3.

9. U.S. Department of Commerce, Bureau of Economic Analysis, National Income and Product Accounts Table 2.1: Personal Income and Its Disposition. See savings rate since 1959: *research.stlouisfed.org/fred2/data/PSAVERT.txt.*

10. Brian Bremmer, "Japan's Dangerous Savings Drought," *Business Week,* June 9, 2003. See also "Germany, Monthly Economic Report," British Embassy Berlin, February 2004, *www.britische-botschaft/de/en/embassy/eu/pdf/MERFeb_04.pdf.*

11. Lawrence Mishel and Ross Eisenbrey, "What's Wrong with the Economy," a fact sheet published by the Economic Policy Institute (Washington, D.C.: December 15, 2005).

12. Credit Card Facts and Debt Statistics, October 11, 2006. See *www.creditcards.com/statistics/statistics.php.* See also Christian E. Weller, Ph.D., and Alanna Gino, "Rising Personal Bankruptcies: A Sign of Economic Strains on America's Middle Class" (Washington, D.C.: Center for American Progress, February 18, 2005). *www.americanprogress.org.* The number of personal and business bankruptcies exploded in the second quarter of 2005, in anticipation of the new federal law that went into effect in October 2005. Administrative Office of U.S. Courts, "Number of Bankruptcy Cases Filed in Federal Courts," news release from U.S. Courts, August 24, 2005. See *www.uscourts.gov/Press_Releases/bankruptcyfilings82405.html.*

13. Joanna Stavis, "Credit Card Borrowing, Delinquency, and Personal Bankruptcy," *New England Economic Review* (July–August 2000).

14. David U. Himmelstein, Elizabeth Warren, Deborah Thorne, and Steffie Woolhandler, "Illness and Injury as Contributors to Bankruptcy," *Health Affairs* (January 2005).

15. Elizabeth Warren, "Sick and Broke," *Washington Post,* February 9, 2005, A23.

16. Rebecca Lindsey, "Got Mail? A Record Six Billion Credit Card Offers Were Mailed Last Year," *CardRatings.com.*, June 3, 2006. Mail Monitor, the direct mail offer tracking service from the global market research firm Synovate, announced that over 6 billion credit card offers were mailed to U.S. citizens in the year 2005. See *www.creditboards.com.*

17. Statistics compiled and kept up to date by *creditcards.com,* an industry website. See *www.creditcards.com/statistics/statistics.php.*

18. See *www.familiesusa.org/resources/newsroom/story-bank.* Families USA provides a story bank of people's health care experiences.

19. CBS News, "46 Million Lack Health Insurance," August 30, 2005, reporting on release of U.S. census data, *www.cbsnews.com/stories/2005/08/30/health/webmd/main806291.shtml.*

20. Government Accounting Office, "Long-Term Care: Aging Baby Boom Generation Will Increase Demand and Burden on Federal and State Budgets GAO-02-544T" (Washington, D.C.: Government Accounting Office, March 2002). For a broader estimate of costs see Marc Freiman, "A New Look at U.S. Expenditures for Long-Term Care and Independent Living Services, Settings, and Technologies for the Year 2000" (Washington, D.C.: American Association of Retired Persons Public Policy Institute, April 2005).

21. Families USA, "Sticker Shock: Rising Prescription Drug Prices for Seniors," Publication no. 04-103, 2004 (Washington, D.C.: Families USA Foundation).

22. In a December 2005 Business Roundtable survey, CEOs cited health care costs as corporate America's number one cost pressure (42 percent) for the third year in a row. This topped energy costs (27 percent) and litigation costs (9 percent). Robert W. Lane, CEO of Deere & Company, "Checkup on the Nation's Health Care Tax Policy: A Prognosis," Testimony before the Senate Finance Committee, March 8, 2006. See *www.deere.com/en_US/compinfo/speeches/2006/06 00308_lane.html.*

23. Jeremy Peters and Milt Freudenheim, "G.M. Retirees Confront Co-Pays and Deductibles," *New York Times,* October 18, 2005.

24. Ibid.

25. John Ellsberry, "Moving on Down: One Month in the Lives of a Homeless Couple Just Trying to Get By," *Baltimore City Paper,* April 12, 2006.

26. See Janny Scott and Randal C. Archibold, "Across Nation, Housing Costs Rise as Burden: Middle Class Squeezed by Stagnant Incomes," *New York Times,* October 3, 2006.

27. Martha Burt, "America's Homeless II: Populations and Services." PowerPoint Presentation (Washington, D.C.: Urban Institute, 2004). Available online at *www.urban.org/publications/900344.html.*

28. Michael E. Stone, "Shelter Poverty: The Chronic Crisis of Affordable Housing," 2004, a condensed version of the chapter "Housing Affordability: One Third of a Nation Shelter Poor," in *Housing Foundation for a New Social Agenda,* ed. Rachel Bratt, Michael E. Stone, and Chester Hartman (Philadelphia: Temple University Press, 2005).

29. Co-author Chuck Collins was a housing activist in Boston's South End in the 1970s and 1980s and witnessed the impact of losing over ten thousand units of single-room occupancy housing.

30. Cushing Dolbeare, Basloe Saraf, and Sheila Crowley, "Changing Priorities: The Federal Budget and Housing Assistance, 1976–2005" (Washington, D.C.: National Low Income Housing Coalition, 2004).

31. Daniel Gross, "Location, Location — Deduction" from *Slate.com,* April 14, 2005. See *www.slate.com/id/2116731/.* Gerald Prante, "Who Benefits from the Home Mortgage Interest Deduction?" Tax Foundation, February 6, 2006, Fiscal Fact 49, *www.taxfoundation.org/news/show/1341.html.*

32. Kenneth Jackson, *Crabgrass Frontier: The Suburbanization of the United States* (New York: Oxford University Press, 1985), 190–209.

33. The math book is *Mathematics: Applications and Connections* (New York: McGraw-Hill, 1995, 1999) as reported in Constance L. Hays, "Math Book Salted with Brand Names Raises New Alarm," *New York Times,* March 21, 1999.

34. Eleanor Randolph, "The Big, Fat American Kid Crisis...And 10 Things We Should Do about It," *New York Times,* May 10, 2006. From the "Talking Points" provided to TimesSelect subscribers.

35. Juliet Schor, *Born to Buy* (New York: Scribner, 2004).

36. See the entire Parents' Bill of Rights at *www.demaction.org/dia/organizations/commercialalert.*

37. This account is taken from a collection of interviews and stories published on a website dedicated to discouraging outsourcing. See *www.outsourceoutrage.com/workers-stories/natasha.html.*

38. Lawrence Mishel and Ross Eisenbrey, "What's Wrong with the Economy," a fact sheet (Washington, D.C.: Economic Policy Institute, December 15, 2005).

39. See Tom Brokaw, *The Greatest Generation* (New York: Random House, 1998), and Tom Brokaw, *An Album of Memories: Personal Histories from the Greatest Generation* (New York: Random House, 2001).

40. Project on Student Debt at the National Center for Education Statistics (NCES), National Postsecondary Student Aid Study (NPSAS), Data Analysis System (DAS). Adjustments for inflation are based on the Consumer Price Index. See Nellie Mae, "The College Board," as reported in *Boston Globe,* October 23, 1997. See also Dr. Sandy Baum and Marie O'Malley, "College on Credit: How Borrowers Perceive Their Educational Debt, Results on the 2002 National Student Loan Survey," Nellie Mae, February 6, 2003. This information can be found at *www.nelliemae.com/library/research_10.html.* The data indicates that while the average student debt is $18,900, the average debt for students who attend a four-year private college is $21,200.

41. Pell Institute Statistics on Opportunity in Higher Education. 2004. See online *www.pellinstitute.org/statusreport/5b_Indicators_cvrsTxt.pdf.*

42. Richard Morin, "Misperceptions Cloud Whites' View of Blacks," *Washington Post,* July 11, 2001. See also U.S. Bureau of the Census, "Hispanic Population in the United States," March 2002 Current Population Survey, June 2003, Washington, D.C.: U.S. Census Bureau, Annual Demographic Supplement to the March 2002 Current Population Survey, 20–545.

43. U.S. Department of Commerce, Bureau of the Census, Current Population Survey, October 2005. From "Percentage of High School Completes Ages 16–24 Who Were Enrolled in College after Completing High School, by Type of Institution, Family Income, and Race/Ethnicity: October 1972–2004."

4. Signs of the Times #2

1. "Hourly and Weekly Earnings of Production and Non-supervisory Workers, 1947–2005," in 2005 dollars, Table 3.3., in Lawrence Mishel, Jared Bernstein, and Sylvia Allegretto, *The State of Working America 2006–2007* (Ithaca, N.Y.: Cornell University Press, 2007).

2. U.S. Census Bureau, Historical Income Tables — Families, Table F-3, "Mean Income Received by Each Fifth and Top 5 Percent of Families, All Races: 1966 to 2004." See *www.census.gov/hhes/www/income/histinc/f03ar. html,* accessed May 2006.

3. U.S. Census Bureau, Historical Income Tables — Families, Table F-1, "Income Limits for Each Fifth and Top 5 Percent of Families, All Races: 1947 to 2004," *www.census.gov/hhes/www/income/histinc/f01ar. html,* accessed May 2006.

4. David Cay Johnston, "Richest Are Leaving Even Rich Behind," *New York Times,* June 5, 2005.

5. Sarah Anderson, John Cavanagh, Chuck Collins, and Eric Benjamin, "Executive Excess 2006" (Washington, D.C.: Institute for Policy Studies and United for a Fair Economy, September 2006). Available online at *www.faireconomy.org/reports/2006/ExecutiveExcess2006.pdf.*

6. Eric Dash, "C.E.O. Pay Keeps Rising, and Bigger Rises Faster," *New York Times,* April 9, 2006.

7. Gretchen Morgenson, "Advice on Boss's Pay May Not Be So Independent," *New York Times,* April 10, 2006.

8. Anderson et al., "Executive Excess 2006."

9. Center on Budget and Policy Priorities, "Poverty Remains Higher, and Median Income for Non-Elderly Is Lower, Than When Recession Hit Bottom," Washington, D.C.: revised, September 1, 2006. See *www.cbpp.org/8-29-06pov.htm.* See also Lawrence Michel and Ross Eisenbrey, "What's Wrong with the Economy" (Washington, D.C.: Economic Policy Institute, December 15, 2005).

10. U.S. Census Bureau, Historical Poverty Tables, Table 3, "Poverty Status of People, by Age, Race, and Hispanic Origin: 1959 to 2004," *www.census.gov/hhes/www/poverty/histpov/hstpov3.html,* accessed May 2006.

11. Robert Greenstein, "Statement on . . . New Data on Poverty, Income, and Health Insurance" (Washington, D.C.: Center on Budget and Policy Priorities, August 31, 2005).

12. See especially Jonathan Kozel, *The Shame of the Nation: The Restoration of Apartheid Schooling in America* (New York: Crown Publishers, 2005); Barbara Ehrenreich, *Nickel and Dimed: On (Not) Getting By in America* (New York: Metropolitan Books, 2001); and David Shipler, *The Working Poor: Invisible in America* (New York: Vintage Paperback, 2004).

13. U.S. Census Bureau, "Income, Poverty and Health Insurance Coverage in the United States: 2003," Current Population Reports, August 2003.

14. National Conference of Catholic Bishops, *Economic Justice for All: Pastoral Letter on Catholic Social Teaching and the U.S. Economy,* tenth anniversary ed. (Washington, D.C.: U.S. Catholic Conference, 1997), 47, no. 88.

15. Fred Kammer, S.J., *Doing Faithjustice: An Introduction to Catholic Social Thought,* rev. ed. (New York: Paulist Press, 2004), 26.

16. This story is from the website of the Capital Area Asset Building Corporation. See *www.caab.org/client_stories/edgar_proctor.htm.*

17. Shipler, *The Working Poor.*

18. Thanks to *Sojourners* magazine for permission to reuse parts of a book review published by Chuck Collins.

19. Lawrence Mishel, Jared Bernstein, and Sylvia Allegretto, *The State of Working America, 2006–2007* (Ithaca, N.Y.: Cornell University Press, 2007), 255.

20. Thomas J. Stanley and William D. Danko, *The Millionaire Next Door: The Surprising Secrets of America's Wealthy* (New York: Simon and Schuster, 1996).

21. Typically this "reserve" should not include equity in a home, which is not immediately liquid, although it can be borrowed against.

22. Mel Oliver and Tom Shapiro, *Black Wealth, White Wealth* (New York: Routledge, 1995). See also Dalton Conley, *Being Black, Living in the Red: Race, Wealth and Social Policy* (Berkeley: University of California Press, 1999).

23. Mishel, Bernstein, and Allegretto, *The State of Working America, 2006–2007,* 247–77.

24. See Meizhu Lui et al., *The Color of Wealth: The Story behind the U.S. Racial Wealth Divide* (New York: New Press, 2006).

25. Mishel, Bernstein, and Allegretto, *State of Working America, 2006–2007,* 247–77. See also "Changes in Household Wealth in the 1980's and 1990's in the U.S.," in *International Perspectives on Household Wealth,* ed. Edward N. Wolff (London: Elgar Publishing, 2006).

26. Forbes 400: The Richest People in America, October 9, 2006, at *www.forbes.com/lists/2006/54/biz_06rich400_The-400-Richest-Americans_land.html.*

27. Fred Kammer, S.J., *Doing Faithjustice,* 28.

28. National Conference of Catholic Bishops, *Economic Justice for All,* 43.

29. Cited in Jeff Gates, *Democracy at Risk: Rescuing Main Street from Wall Street* (Cambridge, Mass: Perseus Press, 2000), xii.

30. Samuel Huntington as quoted in Kevin Phillips, *Wealth and Democracy* (New York: Broadway Books, 2002), xv.

31. For example, the concentration of media ownership narrows and cheapens public discourse. When Ben Bagdikian wrote *The Media Monopoly* in 1983, about fifty media conglomerates controlled more than half of all broadcast media, newspapers, magazines, video, radio, music, publishing, and film in the country. Today, fewer than ten multinational media conglomerates dominate the American mass media landscape.

32. The cost of running for office continues to spiral upward. The average U.S. House winner spent $840,300 in 2000, up from $650,428 in 1996. The average winner for U.S. Senate spent $7.3 million in 2000, up from $5.2 million in 1996. That translates into over $23,400 that the candidate senator needs to raise *each week* of his or her six-year term. The 2004 election cycle shattered all the records. In the presidential election, candidates George W. Bush and John Kerry spent a combined $548 million. This does not include the hundreds of millions spent by political parties or advocacy groups. Big money was the winner of the election across the board. The biggest spender was victorious in 415 of the 435 House races and 31 of 34 Senate races. Source: Center for Responsive Politics (*www.opensecrets.org*).

33. Interview with co-author Chuck Collins, April 18, 2004.

34. Edward J. Blakely and Mary Gail Snyder, *Fortress America: Gated Communities in the United States* (Washington, D.C.: Brookings Institution Press, 1997). Justice Policy Institute Study, as reported in Jesse Katy, "A Nation of Too Many Prisoners?" *Los Angeles Times,* February 15, 2000.

35. For a good overview of health and inequality issues, see Sam Pizzigati, *Greed and Good: Understanding and Overcoming the Inequality That Limits Our Lives* (New York: Apex Press, 2004), 311–30. See also Dr. Stephen Bezruchka's website, Population Health Forum, for information on global and U.S. health and inequality information: *www.depts.washington.edu/eqhlth/.* See also Stephen Bezruchka and M. A. Mercer, "The Lethal Divide: How Economic Inequality Affects Health," in M. Fort, M. A. Mercer, and O. Gish, *Sickness and Wealth: The Corporate Assault on Global Health* (Boston: South End Press, 2004), 11–18.

36. British medical researcher Dr. Richard Wilkinson argues that communities with less inequality have stronger "social cohesion," more cultural limits on unrestrained individual actions, and greater networks of mutual aid and caring. "The individualism and values of the market are restrained by a social morality." The existence of more social capital "lubricates the workings of the whole society and economy. There are fewer signs of antisocial aggressiveness, and society appears more caring." See Richard Wilkinson, *Unhealthy Societies: The Afflictions of Inequality* (London: Routledge, 1996).

37. Bill Gates and Chuck Collins, *Wealth and Our Commonwealth: Why America Should Tax Accumulated Fortunes* (Boston: Beacon Press, 2003).

38. Ibid., 19–22.

39. Zandy Minton Beddoes, "Tipping Point," from "The World in 2006," a special issue of *The Economist* (November 2005).

40. Ibid.

41. Riva D. Atlas and Mary Williams Walsh, "Pension Officers Putting Billions into Hedge Funds," *New York Times,* November 27, 2005.

42. Greg Ip and Mark Whitehouse, "Huge Flood of Capital to Invest Spurs World-Wide Risk Taking," *Wall Street Journal,* November 3, 2005.

43. For a perspective downplaying the importance of trade deficits, see Daniel T. Griswold, "America's Maligned and Misunderstood Trade Deficit," from the Cato Institute (Washington, D.C., 2002). See *www.freetrade.org/pubs/pas/tpa-002.html.*

44. Check out the national public debt level at the U.S. Treasury Department's own website: *www.publicdebt.treas.gov/opd/opdpenny.htm.*

5. Root Causes, Part I

1. For an excellent discussion of structures, see Fred Kammer, *Doing Faithjustice: An Introduction to Catholic Social Thought,* rev. ed. (New York: Paulist Press, 2004), 198–209.

2. Pontifical Council for Justice and Peace, *Compendium of the Social Doctrine of the Church,* English ed. (Washington, D.C.: U.S. Conference of Catholic Bishops, 2005), no. 209.

3. North American Alliance for Fair Employment, *www.fairjobs.org/index.php.*

4. Associated Press, "61 Percent Americans Fear Job-Loss Due to Outsourcing," March 17, 2004. Based on a Gallup poll looking at working anxiety and outsourcing. See *inhome.rediff.com/money/2004/mar/17bpo1.htm.*

5. David Sirota, Christy Harvey, and Judd Legum, "Bush Said His Tax Cuts Would Create 1,836,000 New Jobs By Now — He is 1,615,00 Short of His Goal" (Washington, D.C.: Center for American Progress, January 11, 2004). Data from the U.S. Department of Labor, Bureau of Labor Statistics, "National Employment, Hours and Earnings."

6. See George Seldes, *The Great Thoughts* (New York: Ballantine Books, 1986), 166.

7. U.S. Census Bureau, "Facts for Features: Labor Day," 2006, September 4, 2006. See *www.census.gov/PressRelease/www/releases/archives/facts_for_features_special_editions/007125.html*.

8. Janice Fine, *Worker Centers: Organizing Communities at the Edge of the Dream* (Ithaca, N.Y.: Cornell University Press, ILR Imprint, 2006).

9. See the organizing work of the North American Alliance for Fair Employment, which is a network of organizations concerned about the growth of contingent work — including part-time jobs, temping, bus-contracting — and its impact on workers. See *www.fairjobs.org/index.php*.

10. The living wage is determined by dividing $18,100 (Health and Human Services poverty level for a family of four) by 2080 (52 weeks x 40 hours).

11. For a good survey of the impact of minimum wage legislation, see Robert Pollin and Stephanie Luce, *Toward a Living Wage: Building a Fair Economy* (New York: New Press, 1998).

12. View the "Family Budget Calculator" at *www.epi.org/content.cfm/datazone_fambud_budget*.

13. Sylvia A. Allegretto, "Basic Family Budgets" (Washington, D.C.: Economic Policy Institute Briefing Paper, September 1, 2005), *www.epi.org/content.cfm/bp165*.

14. Robert Kuttner, "Boston's 'Living Wage' Law Highlights New Grassroots Efforts to Fight Poverty." *The American Prospect,* 1997. *www.prospect.org/columns/kuttner/bk970818.html*.

15. Living Wage Resource Center, *www.livingwagecampaign.org*, December 2005.

16. Ibid.

17. Pollin and Luce, *Toward a Living Wage*, 68–73.

18. Jared Bernstein and John Schmitt, "The Sky Didn't Fall: An Evaluation of the Minimum Wage Increase" (Washington, D.C.: Economic Policy Institute, October 1996).

19. Associated Press, "Many State Wal-Mart Workers Using Medicaid," *Centre Daily Times,* March 3, 2006. See Arindrajit Dube and Ken Jacobs, *Hidden Cost of Wal-Mart Jobs — Use of Safety Net Programs by Wal-Mart Workers in California* (Berkeley: University of California Labor Center, August 2, 2004).

20. See the work of Good Jobs First (*www.goodjobsfirst.org*). See also Greg Leroy, *The Great American Jobs Scam: Corporate Tax Dodging and the Myth of Job Creation* (San Francisco: Berrett-Koehler Press, 2005). See *www.greatamericanjobsscam.com*.

21. Karen Kraut, Scott Klinger, and Chuck Collins, "Choosing the High Road: Businesses That Pay a Living Wage and Prosper" (Boston: Responsible Wealth and United for a Fair Economy, March 2000). The report is available for download at *www.responsiblewealth.org/living_wage/choosing/html*.

22. Susan Pace Hamill, "An Argument for Tax Reform Based on Judeo-Christian Ethics," *Alabama Law Review* (Fall 2002). The complete article can be found at *www.law.ua.edu/directory/bio/shamill.html*. See also Susan Pace Hamill, "An Evaluation of Federal Tax Policy Based on Judeo-Christian Ethics," *Virginia Tax Review* 25 (Winter 2006).

23. Kraut et al., "Choosing the High Road."

24. "The Lawyer, the Bible, and the Governor: An Interview with Susan Pace Hamill," *Sojourners* 22, no. 4 (April 2004): 12–17.

25. National Conference of Catholic Bishops, *Economic Justice for All*, 55, no. 122.

26. Jan Schakowsky, "At a Time of War, How Dare We Reduce Veterans' Benefits?" *Chicago Sun Times,* April 13, 2003. See also "PA Governor: Bush Budget Cuts for Critical Programs 'Unconscionable,'" *CNN.com,* March 19, 2005. See *www.edition.cnn.com/2005/ALLPOLITICS/03/19/dems.radio.*

27. Grover Norquist made this statement on National Public Radio, in a profile of Norquist done by Mara Liasson for the Bob Edwards show on May 25, 2001. See *www.thenationaldebate.com/blog/archives/2005/02/norquist_sidest.html.*

28. National Conference of Catholic Bishops, *Economic Justice for All*, 79–80, no. 202.

29. Richard Kogan and Robert Greenstein, "President Portrays Social Security Shortfall as Enormous, but His Tax Cuts and Drug Benefit Will Cost at Least Five Times as Much" (Washington, D.C.: Center on Budget and Policy Priorities. February 2005). See *www.cbpp.org/1-4- 05socsec.htm.*

6. Root Causes, Part II

1. Pontifical Council for Justice and Peace, *Compendium of the Social Doctrine of the Church,* English ed. (Washington, D.C.: U.S. Conference of Catholic Bishops, 2005), 156, no. 363.

2. Sunbeam, Inc., 2000 proxy statement.

3. David Sedore, "Teamsters Slam Sunbeam for Closing Mr. Coffee Site," *Palm Beach Post,* June 28, 2000.

4. Philip Dine, "Workers Want Presidential Hopefuls to Stem the Flow of Jobs Out of America," *St. Louis Post-Dispatch,* February 20, 2000.

5. Sabrina Eaton, "Mr. Coffee Story Illustrates How and Why Jobs Here Often End Up Overseas," *Cleveland Plain Dealer*, November 14, 2004.

6. Ibid.

7. Compare this situation with the case of American doctors. For years, the American Medical Association has lobbied Congress to limit the number of foreign doctors who can practice in the United States. These trade rules protect the jobs and high salaries of doctors and raise the cost of health care for everyone. Yet, since doctors are politically powerful, they are able to enact trade rules that lower-wage workers like Joylyn Billy cannot.

8. National Conference of Catholic Bishops, *Economic Justice for All: Pastoral Letter on Catholic Social Teaching and the U.S. Economy,* tenth anniversary ed. (Washington, D.C.: U.S. Catholic Conference, 1997), 23, no. 10.

9. John Paul II, Address in Mexico City, January 23, 1999, excerpted in *New York Times*, January 24, 1999.

10. Jeffrey D. Sachs, *The End of Poverty: Economic Possibilities for Our Time* (New York: Penguin, 2005), 20–25.

11. Ibid., 1.

12. Clearing House Interbank Payment System. Website: *www.chips.org.* The overwhelming majority of currency transactions are conducted in U.S. dollars. The amount may be shrinking because the number of banks participating in CHIPS is shrinking. We have seen citations that $2 trillion a day flows in international currency exchanges. In Doug Henwood's *Wall Street* (London: Verso, 1998), he cites the Bank for International Settlements located in Switzerland as the source of the $2 trillion-a-day number.

13. Sarah Anderson and John Cavanagh, with Thea Lee, *Field Guide to the Global Economy* (New York: New Press, 2005), 38.

14. Ibid., 68–70.

15. Kate Bronfenbenner, *The Effects of Plant Closing or Threat of Plant Closing on the Right of Workers to Organize* (Ithaca, N.Y.: Cornell University Press, 1996). This was included in a report submitted to the Labor Secretariat of the North American Commission for Labor Cooperation; see *www.naalc.org.*

16. U.S. Labor Department, *By the Sweat and Toil of Children* (Washington, D.C.: U.S. Department of Labor, March 1999) as reported by the Associated Press, "Global Child-Labor Abuses Reported," *Boston Globe,* March 26, 1999.

17. Sachs, *The End of Poverty,* 20–25.

18. Anderson, Cavanagh, and Lee, *Field Guide,* 86. See the World Trade Organization's discussion of this dispute at *www.wto.org/english/thewto_e/whatis_e/tif_e/disp3_e.htm.*

19. Chris Kraul, "Avocado Exports to U.S. Booming," *Miami Herald,* Mexico Edition, Wednesday, October 12, 2005.

20. Kevin G. Hall, Janet Schwartz, and Jay Root, "Mexico's Calderon Faces Pressure to Roll Back NAFTA," Knight Ridder Washington Bureau, August 3, 2006.

21. David Morris, "Blame NAFTA," *Alternet,* April 13, 2006. View this story online at *www.alternet.org/story/34768/.*

22. Howard W. French, "Mobutu Sese Seko, 66, Longtime Dictator of Zaire," *New York Times,* September 8, 1997. See *www.partners.nytimes.com/library/world/090897obit-mobutu.html.* See also Carole J. L. Collins, "Congo/Zaire," *Foreign Policy in Focus,* Issue Brief 2, no. 37 (June 1997). See *www.fpif.org/briefs/vol2/v2n37cz_body.html.* Carole Collins writes: "The U.S. also helped funnel World Bank loans and IMF credits to Mobutu's government, even though internal documents reveal that these agencies knew in advance the money was likely to be stolen and the loans unlikely to be repaid. Mobutu used IMF and World Bank loans to repay Zaire's private creditors, thereby transforming private debt into public debt now amounting to almost $14 billion."

23. "Republic of Congo: Enhanced Initiative for Heavily Indebted Poor Countries — Decision Point Document," IMF Country Report no. 06/148, International Monetary Fund, April 2006. See *www.imf.org/external/country/COG/index.htm.*

24. Sarah Anderson, *Debt Boomerang: How Americans Would Benefit From Cancellation of Impoverished Country Debts,* Institute for Policy Studies, October 2005. Available online at *www.ips-dc.org/boomerang/index.htm.* See also Susan George, *The Debt Boomerang: How Third World Debt Harms Us All* (Amsterdam, Netherlands: Transnational Institute, 1992).

25. An interview with David Batstone, March 2, 2005. See *www.rightreality.com/articles/a_model_of_fairness_in_global_trade_03-02-05.html.*

26. Pontifical Council for Justice and Peace, *Compendium of the Social Doctrine of the Church,* no. 370, 159.

27. For information on leading fair trade efforts, see organizations such as Equal Exchange (*www.equalexchange.com*), Pura Vida coffee (*www.puravida.coffee.com*), and Ten Thousand Villages craft exchange (*www.tenthousandvillages.com*). To learn more about fair trade certification organizations, go to *www.transfairusa.org* and the International Fair Trade Association (*www.ifat.org*).

28. See Millennium Development Goals: *www.un.org/millenniumgoals.*

29. Jeff Faux, *The Global Class War: How America's Bipartisan Elite Lost Our Future — and What It Will Take to Win It Back* (Hoboken, N.J.: John Wiley & Sons, 2006), 219.

30. Sachs, *The End of Poverty*, 20–25.

31. From a prayer offered by Cardinal McCarrick on April 10, 2006, at the National Mall in Washington, D.C.

32. From a summary on "Comprehensive Immigration Reform," published by the Office of Migration and Refugee Policy. See *www.nccbuscc.org/mrs/mrp.shtml.*

33. Dennis K. Berman, "Fistfuls of Dollars Fuel the M&A Engine — P&G's $57 Billion Purchase of Gillette Is Year's Biggest; Asia, Europe Volume Soars," *Wall Street Journal,* January 3, 2006. See also Sandra Sugawara, "Merger Wave Accelerated in '99," *Washington Post,* December 31, 1999.

34. See *Strangers No Longer: Together on the Journey of Hope, A Pastoral Letter Concerning Migration from the Catholic Bishops of Mexico and the United States,* issued by U.S. Conference of Catholic Bishops on January 22, 2003. See *www.usccb.org/mrs/stranger.shtml.*

35. From interviews by author Chuck Collins, January 4, 2006.

36. Mark Weisbrot and Luis Sandoval, "Mexico's Presidential Election: Background on Economic Issues" (Washington, D.C.: Center for Economic Policy Research, June 2006). See *www.cepr.net.*

37. For some of this history, see David Korten, *When Corporations Rule the World* (West Hartford, Conn.: Kumarian Press, 1996); and Richard Grossman and Frank Adams, *Taking Care of Business: Citizenship and the Charter of Incorporation* (Cambridge, Mass.: Charter Ink, 1995).

38. Charles Derber, *Corporation Nation* (New York: St. Martin's Press, 1998), 129.

39. David Batstone, "You Cannot Train Employees to Be Ethical," from his website Right Reality. See *www.rightreality.com/articles/you_cannot_train_employees_to_be_ethical.html.* See also David Batstone, *Saving the Corporate Soul* (New York: Jossey-Bass, 2005).

40. Pope John Paul II, Edmonton, Alberta, Canada, September 17, 1984, from the National Conference of Catholic Bishops, *Economic Justice for All,* 49, no. 94.

41. For a good summary of the Sarbanes-Oxley corporate reforms, see the American Institute of Certified Public Accountants, *www.aicpa.org/info/sarbanes_oxley_summary.htm.*

42. The Social Investment Forum, "2003 Report on Responsible Investing Trends in the United States" (Washington, D.C.: Social Investment Forum, January 24, 2006). See the report online at *www.socialinvest.org/areas/research/trends/sri_trends_report_2005.pd.*

43. Evelyn Nieves, "Accord with Tomato Pickers Ends Boycott of Taco Bell," *Washington Post,* March 9, 2005. See information on the Coalition for Immokalee Workers at *www.ciw-online.org.*

44. David C. Korten, *The Post-Corporate World: Life after Capitalism* (San Francisco: Berrett-Koehler Publishers, and West Hartford, Conn.: Kumarian Press, 1998).

45. Ralph Estes, *Taking Back the Corporation* (New York: Nation Books, 2005), 60.

7. The Moral Measures for Our Economy

1. See National Conference of Catholic Bishops, *Economic Justice for All: Pastoral Letter on Catholic Social Teaching and the U.S. Economy*, tenth anniversary ed. (Washington, D.C.: U.S. Catholic Conference, 1997), 53, no. 113. See also nos. 298–99.

2. Pontifical Council for Justice and Peace, *Compendium of the Social Doctrine of the Church*, English ed. (Washington, D.C.: U.S. Conference of Catholic Bishops, 2005), no. 182. John Paul II, encyclical letter *Sollicitudo Rei Socialis*.

3. St. Gregory the Great, *Regula Pastoralis*. As cited in Pontifical Council for Justice and Peace, *Compendium of the Social Doctrine of the Church*, no. 184.

4. Pontifical Council for Justice and Peace, *Compendium of the Social Doctrine of the Church*, no. 193, quoting John Paul II, encyclical letter *Sollicitudo Rei Socialis*, 38, AAS 80 (1988): 565–66.

5. National Conference of Catholic Bishops, *Economic Justice for All*, 125, no. 328.

6. Gregory Baum, *Compassion and Solidarity* (New York: Paulist Press, 1990), 58. Thanks to Fred Kammer for pointing this out in his excellent book *Doing Faithjustice: An Introduction to Catholic Social Thought*, rev. ed. (New York: Paulist Press, 2004).

7. One of the last notes left behind by Gandhi in 1948, expressing his deepest social thought. See *Mahatma Gandhi, Last Phase*, vol. 2 (London: Greenleaf Press, 1958), 65.

8. *Quadragesimo Anno*, no. 79. As cited in National Conference of Catholic Bishops, *Economic Justice for All*, 50, no. 99.

9. Pontifical Council for Justice and Peace, *Compendium of the Social Doctrine of the Church*, no. 351.

10. Mary Jo Bane and Lawrence Mead, *Lifting Up the Poor: A Dialogue on Religion, Poverty and Welfare Reform* (Washington, D.C.: Brookings Institution Press, 2003).

11. David Bollier, *Brand Name Bullies: The Quest to Own and Control Culture* (Hoboken, N.J.: Wiley & Sons, 2005), 14–15.

12. The image of "enclosure" comes from the historical "enclosure" movement of the 1600s in England. At the time, common lands that the poor depended on for crops, firewood, grazing were "enclosed" by private owners, who denied access to the lands. In modern times, corporations are trying to "enclose" parts of the "information superhighway," which is the technological basis for the new economy.

13. Peter Barnes, "Capitalism, the Commons and Divine Right," address to the E. F. Schumacher Society, October 25, 2003.

14. U.S. House Committee on Education and the Workforce, "New Report Details Wal-Mart's Labor Abuses and Hidden Costs," February 16, 2004. See online *www.edworkforce.house.gov/democrats/releases/rel21604.html*.

15. Good Jobs First, "Shopping for Subsidies: How Wal-Mart Uses Taxpayer Money to Finance Its Never-ending Growth" (Washington, D.C., 2004). See online *www.goodjobsfirst.org*.

16. Stanley Holmes and Wendy Zellner, "The Costco Way: Higher Wages Mean Higher Profits," *Business Week*, April 12, 2004.

17. These examples come from Bollier, *Brand Name Bullies*, 7.

18. Harvey Cox, "The Market as God," *Atlantic Magazine,* March 1, 1999. See also Harvey Cox, "The Market Is My Shepherd, and I Shall Want and Want and Want," *U.S. Catholic,* February 1, 2000.

19. Most of these examples come from "The Commons Rising," a report from the Tomales Bay Institute and available at *www.onthecommons.org.*

8. Solidarity in Action

1. An Interview with Gar Alperovitz, "Our Updated Challenge: Building the (Co-)Ownership Society," *Nonprofit Quarterly* 12, no. 2 (Summer 2005).

2. For information on the Catholic Campaign for Human Development Economic Development Program, see *www.usccb.org/cchd/economicdevelopment.shtml.*

3. Co-author Chuck Collins researched this neighborhood in 1987 as part of writing *The Community Land Trust Legal Manual* (Springfield, Mass.: Institute for Community Economics, 1998).

4. Gar Alperovitz, *America beyond Capitalism* (Hoboken, N.J.: John Wiley & Sons, 2005), 99–100.

5. Ibid., 93. See also information about community land trusts and the Institute for Community Economics, *www.iceclt.org.*

6. Information for this profile was compiled from the website of the Sawmill Community Land Trust (*www.sawmillclt.org*) and an article by Jennifer W. Sanchez, "Onboard at Sawmill," *Albuquerque Tribune,* December 2, 2004.

7. On Community Supported Agriculture (CSAs), see *www.localharvest.org.*

8. Tahree Lane, "Fresh Food, from Farm to Your Table," *Toledo Blade,* May 14, 2006.

9. "Building Wealth: The New Asset-Based Approach to Solving Social and Economic Problems" (The Aspen Institute, May 22, 2005), 8.

10. Corey Rosen, "That Sort of Sounds Like Socialism to Me," *Owners at Work,* the publication of the Ohio Employee Ownership Center, 18, no. 1 (Summer 2006).

11. Mondragón Cooperative Corporation, "Frequently Asked Questions," from their website: *www.mcc.coop.es.*

12. See research on enterprising cities in Alperovitz, *America beyond Capitalism,* 90–98.

13. See the information about ShoreBank at *www.sbk.com.*

14. Credit Union National Association, "Long-run Trends: 1939 to Present: Aggregates," *www.advice.cuna.org/econ/long_run.html,* accessed May 2006.

15. Data from the National Federation of Community Development Credit Unions: *www.natfed.org.*

16. See the information about TRF, one of the earliest community development loan funds, at *www.trfund.com.*

17. CDFI, Coalition of Community Development Financial Institutions, see online at *www.cdfi.org.*

18. Co-author Chuck Collins wrote the first grant and served as initial board chair for the Anti-Displacement Project. Some of this information comes from the organization's website at *www.a-dp.org/.* See also John Hogan, "Credible Signs of Christ Alive," from *Helping People Help Themselves,* the newsletter of the Catholic Campaign for Human Development, no. 1, 2004.

19. Miriam Axel-Lute, "Don't Start Small: Tenants Organize for Ownership," *Shelterforce Magazine* (May/June 2001).

20. Beth Griffin, "Giving San Antonio's Residents a Voice," from *Helping People Help Themselves,* no. 2, 2005.

21. Beth Griffin, "Helping Save the Family Farm," from *Helping People Help Themselves,* no. 2, 2004.

22. Sue Kirchhoff, "Manufactured Homes — and Owners — Gain Respect," *USA Today,* August 7, 2005.

23. Beth Griffin, "No Longer Mobile: People of Hope Create Permanently Affordable Homes," from *Helping People Help Themselves,* no. 1, 2005.

9. Preparing for Discipleship

1. See Fred Kammer, S.J., *Doing Faithjustice: An Introduction to Catholic Social Thought,* rev. ed. (New York: Paulist Press, 2004), 27. For an interesting reflection, see his cycle of Baal.

2. In the cycle of Baal, this leads to exile, the return of prophetic voices, and the killing of the prophets, those who raise their witness against the false idols. Eventually this leads those who are alienated from God to cry out for deliverance — and to receive forgiveness and the eventual restoration by Yahweh.

3. See Chuck Collins, Scott Klinger, and Mike Lapham, "I Didn't Do It Alone: Society's Contribution to Individual Wealth and Success" (Boston: United for a Fair Economy, 2004). See *www.responsiblewealth.org/press/2004/NotAlone_pr.html.*

4. "Bridging the Gap," *PBS Lehrer News Hour,* March 20, 1996.

5. Jennifer Reingold, "Executive Pay: Special Report," *Business Week,* April 17, 2000, 108.

6. National Conference of Catholic Bishops, *Economic Justice for All: Pastoral Letter on Catholic Social Teaching and the U.S. Economy,* tenth anniversary ed. (Washington, D.C.: U.S. Catholic Conference, 1997), 54, no. 115.

7. Encyclical letter of Pope Paul VI, *Populorum Progressio, On the Development of Peoples,* 1967, no. 23.

8. According to economist Lester Thurow, over half the growth in the economy each year is related to technology-induced productivity gains. Lester Thurow, *Building Wealth: The New Rules for Individuals, Companies, and Nations in a Knowledge-Based Economy* (New York: Collins, 2000).

9. See Good Jobs First (*www.goodjobsfirst.org*).

10. Gar Alperovitz, "Distributing Our Technological Inheritance," Fourteenth Annual E. F. Schumacher Lectures, Yale University, New Haven, Connecticut, October 2004. See *www.schumactersociety.org/publications/toc_alperovitz.html.*

11. National Conference of Catholic Bishops, *Economic Justice for All,* 44, no. 76.

12. United for Fair Economy, "Born on Third Base: The Sources of Wealth of the 1997 Forbes 400" (Boston: United for a Fair Economy, October 1998).

13. Richard Conniff, *The Natural History of the Rich* (New York: W. W. Norton, 2002), 266.

14. United for Fair Economy, "Born on Third Base."

15. Quote gallery, *www.inequality.org.*

16. Thomas Shapiro, *The Hidden Cost of Being African American: How Wealth Perpetuates Inequality* (Oxford: Oxford University Press, 2004), 13.

17. Brian K. Bucks, Arthur B. Kennickell, and Kevin B. Moore, "Recent Changes in U.S. Family Finances: Evidence from the 2001 and 2004 Survey of Consumer Finances," *Federal Reserve Bulletin*, 2006, Table 3, *www.federalreserve.gov/pubs/bulletin*, accessed May 2006.

18. U.S. Census Bureau, Housing Vacancies and Homeownership 2005 Annual Statistics, Table 20, "Homeownership Rates by Race and Ethnicity of Householder, 1994–2005," online at *www.census.gov/hhes/www/housing/hvs/annual05/ann05t20.html*, accessed May 2006.

19. As the U.S. bishops commented, where the impact of past discrimination continues, "society has an obligation to take positive steps to overcome the legacy of injustice." National Conference of Catholic Bishops, *Economic Justice for All*, 43, no. 73.

20. Martin Rothenberg, White House press briefing, August 31, 2000.

21. Ibid.

22. As the U.S. bishops observed in their pastoral letter on the economy, "Americans are challenged today as never before to develop the inner freedom to resist the temptation constantly to seek more." National Conference of Catholic Bishops, *Economic Justice for All*, 43, no. 75.

23. Ibid., 127, no. 334.

24. For information on ecological footprints and programs for reducing consumption, see online:

>*www.redefiningprogress.org*
>*www.kidsfootprint.org/index.html*
>*www.mec.ca/Apps/ecoCalc/ecoCalc.jsp*
>*www.naturalstep.org/home.php*

10. Making a Difference

1. These polling results come from the work of Culture Logic and the Demos Center for the Public Sector. They are summarized in a briefing paper: Patrick Bresette and Marcia Kinsey, "Making It Real" (New York: Demos Public Briefing, October 2005), no. 3.

2. Ibid.

3. From the Catholic Campaign for Human Development, "Basic Principles of Catholic Mission as They Are Applied by the Catholic Campaign for Human Development," from the website: *www.usccb.org/cchd*.

4. National Conference of Catholic Bishops, *Economic Justice for All: Pastoral Letter on Catholic Social Teaching and the U.S. Economy*, tenth anniversary ed. (Washington, D.C.: U.S. Catholic Conference, 1997), 55, no. 120.

5. Canadian Auto Workers Union, "Big Three Bargaining Backgrounder Issues" (Toronto, October 1996).

6. Take Back Your Time, *www.timeday.org*.

7. See Sojourners/Call to Renewal at *www.sojo.net*.

8. On the Covenant for a New America see *www.covenantforanewamerica.org*.

Conclusion

1. National Conference of Catholic Bishops, *Economic Justice for All: Pastoral Letter on Catholic Social Teaching and the U.S. Economy*, tenth anniversary ed. (Washington, D.C.: U.S. Catholic Conference, 1997), 11.

Resources

The Short List

For an expansive, periodically updated, and comprehensive resource list, see *www.ips-dc.org/projects/Inequality/MoralMeasure*.

Organizations

Catholic Campaign for Human Development

Founded in 1969, the Catholic Campaign for Human Development is the domestic anti-poverty, social justice program of the U.S. Catholic bishops. Its mission is to address the root causes of poverty in America through promotion and support of community-controlled, self-help organizations and through transformative education.

> 3211 4th Street, NE
> Washington, DC 20017-1194
> 202-541-3000
> *www.nccbuscc.org/chd/*

Catholics in Alliance for the Common Good

Catholics in Alliance for the Common Good was formed in 2004 and is dedicated to promoting the fullness of the Catholic social tradition in the public square. They provide information to Catholics about church social teaching as it relates to public participation in our society, and they are committed to advance the prophetic voice of the Catholic social tradition. They characterize themselves as an "open-source" organization, meaning that participants contribute ideas, content, and activities — to build and support the Catholic social justice movement through communication, grassroots outreach, and coordination.

> Washington, D.C.
> Phone: 202-822-5105; Fax: 202-822-5107
> *http://thecatholicalliance.org/new/*

JustFaith Ministries

JustFaith Ministries strives to provide faith formation processes and resources that emphasize the Gospel message of peace and justice, Catholic social teaching, and the intersection of spirituality and action. The aim of JustFaith Ministries is to enable people of faith to develop a passion for justice and to express this passion in concrete acts of social ministry.

> 7409 Greenlawn Road
> Louisville, KY 40222
> 502-243-9287
> *www.justfaith.org/*

Network: A National Catholic Social Justice Lobby

Founded in 1971 by Catholic sisters, NETWORK works for peace and justice. Through Congressional lobbying and legislative advocacy, it strives to close the gap between rich and poor and to dismantle policies rooted in racism, greed, and violence.

> 25 E St. NW, Suite 200
> Washington, DC 20001-1630
> Phone: 202-347-9797; Fax: 202-347-9864
> *www.networklobby.org*

Education for Solidarity

Education for Solidarity partners with Catholic congregations to discuss the changing economy, growing inequality, and what we can do together. Through a deep exploration of Catholic social teachings, participants explore meaningful actions.

> *www.ips-dc.org/projects/Inequality/Solidarity*

Sojourners/Call to Renewal

Sojourners was founded in 1971 to articulate the biblical call to social justice, inspiring hope and building a movement to transform individuals, communities, the church, and the world. They publish *Sojourners* magazine. Call to Renewal seeks to build a movement that puts faith to work for justice.

> 3333 14th St. NW, Suite 200
> Washington, DC 20010
> 202-328-8842
> *www.sojo.net* and *www.calltorenewal.com*

Books

On Catholic Social Teaching and Economics

See the publishing house and resources of the National Conference of Catholic Bishops: *www.usccbpublishing.org*.

Curran, Charles. *Catholic Social Teaching: A Historical, Theological and Ethical Analysis*. Washington, D.C.: Georgetown University Press, 2002.

Hogan, John. *Credible Signs of Christ Alive: Case Studies from the Catholic Campaign for Human Development*. Lanham, Md.: Rowman and Littlefield, 2003.

Kammer, Fred, S.J. *Doing Faithjustice: An Introduction to Catholic Social Thought*. Rev. ed. New York: Paulist Press, 2004.

Massaro, Thomas, S.J. *Living Justice: Catholic Social Teaching in Action*. Lanham, Md.: Rowman & Littlefield, 2000.

National Conference of Catholic Bishops, *Economic Justice for All: Pastoral Letter on Catholic Social Teaching and the U.S. Economy*. Tenth anniversary edition. Washington, D.C.: U.S. Catholic Conference, 1997.

Pennock, Michael. *Catholic Social Teaching: Learning and Living Justice*. Notre Dame, Ind.: Ave Maria Press, 2000.

Pontifical Council for Justice and Peace. *Compendium of the Social Doctrine of the Church*. Washington, D.C.: U.S. Conference of Catholic Bishops, 2005.

On Economics and Poverty

Ackerman, Bruce, and Anne Alstott. *The Stakeholder Society*. New Haven: Yale University Press, 1999.

Alperovitz. Gar. *America beyond Capitalism: Reclaiming Our Wealth, Our Liberty and Our Democracy*. Hoboken, N.J.: John Wiley & Sons, 2005.

Anderson, Sarah, John Cavanagh, with Thea Lee. *Field Guide to the Global Economy*. New York: New Press, 2005.

Bane, Mary Jo, and Lawrence M. Mead. *Lifting Up the Poor: A Dialogue on Religion, Poverty and Welfare Reform*. Washington, D.C.: Brookings Institution, 2003.

Barnes, Peter. *Capitalism 3.0: A Guide to Reclaiming the Commons*. San Francisco: Berrett Koehler, 2006.

Collins, Chuck, and Felice Yeskel. *Economic Apartheid in America: A Primer on Economic Inequality and Insecurity*. New York: New Press, 2005.

Ehrenreich, Barbara. *Nickel and Dimed: On (Not) Getting By in America*. New York: Metropolitan Books, 2001.

Gallagher, Vincent A. *The True Cost of Low Prices: The Violence of Globalization*. Maryknoll, N.Y.: Orbis Books, 2006.

Gates, William H., Sr., and Chuck Collins. *Wealth and Our Commonwealth*. Boston: Beacon Press, 2003.

Newman, Katherine. *No Shame in My Game: The Working Poor in the Inner City*. New York: Knopf, 2000.

Pizzigati, Sam. *Greed and Good: Understanding and Overcoming the Inequality That Limits Our Lives*. New York: Apex Press, 2004.

Shipler, David. *The Working Poor: Invisible in America*. New York: Knopf, 2005.

Wallis, Jim. *God's Politics: Why the Right Gets It Wrong and the Left Doesn't Get It*. New York: HarperCollins, 2005.

Acknowledgments

Mary: I wish to thank the thousands of members and leaders of projects funded by the Catholic Campaign for Human Development (CCHD) for sharing their lives, struggles, hopes, failures, and many accomplishments with me; for sharing their economic struggles with parishioners across the United States year after year; and for helping those who are not poor or low-income understand the effects of the U.S. economy on the lives of the poor. I thank the CCHD leaders and members for their courage to speak up and participate in efforts to create a nation where the economy works for everyone. These leaders and members of CCHD-funded projects have long been a key source of economic knowledge, optimism, and hope for me.

I also want to thank those leaders of the Catholic Church who had the courage to listen long and hard and publish what they heard in the document *Economic Justice for All*. This document challenges us to weigh productivity on a scale with distributive justice and to always ask how the poor and vulnerable are faring in our economy.

In addition, I thank my Republican friends and family members who stay in endless conversations with me in my struggle to learn about the ever changing economy and its effect on the poor of the world.

Finally, I thank Chuck Collins, for his friendship, inspiration, and economic guidance. He truly is a role model for the common good.

Chuck: I wish to thank my colleagues at the Institute for Policy Studies and United for a Fair Economy for their solidarity over the years. Thanks to the members of St. Mary of the Angels in Roxbury, Massachusetts, and First Church in Jamaica Plain for being remarkable communities of worship and works of justice.

Many thanks to the various individuals who provided spiritual and intellectual inspiration for this book including Bishop Peter Rosazza, Bishop Rembert Weakland, Sister Margaret Leonard, Rev. Terry Burke, Sister Monica McGloin, Rev. Jim Wallis, David Batstone, Scott Klinger, Ched Meyers, Father Philip Pitya, Dave and Karen Hinchen, Rev. Kate Stevens, Rev. John Buehrens, Rev. Carl and Faith Scovel, Felice Yeskel, Daniel Moss and Tyler Haaren, and Uncle Walt and Aunt Julianne Sullivan.

I owe a special debt to the late Chuck Matthei, who introduced me to the Catholic Worker movement and the writings of Dorothy Day. Thanks to the CCHD team for the fun we had doing "Education for Solidarity" programs across the country. I'm most thankful to Mary Wright, who has made this an inspiring and enjoyable project, and I look forward to our future work bringing these ideas into the world.

Both authors wish to thank Robert Ellsberg at Orbis Books. He is no ordinary editor. He is also a gifted writer and thinker whose contributions greatly improved this book. Thanks to the entire team at Orbis Books.

Thanks to our readers, who gave us invaluable feedback, including: Patricia Brennan, Chris Hartman, Scott Klinger, Alice O'Rourke, Mike Evans, Jack Jezreel, Chris Breu, and Martha Miller. Special thanks to Chris Hartman, who did fact checking and designed our graphics.

Index

Numbers in *italics* indicate figures.